Our Way to Fight

OUR WAY TO FIGHT

Peace-Work Under Siege
in Israel–Palestine

Michael Riordon

PlutoPress
www.plutobooks.com

Between the Lines
TORONTO

First published 2011 by Pluto Press
345 Archway Road, London N6 5AA
www.plutobooks.com

First published in Canada in 2011 by Between the Lines
401 Richmond Street West, Studio 277, Toronto, Ontario, M5V 3A8, Canada
1-800-718-7201
www.btlbooks.com

British Library Cataloguing in Publication Data
A catalogue record for this book is available from the British Library

Library and Archives Canada Cataloguing in Publication
Riordon, Michael, 1944–
    Our way to fight : peace-work under siege in Israel–Palestine / Michael Riordon.
ISBN 978-1-897071-72-4
1. Arab–Israeli conflict—1993–   —Personal narratives. 2. Pacifists—West Bank.
3. Pacifists—Israel. I. Title.
DS119.76.R56 2011   956.9405'40922   C2010-903011-7

ISBN   978 0 7453 3023 5   Hardback
ISBN   978 0 7453 3022 8   Paperback (Pluto)
ISBN   978 1 897071 72 4   Paperback (Between the Lines)

Between the Lines gratefully acknowledges assistance for its publishing activities from
the Canada Council for the Arts, the Ontario Arts Council, the Government of Ontario
through the Ontario Book Publishers Tax Credit program, and the Government of
Canada through the Canada Book Fund.

Canada Council
for the Arts

Conseil des Arts
du Canada

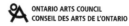

ONTARIO ARTS COUNCIL
CONSEIL DES ARTS DE L'ONTARIO

Canadä

10   9   8   7   6   5   4   3   2   1

Designed and produced for Pluto Press by
Chase Publishing Services Ltd, 33 Livonia Road, Sidmouth, EX10 9JB, England
Typeset from disk by Stanford DTP Services, Northampton, England
Simultaneously printed digitally by CPI Antony Rowe, Chippenham, UK
and Edwards Bros, USA

Contents

Acknowledgements   vi

Introduction   1
 1 A Day in the Country   5
 2 My Way to Fight   17
 3 The Jerusalem Syndrome   29
 4 Bridge to the World   42
 5 Witness   54
 6 There is a Law   68
 7 This is My Homeland   80
 8 Facts Under the Ground   89
 9 A Drop in the Sea   100
10 Dreams Have Their Uses   113
11 Civil-izing Israel   126
12 The Generation that Matters   139
13 Naming Palestine   152
14 A Cure for Amnesia   164
15 The Tempo of History   177
16 Hello?   190
17 Cracks in the Wall   199
18 The Safety of Sleep   215

Index   231

Acknowledgements

My deep, enduring gratitude goes to:

Many good people who shared stories, contacts, hospitality, encouragement, comment, and other invaluable support.

The Canada Council for the Arts, the Ontario Arts Council, and people who struggle to keep them a safe distance from the shifting will of governments.

Introduction

What can I say? Surely there can't be anything new, nothing that Israelis and Palestinians haven't already said about the horrors of the occupation, the devastating impact on Palestinians, the corrosive effect on Jews and Judaism.

Yet in the face of overwhelming harm, the question arises: "What can I do?" The victims ask, our conscience asks. So does a shared interest in a liveable world. What can I do?

During Athens street protests in 2008, a Greek blogger answered, beautifully: "We have a duty to move here, there, anywhere except back to our couches as mere viewers of history, back home to the warmth that freezes our conscience."

This book emerges from a journey and a search, to see what grounds for a just peace I could find in the tormented land that many call holy. In a world of spin where "peace" can mean anything, including war, it's essential to specify: a *just* peace. Peace without justice is hollow, a sham, the deathly stillness of tyranny triumphant. By contrast, a just peace is alive, clamorous, and vibrant with possibilities. Of course, in a world of spin, "justice" can mean anything too. This book explores what it might look like, and how people imagine building it.

Our Way to Fight offers no solutions, only stories of extra/ordinary people fighting for such a peace, on whichever side of the wall they happen to have landed by accidents of birth.

Stories are one way of sharing the belief that justice is imminent. And for such a belief, children, women and men will fight at a given moment with astounding ferocity. This is why tyrants fear storytelling: all stories somehow refer to the story of their fall. (John Berger)

OUR WAY TO FIGHT

For the title I thank Mustafa Staiti, a young Palestinian who makes and teaches film at the Freedom Theatre in the Jenin refugee camp. At one point in our conversation he said, "This is my way to fight."

Like other people featured in this book, Mustafa is a peace activist. Like them, he is also, in his own way, a freedom fighter. Because none of the people in this book fights alone, "my way to fight" became "our way to fight".

What constitutes a peace activist? It depends where you are, at which end of the gun. If you're at the shooting end, you have to stop shooting, and let go of the gun long enough to risk facing the other as an equal. If you're at the getting-shot end of the gun, you have to live as if you were not. Which is more difficult?

WHY ME?

I'm not Israeli, not Palestinian, not Muslim or Jewish. Then why write such a book?

I spoke my doubts to people on my travels. Often they replied that if I watched and listened closely enough, my distance would not be a deficit, but an asset.

In fact my distance is less than it might seem. I grew up colonized. Not knowing better in 1950s and 1960s Canada, I swallowed the official version that I was fed from birth by family, church, school and media: As a homosexual, I was a criminal, a sinner, a degenerate. I was one of *them*. Offered salvation through electric shocks – basically torture by consent – I consented.

Eventually nature triumphed over mad science, and I emerged intact, with a deep suspicion of official versions, and a growing identification with people, and peoples, who had also been designated *them*, the other. As *they* become *we*, everything changes.

Much of my work explores the worlds of people who live and die beneath official notice, or who suffer from too much of it: First Nations (aboriginal) youth, Mozambican farmers, inmates in Canadian prisons, traditional healers in Fiji, queer folk across Canada, Guatemalan labour activists. This approach to history-telling challenges the noisy monotone of the official version, and honours the riotous diversity of human life.

In cultures that glorify war, the voices of authentic peace-makers are seldom heard. Sadly, war is so much easier to sell than peace. Even Canada, which used to be seen as a peace-maker, now has military forces occupying another country, with all the attendant cruelties and lies.

So then, why Israel–Palestine? Or, as some will say, why pick on Israel?

THE OFFICIAL VERSION

Like many people in North America, I grew up on the official version of Israel: the Holy Land, the Promised Land, the Holocaust, *Exodus* (Paul Newman and the other beautiful, tanned freedom fighters), the Six Day War – brave little Israel, surrounded by hordes of Arabs bent on driving the Jews into the sea.

I had also absorbed the official version of Arabs: the enemies of Christianity, the target of the Crusades, exotic and cruel. We are still told the same story, to justify current crusades. But Palestinians – I had never heard of them. In my *Bible Reader's Encyclopedia*, a Sunday school prize from 1956, black and white photos depict people of the Holy Land, Bible country, clothed as they might have been 20 centuries ago, barefoot in stony places, unsmiling, bent under heavy bundles or water jars on backs and heads. The photos have no colour, no life. To the eyes of a Canadian child the people look timeless, or fixed in time, unevolved, quite unlike those dynamic Israelis who, we kept hearing, made the desert bloom. I had no name for the timeless, burdened people, not until the 1960s when some of them hijacked airplanes. Even then, all I learned was that they called themselves Palestinians; and where I lived, they were called terrorists.

In the summer of 2001, I met my first actual Israeli, an anthropologist, at an oral history conference in New York. We discovered a shared interest in complicating the official version with stories from the ground, in her case the stories of Palestinian villagers who had lost their homes and their land in 1948. While she evolved from travel acquaintance to friend, she also changed from observer to activist in Israel–Palestine, and became my first trusted guide to its travails.

Learning more, I wanted to know more. I went to see for myself, both sides of the wall. Over time, I began to see parallels.

On my second trip to gather material for this book I was invited by an Israeli organization called Zochrot to give a public talk in Tel Aviv. Titled 'Living on Indian Land', it explored an oral history project in which I worked with First Nations youth whose homes are not far from mine in rural Canada. They interviewed Mohawk elders about the long struggle to defend their land and culture from – well, from my people. The Tel Aviv talk included a brief account of indigenous resistance to the colonization of the entity now called Canada. Several times people interrupted to ask, with lively irony, "Are you sure you're not talking about Israel?" I was not. The parallels were not mine, but history's.

Aware of empire's dark history, I can see why the people who run Canada, the United States, Britain and Australia would be so comfortable with Israel's occupation of Palestine.

Seeing parallels is another reason to write this book.

> The trouble is that once you see it, you can't unsee it. And once you've seen it, keeping quiet, saying nothing, becomes as political an act as speaking out. There is no innocence. Either way, you're accountable. (Arundhati Roy)

PEOPLE OF THE BOOK

My Israeli anthropologist friend speaks of two world-views, the macro and micro. To me the macro view is an overview, from the war room, the cabinet room, the CEO's suite. The micro view is close up, on the street, on the wrong side of the wall, under the bombs. It is the view of this book.

Acts of resistance and solidarity are often so small that unless you look closely you may never see them. At some point a person thinks, I can no longer remain silent. She risks talking to others, and, sometimes, something happens.

These are just people. For a variety of reasons, which the book explores, they wanted to see more, to know more. They insist on seeing beyond the wall. Despite the overwhelming persuasive and punitive power of the tyrant, still they refuse his terms: to not know, to not care, to regard The Other as enemy, to accept that there is no alternative, to settle into the easy refuge of cynicism.

At the darkest times in human history, it is people like these who stand – at risk to themselves – against the crimes of tyrants. If ever a just peace is to grow in Israel–Palestine, it is people like these who will have planted and nurtured the seeds. The darker the weight of facts on the ground, the more urgent it is that their stories be told.

My Israeli friend urged me not to make heroes of the people in this book. I don't. It is context that renders them heroic. They aren't perfect. They are as vulnerable and flawed as the rest of us. Under normal conditions, I imagine they would be doing what normal people ought to be doing – living, loving, thinking for themselves, treating their neighbours with respect. But under abnormal conditions, what they do is exceptional. As conditions get worse, their actions become more exceptional. Eventually they become heroic.

1
A Day in the Country

From Jerusalem the train winds slowly north through the olive and cypress-pillared Soreq River valley, dust-dry in late summer. The track follows a late nineteenth-century Ottoman route, one of countless marks left by earlier empires on this land.

Facing me sit two soldiers in olive green. With buds in ears, he nods to music in his head; she dozes behind high-fashion sunglasses. Across the aisle, three soldiers play cards, sleeves rolled neatly to the elbow. All have assault rifles propped beside them or nestled in laps.

We pass a hillside village, children in dark blue uniforms walking to school; a sand quarry, orchards, towns, a forest of construction cranes, crimson bougainvillea spilling over a wall, one gaunt cow grazing in a field of rubble.

DOROTHY NAOR

The train terminates at Tel Aviv, Israel's metropolis. In the Central Station hall, more soldiers sprawl among their packs. Outside, the city quavers under a blanket of humid heat. Through ranks of buses I see an older-model green Volkswagen Passat, a woman waving, short grey hair – this would be Dorothy Naor.

Introductions done, I launch into small talk about the weather, a Canadian habit. But Dorothy interrupts, "I want to get on the road right away. We have a long day ahead of us." She doesn't seem so much rude as driven.

She lives up the Mediterranean coast in Herzliya, named for Theodor Herzl, a revered founder of Zionism. Dorothy was born in San Francisco in 1932. At 18 she flew to the new state of Israel, then only two years old, for a Zionist leadership training course. "Like many of us who grew up during the Holocaust, I was convinced that the only place where Jews could be safe would be in a country of our own. And now suddenly here it was! Of course I was quickly enamoured with lots of Israelis I met, including the one I married." They met at university in California.

With help from a Hungarian uncle, Eric Naor had slipped out of Austria at age ten with an older brother, after the Nazi coup in 1938. They made their way to Palestine, then under British rule. Of their immediate family, Eric and his brother were the only survivors; the others died in concentration camps.

After fighting in the 1948 war of independence, and proudly taking the name of his new country, Israel Naor went to California to study water engineering. There he met Dorothy, working on a PhD in English. They married in 1952, and four years later they emigrated, or made *aliyah* – Hebrew for "ascending" – to the promised land.

"I thought it would be the perfect place to raise our kids," says Dorothy, "a place of our own where Jewish customs, holidays and culture would be the norm." Working for an Israeli engineering company, Israel Naor specialized in international waterworks, dams and canals. Dorothy raised the kids, completed her PhD at Tel Aviv University, and taught English in several countries where they went for Israel's work.

East of Tel Aviv the air clears visibly, as if the windshield had been washed. Under a cloudless sky, the land here looks hard and white, scraped bare.

THE GREEN LINE

"Now pay attention here," Dorothy says with pointed emphasis – I can hear the teacher. "We've just crossed the so-called Green Line. That means we have left Israel and are now in the Palestinian territories. But do you see any sign to that effect, 'Welcome to the West Bank?' Of course not, the Israeli government would never allow it. This is psychological expansion. We're meant to regard all of this land as part of Israel."

The "Green Line" refers to the truce line between Israel and its older neighbours – Egypt, Jordan, Lebanon and Syria – after the 1948 war. It left the new state with almost 80 per cent of the land that had constituted the British colony of Palestine.

As Israel expands, the Green Line has become little more than a historical footnote, a myth. Dorothy tells me that Israel is the only country in the world that refuses to define its borders.

We're flying east on newly built Road 5, wide and smooth. It links Tel Aviv to massive Israeli settlements deep in the northern West Bank. "This used to be Palestinian farmland," my guide explains, "but hardly any of the colonists are farmers. They all work in the city – morning and afternoon you'll see long lines of commuters on this road. Not only are we stealing the land, we're also urbanizing it, the way we've done with so much of Israel."

Why does she say "colonists" instead of the usual "settlers"? "I prefer to call them what they are", Dorothy replies crisply. "The distortion of words is another form of occupation, one that should offend anyone who cares about language. 'Settlement' sounds much nicer, especially to Americans who did exactly the same thing. But when you occupy other people's land and build towns on it, that's a colony."

I watch her as she drives, face set, a little fierce, but with enough laugh lines to imply the delight she takes in her eight grandchildren. She wears sturdy sandals, jeans and a white shirt, long-sleeved for modesty because we'll be visiting Palestinians during Ramadan, the holiest time of the year. To respect our hosts who will be fasting dawn to dusk, we won't eat or drink.

Dorothy makes this journey often, either to educate foreigners like me or to transport Palestinians from the West Bank, often children with serious illness, to hospital in Israel. I suspect this formidable grandmother would not be easy for young Israeli soldiers to turn back at the checkpoints.

How did she first encounter Palestinians? "For many years I never met any. We weren't supposed to, you know, except maybe the occasional gardener. Of course there were things that bothered me, but with the kids, the PTA [Parent-Teacher Association], teaching and everything, who had time to ask questions?"

What things bothered her? "Oh, lots of things, things you have to work harder each time to ignore. Probably the first big shock I couldn't ignore was when Goldstein murdered all those people in the mosque." On 25 February 1994, American-Israeli settler Baruch Goldstein entered a mosque in the West Bank city of Hebron, in army uniform and carrying an assault rifle. Unimpeded by Israeli soldiers on duty there, he opened fire on the worshippers, killing 29–52 (Israeli and Palestinian sources differ on the count), and wounding more than 100, before survivors beat him to death.

Dorothy says, "What disturbed me almost as much as the massacre was the fact that, instead of removing the colonists from Kiryat Arba, Rabin locked up the Palestinians." On orders from Israeli Prime Minister Yitzak Rabin, the army imposed a two-week curfew, 24 hours a day, on the 120,000 Palestinian residents of Hebron. Caught outside their homes they could be shot on sight. The 400 Jewish residents of Kiryat Arba remained free to move about at will. "Sadly, the injustice of that wouldn't surprise me now," says Dorothy, "but at the time it shocked me deeply. It's like being rudely awakened from a long sleep."

The next shock hit Dorothy and Israel – her husband and the country – in autumn 2000, when the second intifada erupted. Intifada translates as "awakening", or "shaking off". Essentially an uprising after four decades of military occupation, it spread quickly from East Jerusalem to Palestinian towns and villages across the West Bank and inside Israel. In October, during protests in northern Israel, 13 Palestinians – or Arab-Israelis as they are called here – were shot by Israeli police.

"For me this was a turning point", says Dorothy. "Until then, as far as we knew the police had never used live ammunition against Israeli citizens. I became obsessed, as did many of us – how did we come to this, what are we doing? I started searching, looking at the early Zionist works, the congresses, the history of Palestine, the UN partition. Did you know that the Jewish population, despite being less than a third of the total in 1947 and very few of them farmers, were given more than half the land by the UN, including the best farmland and nearly all the seafront? Just like that. The Palestinians, most of them farmers, got the leftovers. How could such a thing happen?"

THE WALL

We pass the Rosh Ha'ayin industrial zone, built on land that belonged to the village of Kafr Qassem, which figures in the story of the first Palestinian we'll meet today. Hani Amer's grandfather farmed there until 1948, when advancing Israeli forces killed him as he fled with his family. For ten years Hani's grandmother and her children lived as refugees under the trees by Mas'ha village, until they were able to build a house.

We turn off the multi-lane highway onto a narrower road, pitted and cracked. "Welcome to the West Bank", says Dorothy. "When you're barely surviving, road maintenance isn't a high priority."

With Israel's web of high-speed roads, everything seems next door; my friends in Jerusalem say it's five hours' drive, top to bottom. But here in the West Bank, geography is trumped by the dictates of the occupation. Though we are almost within shouting distance of Mas'ha, we will have to twist and bump through a tangle of small roads to get there.

After their rude awakening in the second intifada, Dorothy and her husband began to join protests against the occupation, in Israel and the West Bank. Now they would stand beside Palestinians, facing Israeli soldiers and border police. The stark boundaries, us versus them, began to blur.

In 2002, a series of Palestinian suicide bomber attacks within Israel were followed by a full-scale Israeli invasion and re-occupation of the West Bank. In the belligerent atmosphere of the time, Jewish protesters were denounced in the Knesset, the Israeli parliament, as traitors and self-hating Jews. For Dorothy this was a time of deep questions. "At each step you have to decide, are you going to be intimidated, back down, keep quiet? It's tempting. But by then it felt as if we knew too much." A moment later she adds, with a sideways glance and a trace of smile, "In case you haven't noticed, Israelis aren't famous for backing down."

Early in 2003, she joined protesters in the village of Mas'ha. In February, military officers had notified villagers that the "Separation Fence" would soon arrive. Construction on the gigantic project had begun the year before. According to location and topography, its form varies from multiple layers of wire fence with electronic monitors and patrol roads to concrete slabs six to eight metres high. Supporters call it the security fence, and say it's designed to protect Israel from Palestinian terrorism. Opponents call it the segregation or apartheid wall, and say it's designed to imprison Palestinians in ghettos, to steal more of their remaining land, and to fragment Palestine, destroying any chance for a viable state. In 2004, the International Court of Justice declared that the barrier violates international law.

Dorothy has no illusions about it. "They say it's for security – nonsense. There are ways to get around it. For every Palestinian they catch in a spot-check on the road, there are hundreds who get into Israel without permits. Obviously they're not terrorists, they're desperate for work. A Palestinian friend said there are two types of force: one is the use of weapons, the other is the use of hunger. If you read first-hand accounts of the Warsaw Ghetto, it was the same thing, people would climb the wall – they were so hungry, they were willing to risk their lives. If you have seven or eight mouths to feed, you'll do whatever you have to."

As the wall cut deep into Palestinian territory to embrace the growing Israeli settlements, almost every village along the way has resisted its advance. In Mas'ha, resistance took the form of a tent camp in the path of the wall. Villagers were joined by supporters from abroad and from within Israel, including Dorothy. "In Mas'ha they've lost 92 per cent of their land, mostly olive groves, pretty much their only source of income. The villagers were told they'd be given permits to go to their groves. Bullshit. It never happened anywhere else, and it never happened here."

HOME IS PRISON

We arrive at the modest home that Hani Amer built for his family in 1972. Over it looms the wall and a mesh fence capped with razor wire. The only access to the house is through a narrow locked gate; there is no space for garden or yard.

Construction began on the nearby Elkana settlement in the early 1980s. Soon it began to swallow Mas'ha village land. Still, Hani, his wife Munira and their four children built a plant nursery behind the house, growing olive and citrus saplings, grapevines, flowers and decorative trees for sale. Elkana continued to press closer.

In 2003, military officers arrived with two choices: hand over the house for demolition – they offered a token payment – or it would be cut off from Mas'ha by the advancing fence. The Amers refused to sell, refused to move. They had learned a fundamental lesson of modern Palestinian history: if you leave your land, you will never get it back. Now they would learn what happens if you don't.

Soldiers destroyed the plant nursery. When the Amers bought a small poultry farm in a neighbouring village, soldiers prevented him from getting there until he was forced to sell it. They also demolished the Amers' own chicken coop and goat shed. Settlers stoned their house, destroyed solar panels and water tanks, and stoned the children. Now Hani works a farm that should be ten minutes' drive from here, but due to military checkpoints it can take two hours.

All these assaults occurred before the wall was built. "Through all of it I never heard Hani cry, not once," says Dorothy. "But then one day he called me in tears, he said they're going to build the fence. It nearly finished him. But he goes on – what else can he do?"

She points at a car-sized boulder that juts through the wire fence. "You can see places where Palestinians have broken through. They keep trying, but the army comes and repairs it, or they block it with huge boulders like that. In Israel we have no money for Holocaust survivors, one in three children is hungry, but there is never a shortage of funds for the occupation."

Just before we leave, Dorothy mentions that Munira Amer is probably in the house right now. "She hardly ever leaves it, fearing that if she does, the colonists will come and take it."

HANI AMER

To meet Hani where he farms, we pass through the checkpoint, unhindered. Dorothy says the soldiers don't like it when Israelis are friendly with Palestinians, but usually they don't harass Israeli cars, identifiable by their yellow licence plates. We drive down a cratered dirt road to a pile of rubble that the soldiers have bulldozed into a roadblock. A year later, this rough obstacle hardens into a guard tower.

We clamber over the barrier, continue on foot, then climb onto the roof of a small outbuilding surrounded by olive trees. At midday the air is still and baking hot. A sparse woody vine offers thin but welcome shade. Among the silver-grey olive leaves I see the precious fruit, still green but tinged with blue, a month before harvest. Then Hani arrives in a rusty Toyota that's burning oil.

He's broad and sturdy, walks heavily, supported by a stick. Black hair under a white cotton cap, moustache on a sun-browned face deeply etched by weather and history. Hard hands, a gentle grip. We set out three plastic chairs on the roof. Dorothy asks for an update on his attempts to get fuel for the diesel pump that draws water from his well. She explains, "There is no electricity here. Hani has been trying to get it for ten years now, he paid thousands of shekels to have the lines put in, but the army won't allow it. You see, there are many ways to choke people."

Hani replies in Hebrew, which he learned to negotiate with the occupier. Dorothy translates. "The fuel is available in Nablus, but to get it both the driver and the car need permits. I got both permits from the military adminstration, then they told me the driver needs a second permit to deliver here. I requested it a week ago. They said it would definitely be ready by Wednesday. *Definitely*", she repeats, with a short sardonic laugh. Hani sighs.

I ask how long he has farmed. "All my life," he says, "like my father, my grandfather and before. The Israelis make it harder all the time. I'm only 51, but I've seen more destruction in my lifetime than you would in 1,000 years living somewhere else. The only thing that doesn't change is the olive trees. They are still here, thanks to Allah."

What does he grow? "Olives, figs, apples, grapes, avocados, lemons, clementines, peppers, cucumbers, tomatoes." Where does he sell them? "Nablus, Qalqilya. It's hard to get there – you need permits, and sometimes you get them, sometimes you don't, so transport is very expensive. With the fence it's also difficult to get workers for the farm, often they can't get here."

An ancient farmer in a faded grey *djellabah* emerges from the olive grove, on a wagon pulled by a donkey. "*Marhaba* (hello)", he and Hani call to each other. He needs water. Hani replies that he doesn't have any, but he's working on it.

I ask Hani if water is getting scarce here, as I've heard. He nods. "For the past ten years it's drier than it used to be – last winter there was hardly any rain. A few more years like this and there won't be any water left to pump." Are there no other sources? "There used to be a river by Rosh Ha'ayin with lots of water, but it's been diverted by the Israeli water company, and now it's barely a trickle."

Here the weather is shared, but not the water. According to a 2009 study by the World Bank, Israel controls all the water sources, but allocates to Palestinians only 20 per cent of the water. It is forbidden for Palestinians to drill new wells, forcing them to buy water from the Israeli national water company, Mekorot. The World Health Organization reports that water consumption in many parts of the West Bank has fallen below basic needs.

Dorothy tells Hani that we have to move on. She wants to bring a group from Austria to meet him next week, would that be all right? "*Beseder*", he says, Hebrew for "okay". I ask him, does he get tired of telling his story to foreigners year after year? "It's easier for me", he says. "This way I get my pain out, instead of keeping it to myself."

ISSA SOUF

The broken road into Hares is blocked by a pile of bulldozed rubble. "You never know", says Dorothy. "The army closes and opens roads without warning, at their whim." We circle the village, eventually finding an even rougher track. In the village she calls out "*Marhaba*" to boys and men we pass on the street. "It's not for my safety", she says. "I don't feel unsafe here. It's to give them the feeling that I'm not here to do any harm. Usually the only Israelis they see are soldiers or armed settlers." Some of the men return the *Marhaba*, or other words that neither of us can translate.

A tall, grey concrete tower overlooks the village, with dark window-slits at the top. The army is watching.

Issa Souf's house has two storeys, the upper one under construction – tools and bags of cement sit by the entrance. Issa welcomes us into a cool, slate-floored vestibule, greeting Dorothy in Hebrew and me in capable English. He's tall and well-built, clean-shaven, with thinning brown hair. A small wide-eyed girl stares at us from behind Issa's wheelchair, and a young boy who could be five or six grabs at his hand. Issa speaks quietly to him, and the boy disappears into an inner room, followed shortly by his sister.

Born here in 1971, Issa Souf trained as a journalist, then switched to physical education. When the second intifada erupted, Israeli military raids escalated. "The situation here was very dangerous", he says. "The settlers and the army cut down more than 3,000 olive trees, they killed seven people from the village and wounded more than 50. We were not allowed to drive or walk on the settlers' roads. We couldn't go to work, to the doctor, we couldn't go anywhere without a permit. Me, my brother and my friends, we said, 'Look, it would be easy to take a gun, go to the settlers' road and shoot.' But life is a gift from Allah, and no one has the right to end it. Also we knew that if we did that, we would either be killed or arrested, and our message would end, we would be forgotten like the 11,000 Palestinian prisoners in Israeli jails. To keep our message alive, we chose non-violent resistance." They invited Israelis to join them. "We hosted them for many nights in my house and my brother's house. All of us ate from the same plate, and we slept in one room together."

Issa also invited international media to report what was happening to Hares. "Israel has occupied not just our land, but also – this is what I think – the brains of western people through the media. They show the Israelis always as victims, they never show how the Palestinian people suffer. This is why we invited CNN, BBC, to come and see for themselves how it is here. We gave them complete independence to photograph what they saw, with no limits from us."

Did they come? "They came, yes, but they didn't report what they saw. I joined CNN for a trip to one farm. At the time the Israelis didn't allow Palestinians to pick their own olives. While the car was stopped, two settlers came and shouted at us. The reporter said, 'It's ok, we're CNN', and they went away. He shot all this with his camera. But when I saw his report, there was no mention of the settlers, no footage – they hid that. From that time, I lost trust for those media."

BE HUMAN, PLEASE

On the morning of 15 May 2001, Issa's brother called to say an army squad had just entered Hares, and they were firing tear-gas grenades. Issa ran to gather children off the street. "I heard automatic weapon fire behind me, tack tack tack, I don't know what happened but I fell down. Two soldiers stood over me, one of them with his boot on my chest. They shouted at me to stand up. I couldn't. I tried to ask for help, but nothing worked. It became hard to breathe, I was losing consciousness. I think I whispered to the soldiers, 'Be human, please help me, I'm going to die.' When I woke up in the hospital, the first words I remember were from the physician to my brother: 'If he lives, he will live in a wheelchair.'" Issa's delivery is muted, almost flat.

From his medical records he learned that he had been shot with a dum-dum bullet, which penetrated his right shoulder and exploded in the spinal column. A British colonial invention, these bullets are designed to produce a wider, more damaging wound than regular bullets. Since their use is prohibited by international law, Issa sued the army. As is their custom, Dorothy tells me later, the military authorities settled quietly out of court, providing the means to make Issa's house wheelchair accessible and to purchase a suitable vehicle for his tranport.

I ask him how he's doing. "Thanks to God I have my life. It's not 100 per cent, but it goes on. The treatment is long and hard, until now in Jordan, in Britain and here." Dorothy asks if there's been any progress with Physicians for Human Rights. They are trying to arrange rehabilitiation treatment for Issa at an Israeli hospital. "Until now there is no decision", he replies.

Dorothy explains, "He has to go to Israel because he can't get a permit to go to the Palestinian hospital in Nablus. It can't be more than 20 or 30 kilometres from here, but he would either need to get a special permit for his own car, which they won't give him, or he would have to change cars three times to get through the checkpoints." He adds, "It is hard to do that with a wheelchair."

HALF JUSTICE

Despite everything that's happened here, Issa still believes in peace and hopes to instil this belief in others, especially the children of Hares. "What else can I do?" he says. "We have to find some way to live together – without walls. To do this there are only two choices, one state or two. But Israel refuses both. They say they support two states, but they do everything on the ground to make it impossible. I keep asking myself, do they really want peace, or do they just say that for the outside, for the Americans?" He leaves the question hanging.

In March 2009, hundreds of soldiers invaded the village again, and arrested more than 150 people. Most were blindfolded and bound, some beaten. When witnesses from the International Women's Peace Service asked why, an army officer replied that they wanted to update their database on the village.

How do you promote peace and non-violence among people who have to endure so much routine brutality? Issa looks at me steadily, silent for a moment.

"I think peace is not something you get by pushing a button. War you can have by pushing a button, but not peace. Peace comes as a result of justice, which you have to build. But the situation here is so complex, we have to work double to build justice. For complete justice, you would have to transfer from here all Israeli people except the ones who were here before 1948, like the Jews in Nablus, like the Christians in Bethlehem. But now we don't think about complete justice any more. Israel is a fact. Palestinians are a fact. That leaves us with only one choice, half justice – we accept them to live here, they accept us to live here. We live here together, in equality. With equality you can have justice, and with justice you can have peace. Is this possible? I don't know. But I also don't know that it is not possible. So I must live as if it is possible."

The afternoon is fading, and we still have one more stop. As we walk outside into the hot light, Issa's smiling face recedes into shadow. I feel a pang of shame at my freedom, such a luxury here. "Of course," says Dorothy, "we all feel that."

LORDS OF THE LAND

Our last stop will be Ariel, a showcase for the Israeli settlement enterprise in Palestine. But first we break our fast, at an outdoor felafel café and grocery store next to the Ariel security barrier. We order hummus with pitta, and a tomato-cucumber-parsley salad. The hummus is fresh and lemony, ringed by a little moat of local olive oil. The owners and staff here are Palestinian, the customers Israeli. "This is how it could be here", says Dorothy, "if only the Israelis would allow it."

At the Ariel barrier we are waved through by private security guards in black T-shirts and khaki trousers, the usual assault rifles across their chests.

Ariel is built on a mountain. It was founded in 1977 as a stategic outpost between the coast and the Jordan River. As it happens with outposts, caravans housing 40 Zionist families grew into a modern city with a college, shopping, sports and community centres, and its own industrial park, the hub of an expanding bloc that already incorporates a dozen settlements housing close to 40,000 people and covering over 120 square kilometres, all of it built on Palestinian land. Its east-west stretch also serves as a bulwark between two areas nominally under full or partial Palestinian control.

Because the area is designated a strategic national priority, Israelis are offered generous government subsidies to move here, including lower taxes and subsidized mortgages. Driving slowly through wide, curving streets of tidy, gated townhouses, parks and shops, we see signs in Hebrew and Russian. Dorothy tells me that almost half the residents here are Russian immigrants.

She stops the car on a quiet street near the crest of the mountain. The air up here is breezy and clear. To the west, Tel Aviv smog blurs the horizon. We look down on a range of hills, distant villages scattered on the lower slopes. Directly below are the grey roofs of Marda, a Palestinian farming village of about 2,000 residents. Over three decades they've watched their land shrink, confiscated piece by piece for settlement construction, a fenced road for the exclusive use of settlers, and the wide swathe of the separation barrier, which snakes into the West Bank to incorporate Ariel and its satellites. Like many other villages, Dorothy tells me, Marda is subject to nocturnal invasions by both settlers and the army.

"Who wouldn't want to live up here?" she says. "Imagine how easily you could come to believe that you really are lords of the land."

On the wide, smooth road back to Tel Aviv, both of us are silent with our own thoughts. Suddenly Dorothy takes in a sharp breath, startling me. "When we created Israel," she says, "the idea was to have a place where we Jews would be safe. But 61 years later, after so many wars and battles and campaigns, so many killed and injured, what we've created is probably the least safe place on earth for Jews. I think that is so sad. Don't you?"

2
My Way to Fight

From the shaded courtyard of the Freedom Theatre we walk into the Jenin refugee camp. With no gate or sign, it is just another a neighbourhood in Jenin city, though more densely packed, and in some streets the pavement is more broken.

"Thirty-seven degrees today", says Mustafa Staiti, our host and guide. "Let's walk in the shade." Mustafa teaches photography and film at the Freedom Theatre. He's 23, tall, in black T-shirt and jeans, cool sunglasses perched in a mass of curly black hair. As he talks, a smile often starts on his face and plays there for a moment.

Four guests tag along in his wake: a trio from Belgium – videographer, theatre-maker, social worker – and a writer from Canada.

The sloping streets are almost empty due to midday heat and Ramadan, the Islamic holy month. People will come out later to walk, when the sun goes down and they've finished the meal that breaks the fast.

The streets in this part of the camp seem unusually wide for cities here. "It wasn't like this before the invasion", Mustafa explains. "These used to be alleys, but when they were rebuilt they made them wide enough for tanks to come through. If they are narrow like before, the tanks will break the walls of houses again."

MUSTAFA'S LANDSCAPE

Established in 1953, Jenin refugee camp houses some 18,000 Palestinian refugees in less than half a square kilometre. Almost half of them are under 18, the third generation to live without secure homes in their own land. The camp was originally intended to be temporary, the refugees to return to their homes in what had been Palestine. As part of the West Bank, Jenin was occupied by Israel in 1967, and eventually handed over to the Palestinian Authority in 1996. Claiming that the refugee camp had produced suicide bombers, the Israeli army reinvaded it in 2002, leaving a substantial portion of the camp in ruins.

We have arrived at the centre of it, our guide tells us. The large building on our left is the UNRWA (United Nations Relief and Works Agency) health centre. It too was originally meant to be temporary. "UNRWA takes care of health, education and food supplies for people in the camp", Mustafa says. "It's not enough, but at least it exists." The Belgian videographer asks him to clarify. "There are not enough medicines or qualified doctors. In school, there are 45 students in each classroom, which is not good for education. And food supplies are enough to stay alive, but not enough to feed a whole family."

The rural Canadian asks if people can grow their own food. "There is no space," says Mustafa, "so they have to buy at the market. The Jenin area used to be agricultural, but now there is not enough water. Even Jenin city has a lot of problems getting water, they have to buy it back from the Israelis who stole it. We are not allowed to make wells deep enough to get the water, it is only for the settlements – so you see huge fucking swimming pools in the settlement, and in the village next to it they cannot take showers." He says this calmly, without discernible heat.

We arrive at what Mustafa calls the zero area. The small concrete block houses look newer here. "It was completely destroyed in the Israeli invasion", he says. "This was the last point for Palestinian resistance. All of the fighters still alive collected here, then the Israelis surrounded the area and started to destroy the houses, roads, everything, zeroed to the ground."

This is Mustafa's landscape, as familiar to him as forest and meadow are to me back home.

Three boys in their early teens walk by, watching us. Mustafa greets them, "*Salaam aleikum*" ("peace be with you"). Two boys return the greeting with nods, but the third says "Fuck you." Mustafa smiles. "He thinks you are Jewish. Some people think any foreigner who comes here is Mossad [the Israeli spy agency] or CIA; in any case, the enemy."

Between 2000 and 2004, 61 children were killed in Jenin, 676 in the Occupied Palestinian Territories, and some 14,000 injured. Close to 5,000 have seen their homes demolished by Israeli forces. Mustafa is a survivor, his life framed by occupation, resistance and invasion. Born a refugee in 1986, he has witnessed both intifadas. In the second, which erupted in 2000, he wanted to be a fighter, but was considered too young.

No doubt Mustafa has given his account of the Israeli invasion many times, but still it sounds freshly felt: "Many here wanted to fight and even die for the camp, for Palestine. But for our own safety my family went to our relatives' house in Jenin city. We were a lot of people together in one house, with no water, no food. We saw helicopters, tanks, bombs, and shooting, 24 hours a day. This was the hardest time in my life – this camp is my home, my friends are there, my life is there. You don't know what's happening, who is dying. Every day my father blamed himself, 'Why didn't I join the fight, instead I stay home like a woman.' But he's old, I'm sure he wouldn't last a second in the fight. After they allowed us back into the camp, we saw that big parts were destroyed, it looked like an earthquake. We saw bodies burned, children looking for their parents, people lost, homes destroyed, including my aunt's, but not mine."

As it happens after catastrophe, people began immediately to sift through the rubble, and rebuild as they could. "You have to live", Mustafa says. "When the Israelis invaded the camp, they wanted not just to kill people but to kill our spirit too, they wanted us to feel there is nothing we can do against this superman. But the camp held out for many days in front of them, and the only way they could destroy it was by bulldozers. After that I felt I had to do something. Some want to fight by gun but also there are people who want to fight by their intelligence, their talent. This is what I am doing at the Freedom Theatre."

CULTURAL INTIFADA

The foundations for the Freedom Theatre sprang from the life and passion of a Jewish woman, Arna Mer, who had already fought to establish a homeland for her own people. Born in 1929 to Jewish parents in Palestine, she served in an elite brigade during the 1948 war, then carried on fighting for freedom and justice until she died of cancer in 1995. Following the 1967 war, Arna Mer Khamis (she had married Saliba Khamis, the Palestinian secretary of the Israeli Communist Party) was imprisoned several times for protesting the Israeli occupation of the West Bank and Gaza.

During the first intifada (the popular uprising that swept through the Occupied Territories in 1987) she established the Care and Learning project to advocate for Palestinian children in Israeli prisons, and to provide education when the military occupiers shut down all Palestinian schools for two years. Care and Learning opened four children's houses in Jenin, offering a range of creative outlets to mitigate the trauma of conflict and occupation. After

Arna Mer Khamis won the 1993 Right Living Award (a people's alternative to the Nobel Peace Prize, also based in Sweden), she established the Stone Theatre in Jenin, working with her son Juliano, an Israeli actor-director. In the 2002 invasion, Israeli armoured bulldozers demolished the theatre; several former acting students of Arna's died fighting in the resistance or in suicide attacks, and others were imprisoned. Arna's life and theirs are featured in the documentary *Arna's Children*, co-directed by Juliano Mer Khamis.

In 2005 Juliano abandoned a prominent acting career in Israel, returned to Jenin, and worked with Swedish-Israeli musician Dror Feiler, Swedish-Jewish peace activist Jonatan Stanczak, and a team of Palestinians, Israelis and internationals, to launch the Freedom Theatre. The peace/justice movement in Israel–Palestine is a relatively small world. I met Dror Feiler's 80-year-old Israeli mother, Pnina, working as a nurse in a mobile clinic in the Tulkarem refugee camp (see Chapter 9). Now operations manager of the theatre, but currently in Sweden to meet with funders, Jonatan Stanczak organized today's encounter with Mustafa.

The Freedom Theatre aims to provide young people of both sexes – a conscious, even provocative choice in a male-dominated society – with a safe space to express themselves, and to develop skills, self-knowledge and confidence through art-work. It also offers people of the camp and surrounding areas the fantasy and humour of theatre as temporary relief from the constant burden of military occupation, poverty and isolation. Its ambitious programme includes theatre, dance, circus, theatre training, drama therapy, film and video, photography, English classes, an online magazine, a summer camp, festivals and field trips. In 2008, more than 16,000 children took part in activities at the theatre.

Before the Belgians joined us for the camp tour, I sat awhile with Mustafa Staiti in a small film-editing suite at the theatre. He smoked. With sunglasses up in his dark hair, he looked very much the cinéaste. I asked how he had found his way here. He knew of Arna and Juliano through his mother, he says, who worked with Arna in the Stone Theatre. Four months after the new theatre opened, Mustafa signed on as accountant. He explains, "I studied management informations systems at university, but later I realized that accounting was not what I want to do with my life. I want to work in art, especially film-making. I learned from Juliano, and film-makers who came here to volunteer, also through the internet and books."

What does he do here? "I give courses for children, working mostly with film and still photography", he replies. "We've done exhibitions, and a lot of short films. I love theatre, but I believe cinema is an easier way to talk to people about things. You have to get people to come to the theatre, but with cinema you can go to their homes. Cinema is my way to send messages, my way to fight. We can't fight tanks, but we can educate ourselves to tell the world the truth about who we are. This is cultural intifada."

Yearning to share their reality with outsiders is a theme I encountered often in occupied Palestine. People who live here are constantly shocked by the gap between what they see on the ground and what they see on satellite TV, images and information beamed to viewers around the world.

Given the opportunity, what messages would Mustafa like to send? He lights another cigarette, takes a deep drag, then replies, "Here in the refugee camp we live in a small, closed culture. First, I want to send a message to people living here about woman oppression, about children oppression, and how to deal with each other in a better way. Through films, I want to show that girls have the right to ride a bicycle, go to college, go to work. Also I want to send a message to people around the world: 'Hello, we are human beings.' People from outside, in Europe and America, they think we're not normal, we're strange, maybe less than human. They learn it from the media. But we are human beings. 'We want to live. We are just like you, we have intelligence, we have talents.' These are things I want to say with short films."

To pursue his dream, Mustafa faced a series of obstacles. First, his parents' disappointment that he chose film over university – this he believes he has overcome. Next, he has to deal with his fellow inmates in the camp. "People here are becoming more religious", he says. "They are taking religion as a wall to protect them against the world. It can make them blind, unable to see that theatre, art is a way to fight. They are not used to seeing art, and people on stage. Dancing, mixing girls with boys, oh, that's bad. We wanted to make a short film about a girl, she dreams of riding a bicycle. We had to shoot that scene in the camp, but they stopped it, they said bad things to me in front of the girl, and sent me back to the theatre. Then they talked about me and the theatre in the mosque – this guy who wants to film a girl riding a bicycle, what the hell is he doing? So the film isn't finished. Every day we have challenges like this."

While Mustafa shepherded our little group through the refugee camp, a few young men tossed remarks at us that didn't seem friendly. Mustafa told me later that quite often he gets taunted for his long, unruly hair. "Sissy-boy", they call him. All the young males I saw here have uniformly close-cropped hair. Though I saw several pairs of adolescent men walking hand-in-hand – male intimacy is common and acceptable here, before and after marriage – a man with longer hair is called a sissy-boy.

What about the other wall that people have to endure, the occupation? "Many youth live here in the camp, and they don't leave", Mustafa says. "To go even to Ramallah, it's a big thing, only 40 kilometres, but it could take five, six hours each way. The checkpoints make walls in our minds, it's hard to get out. You want to see other things, to open your mind, but you can't. Also, you don't know when the soldiers will come into the camp, shooting and arresting people. We have drama therapy sessions here, so the children can open their minds and feel better about themselves, but when they go home to sleep, they hear Israelis shooting, and they forget everything they've learned here, they go out and throw stones at the Israelis, then they come back to us the next day at zero. This is something not easy to deal with."

A NEW GATE

At the theatre I also met Rawand Warqawi, a volunteer who teaches English here. She wears jeans, a comfortable shirt, and two layers of headscarf; brown under, and a decorative fabric over it. Rather shy, and unsure of her own English, Rawand speaks quietly.

Born in 1976, she was still quite young when the first intifada broke out. "I saw the soldiers with their guns and their tanks," she recalls, "and the Palestinian fighters with stones, only stones. Many people were killed, many injured and put in prison, they had no way to defend themselves. This is when I learned about the Israeli occupation."

I asked her to tell me about her education. "I studied English at Al-Quds Open University, it has a branch in Jenin. I dreamed of living as a student, to go to lectures, to have a nice time with your friends at the university. Unfortunately it didn't happen, due to the invasion. We couldn't go to classes or exams because of the curfew, and checkpoints everywhere. The curfew would last for three days, four days. You couldn't go outside, you couldn't open a window or a door. The electricity was often cut. You couldn't get any food or visit your neighbour – if a soldier sees you, he shoots you. My neighbour, an old man, father of five daughters, not a fighter, he opened the window, curious to see what was happening outside, and a soldier shot him in the head, killed him. This is how we lived."

Despite the occupation, life goes on here. Still pursuing her English studies, one day Rawand went to Nablus for some research. It's about 20 miles from Jenin, a little over 30 kilometres. "On my way back to Jenin," she says, "the soldiers called a curfew when I was on the way – sometimes you know there will be curfew, but when you are travelling you don't know. They told me I couldn't go to Jenin. I said to the soldier, 'What shall I do, I have to go to Jenin.' He refused to let me pass. 'Then I will go back to Nablus.' He refused. So I started to cry and shout, 'I can't stay here, please let me go home!' After a long time, they allowed me to go."

Does the occupation have other effects? Rawand nods. "The economic situation is very bad. My father works as a mechanic, he has a shop to fix cars. Before the second intifada his work was very good, he had Arab customers from Israel, even some Jewish people came to him. But now everything is closed, they can't come. We are a big family, six sisters and three brothers, so now my father works just to bring bread, nothing else. Every day he opens his shop so people can see that he's still here."

Before she came to the Freedom Theatre, Rawand worked as a painter with a man who also acted in the theatre. He invited her to see a play that had just opened. "This play was unique and amazing, and I wanted to work here. But what can I do here? I talked with Juliano, he said 'Maybe you can help students to write and speak English.'"

Why English? "English is the second language in most of the world," she says, "so if you want to speak to the world, you need English. This is a way for us to pass through the wall. It is important for us to tell our stories, to tell people about our situation here. They hear only the Israeli story, that they are the victims and we are the criminals."

Who does she teach, and how? "I focus on little girls, because they are very weak in English, but they want to study it. I show them how to read, how to write the alphabet – by singing, movements, drawing, and sometimes we use the internet, to make it fun to learn. It takes a long time, but I'm really patient." She laughs quietly, looking a little embarrassed.

Perhaps to put her more at ease, I comment, "It's important to laugh, isn't it?"

"Oh yes", Rawand replies. "This is life, we say, and what's done is done. So we smile, we laugh, we work hard to keep ourselves and build our community. That's what we do here at the theatre. We have to open a new gate between Palestinian people and Jewish people. We used to work with them, live with them. We need to do that again."

WE HAVE A GIFT

Fans turn lazily over an unfurnished room carpeted in grey. With a high ceiling, it's an airy, open space for imagination to bloom. Present are two women and six men, in their late teens to early twenties. The men wear T-shirts and loose trousers; one woman a black head-covering and long, tailored robe; the other a rumpled orange tracksuit with white stripes. All are barefoot.

They wait in varying degrees of restless motion. In mid-Ramadan they've been fasting since daybreak, and today in Jenin it's close to 40 degrees. Sweat slides down my back, and I'm just watching.

Two acting teachers from Sweden enter quietly, Beatriz and Jan, also barefoot, probably in their fifties, wiry and smiling. When I ask permission to observe and record the class, Jan replies, appropriately, "We will ask the students." With a word – *naam* (yes) – or a nod and a smile at me, they consent.

They arrange themselves in a circle. With a flutter of his hands Jan launches a silent invisible message across the void. The head-covered woman receives it in cupped hands, and hands it off to her neighbour. He lofts it across the circle to another. The pace picks up, the message becomes more urgent. To keep it alive, each member of the circle has to be fully alert and responsive. One lobs it, a hot potato, another releases it softly, setting a bird free to fly. After a few minutes Jan catches the message, enfolds it to his chest, and lays it gently to rest on the floor.

In an old converted stone house, the Freedom Theatre school overlooks the refugee camp. It offers a three-year study programme in all aspects of theatre, funded by the Swedish International Development Cooperation Agency, and Art Action, the philanthropic arm of an investment firm based in Singapore.

The young woman in black translates back and forth between the Swedish trainers' English and the students' Arabic. Later I learn that she is Petra Barghouthi, drama therapy instructor. In a short video made at the theatre, she explains, "Jenin refugee camp is a conservative and traditional community. They still believe that if a person is suffering from psychological difficulties, it is something that is a shame, they have to go and heal, to ask for help even. So drama therapy is a gentle way, an indirect way to bring people to deal with their difficulties and problems without, you know, the classical way of going to a psychiatrist." A young man says in the video, "I pull the fear out of me so I can be free."

During the break, I chat with a few students who speak some English. One man tells me he has an internet friend in Canada. "I can live with the Israelis," he says, "no problem. If only they would live with us."

The woman in the orange tracksuit agrees to a quick interview in the few minutes left before class resumes. We sit on the stone balcony, a light breeze soft and pleasant on overheated skin.

Born here in 1989, Daana came to the school after she saw a friend perform at the Freedom Theatre. "At first I said it's impossible, this thing in my country, in Jenin. But then I saw my friend in this play, and I found it very exciting. My friend told me I too can join if I want, so I came quickly here."

Almost as quickly, she landed her first role, as the Juliet of Shakespeare's famous star-crossed lovers. The Freedom Theatre mixes Palestinian plays with international fare, translated into Arabic and adapted to local realities. It's not hard to imagine the relevance here of a play about young lovers undone by the furies of hatred. "It's a very nice play", says Daana, her eyes glowing.

What does she hope to accomplish here? "I wish to become a big actor, to be famous, and to know everybody." She laughs, blushing a little, then continues, "I wish to change the mind of people in my country, to change how they think about things, like how a girl cannot do anything, but a boy can do everything. I would like very much to change this."

Will it be difficult? "Yes," she replies, "very difficult. In the school we are just two girls, me and my friend Zatour. Boys can come here, but nobody lets the girls come. At first my mother said no, she did not like this idea, because I am a girl and if I do this, people will talk about me. But when she came to see *Romeo and Juliet*, she was surprised and very happy. Then she told me, 'Every day you must go to this school!'" Daana laughs with delight, and so do I.

I wonder if there is anything she might like to tell others in the wider world. She nods vigorously. "Yes, of course. People outside Palestine, in Europe or America, they don't know about us – what is Palestine, the reality here, the things that happen to us. I wish everyone to know." On CNN, Daana sees the same wash of images we see: as Rawand said, no matter what happens here, the Palestinians are always to blame, the Israelis eternal victims.

Her fellow students are heading inside to resume class. Quickly I ask, if she had the opportunity, what would she tell other people about Palestinians? Without hesitation she replies, "I wish for all people to know us. I want to tell them we are a good people, we have a gift, and if we have some support we can do something big in our life."

Sometimes in my work, when I invite so much candour from others it seems unfair to hide behind the role of perpetual questioner. Especially here, where so many have been interrogated. So I ask Daana, "Is there anything that you want to ask me?"

"Um", she says, hesitating. I imagine her gathering confidence as she steps onto the stage. "I want to know what you will do with this interview."

Good question. "I'm writing a book about people who are trying to make peace in this land. In the west, in Canada, we don't hear much about that. I want people to hear voices like yours."

A smile lights her face. "Thank you", she says. "This is what we need, for somebody to hear our voice. Really, thank you." We shake hands, and she returns to class.

For the next exercise, Beatriz explains that each actor must convey to the audience that the open space is a room which he or she is trying to decide whether or not to rent. No words, just the space, their bodies and a few props – a pair of sandals, a chair, a hat. "We need to see you assessing the room", she says. "We need to see you making a decision." Petra Barghouthi translates.

The young man with the internet pal in Canada volunteers to go first. He enters, sniffs the air, looks rather displeased, tries on the hat, examines the chair carefully, and with a slight shake of the head, he exits.

"What happened there?" Beatriz asks the students. "What did you see?"

While they respond, my mind goes to Daana's parting thanks. It strikes me as extraordinarily gracious. All I'm giving here is respectful attention. If gifts were exchanged, hers was the greater – her young face glowing with the prospect of what might still be possible.

Just before I have to leave, the students read poems they've selected. They have the text in Arabic, the trainers an English translation. Jan tells them their task is to read the poem aloud – to *express* it – while maintaining contact with the audience.

Sitting cross-legged and leaning to his attentive audience, two Swedes and one Canadian, a student *expresses* in Arabic a poem by Mahmoud Darwish, who died just a month ago, beloved here in Palestine and renowned abroad. I've seen his photo postered like a rock star's on walls throughout the West Bank. In how many cultures, I wonder, does a poet become an icon?

FREE YOUR MIND

One night in April, 2009, someone set fire to the main door of the Freedom Theatre. The door was destroyed, but apparently it prevented the fire from spreading into the building. Three weeks earlier, a previous arson attempt on the theatre failed; on the same night in Jenin, the Al-Kamandjati Music Centre was destroyed by fire. In both cases the Palestinian Authority police were informed, but to date no suspects have been identified.

As Mustafa Staiti knows, not everyone in the Jenin refugee camp is a fan. The theatre's recent high-energy adaptation of George Orwell's famous novel, *Animal Farm*, played to full houses every night. But it also touched a very sensitive nerve. Though originally about the corruption of revolutionaries in Stalinist Russia, when transferred to the context of Palestine it raised provocative questions about the current Palestinian leadership, and collaboration with the Israeli occupiers.

Israeli army incursions continue here. Mustafa says people are relieved when the armoured jeeps show up only once a week instead of every second night. Sometimes the soldiers shoot, and nearly always they arrest someone; usually someone young, the Freedom Theatre's primary constituency.

On our tour of the camp, the Belgian theatre-maker asked Mustafa how the soldiers treat the Theatre. He replied, "Sometimes when Jonatan goes back to his home, they stop him and interrogate him, then they let him go. But they didn't enter the theatre, not yet. They know there are always foreigners here, people who might call their consulates, so the Israelis don't want to make a big mess."

From its inception, the Freedom Theatre has rented a building from UNRWA. Now that it has outgrown the available space, land has been purchased and plans are evolving to build a new theatre. Building work will begin as soon as sufficient funding has been guaranteed for the project.

Walking through the refugee camp, on bullet-pocked walls we see another model for young people in Jenin, posters of martyrs, fighters killed in battle with the Israelis. Some of the posters are sun-bleached, some half stripped away, some freshly applied.

*   *   *

Our tour concludes at a small graveyard, where we stand in the welcome shade of an olive tree. The graves follow the slope of the land, descending in a series of shallow terraces. "From that step down," says Mustafa, "those people were all killed during the Israeli invasion, 64 of them. Twenty are fighters, the rest civilians. At first all of them were buried in one hole, there was no time to do anything else. But then later they had to be re-buried so their families could communicate with them. Some of them are in pieces, some of them burned." He lets out a soft sigh. I hear it only because I'm standing by his side. "Up there," he concludes, pointing at another terrace, "it's people killed since the invasion."

Earlier I asked Mustafa if he could imagine an end to the Israeli occupation in his lifetime. "This is a hard question to answer", he replied. He took a deep drag on his cigarette. Suddenly I felt foolish for asking it. What can he possibly say?

"Maybe", he says. "Nothing is impossible. But something scares me about this question. Okay, if the occupation is gone, if we got freedom, then what are we going to do? We have been occupied so long, we don't imagine ourselves without it, without being the occupied. It is important for us to think about this – what are we going to do after the occupation? If we get Palestine back, will we have an Islamic country? Will we have a Fatah country? What exactly will we have?"

In the meantime, I asked, how does he find freedom behind the wall? "Which wall?" he asks, with a slight smile. "There is a wall outside, of course, but there is also another one here in our heads." He taps his forehead. "I have in my editing suite a sign: 'Prison is a state of mind; to free Palestine, free your mind.' I read it every day."

3
The Jerusalem Syndrome

In a quiet, time-roughened voice, Meir Margalit asks what I mean by "a just peace". I had told him I'm writing about people who work for a just peace here in Israel and Palestine. "Do you mean Oslo," he asks, "or beyond?" In a context where the word "peace" can mean almost anything, even an excuse for war, it's a reasonable question. "Beyond", I replied. "Far beyond."

We're sitting in the living room of the compact apartment that Meir shares with his wife Sulie and their three children, in the Talbiyyeh neighbourhood of Jerusalem. Before 1948, its tree-shaded streets were lined with elegant villas and lush gardens of wealthy Palestinians. Some of the original residences were demolished, some restored with Moorish and Arabic detail intact. Meir's plain, sturdy limestone building was constructed in the 1960s by Histadrut, the Israeli trade union federation. "They wanted to create cheap, nice housing for workers", says Meir. Crowded with potted plants, their small balcony overlooks a courtyard of trees and shrubs that help to moderate the September heat.

I've caught Meir on the run, between an early morning attempt to thwart the demolition of a Palestinian home in East Jerusalem, and a strategy session for his upcoming municipal election campaign. It is this duality of role, as activist and politician, that drew me to Meir Margalit.

EVERY IDEOLOGY HAS A PRICE

Born Argentinian in 1952, Meir visited Israel in 1968 as a student, then made aliyah – the Zionist dream of ascent to the promised land – in 1972. "It was clear to me that Israel was the only place where Jews could live in safety, and sooner or later all the Jewish people must come."

Three months after he arrived, he joined a Nahal brigade in the Israeli army. Launched in 1948, these Young Pioneer units combined military service with the establishment of new agricultural settlements, usually in isolated locations on the periphery. Their job was to extend and defend new Israeli territory. Meir helped found the Netzarim settlement in the Gaza Strip.

I asked Meir what this dual role of soldier-builder had meant to him. "First I was a soldier", he says. "But for me this was not a job or a duty, it was a mission. I had always dreamed of being a pioneer like the early Zionists, so I was very proud that I had the opportunity to do this for the state of Israel."

In October 1973, Meir's second year in the army, war erupted. Egyptian and Syrian forces advanced rapidly in the early days from the north and southeast, suddenly putting the Gaza settlements on the front lines. Meir was gravely wounded, enough to require hospitalization for several months. He speaks cryptically of a subtle but profound shift that occurred during his long recovery. "I began to understand that every ideology has a price," he says, "and the price of the Greater Israel ideology is very expensive. The war was a catalyst for that."

The horror of war, especially a war that Israel had almost lost, sparked new growth in the small, fragmented Israeli peace movement, which Israelis often refer to as the left. The troubled young veteran was interested, but leery. "All my friends were on the right," Meir explains, "so it was difficult to move from there. For a year I stayed on the right, even after I was already convinced that it will take us to disaster."

He joined a peace group at university, then a new organization, Peace Now, founded in 1978 during peace talks between Israel and Egypt. Meir describes himself in those days as "an ordinary activist" who attended demonstrations against new settlements, and engaged in solidarity activities with Palestinians whose land had been confiscated. As his commitment deepened, he began to find Peace Now too moderate, and in 1998 he helped establish the Israeli Committee Against House Demolitions (ICAHD). Its website describes it as "a non-violent, direct-action group originally established to oppose and resist Israeli demolition of Palestinian houses in the Occupied Territories." As the struggle has broadened and intensified, so have ICAHD's activities.

In parallel, Meir joined one of the three small left-wing parties that later merged into Meretz. Eventually he headed its Jerusalem branch, and won election to the city's municipal council. After a four-year break, he's about to run for office again on the Meretz ticket.

What was it that moved him from right to left? He looks at me for a moment, thinking and, I imagine, translating his thoughts into English. "Maybe it's something I learned from my father, a survivor from the Holocaust – the concept that there are injustices we cannot accept. Maybe it was the feeling that we do to the Palestintians something similar that the *goyim*, the Gentiles, did to the Jewish people in Europe before the Holocaust. It reminds me of stories I heard from my father's childhood and about Polish Jews in the nineteenth and early twentieth centuries. Maybe this opened my eyes to understand that something is wrong in our attitude, our ideology, the way that we manage the state. It became clear for me that this was not the state where I wanted to live, it was not the state of the Bible prophets that I had dreamed of."

Later, in another strand of his life, Meir wrote a PhD thesis about people whose Zionist dream had faded earlier – Jews who left Palestine in the British colonial period, the 1920s to 1948. After years of research, the thesis that emerged was not warmly received. "It was very shocking for the historical establishment here", says Meir. "They are only interested in who came here, not who left. At the Hebrew University in Jerusalem they refused to approve my thesis. I had to go to Haifa University, where the history department is younger and more open-minded." Finally his thesis was approved in 2005, and to his other, more grounded credentials, Meir added Doctor of Philosophy.

THE RIGHT WORDS

As in my own country, in Israel I encountered activists who have abandoned party politics as too fatally corrupt to salvage, and now devote their energies to struggles on the ground. Since Meir continues to function in both realms, I asked him what he thinks can still be gained through the machinery of government.

"I feel that the conflict with the Palestinians is a political conflict," he says, "so the solution must be political. This is why I entered politics. On other hand, I also agree that the conflict is more complicated than it looks, and the political arena is not enough to bring a solution. If you are just a politician, you don't spend time on activities that won't bring more votes to the party. You may not do humanitarian activity in the South Hebron, with the Bedouins who live there – that is not something that will help us to win votes in Israel. Also you may not use words that voters don't like, words like apartheid and ethnic cleansing. But in the movement you can use the right words."

The ICAHD operates on three fronts. The most urgent is the primary focus of Meir's job as field coordinator. Early in the morning, when the army surrounds a village he gets a call from an ICAHD contact in the community. Local people know which houses have demolition orders. Meir contacts solidarity activists to go immediately to the target house. Usually the bulldozers don't arrive before eight, so they have time to enter the house, where they try to prevent the bulldozers from demolishing it. At the same time, ICAHD's lawyers go to court and try to freeze the demolition.

On what grounds can they persuade the court to do that? "We try to get demolition orders frozen for administrative reasons", says Meir. "It's useless to say it's not fair, to claim that people have no choice but to build without permits – the court isn't interested in these arguments. Instead we try to convince the judge that the specific house has a good chance to get a permit in the future. The government will never say it refuses because you're Palestinian, it refuses because there is no master plan for the area. So we come to the judge and we say, 'Okay, there is no master plan now, but we promise we will help to make a master plan for the area, then this family will have a chance to ask for a permit.' In some cases this has worked. The problem is, to make a master plan is very expensive, so we can do this in some places, but not everywhere."

They do have occasional successes. In the East Jerusalem neighbourhood of Al-Bustan, 88 houses were slated for demolition, threatening to evict up to 1,500 Palestinians to make way for a Jewish historical theme park. "In this case," says Meir, "we succeeded not because we are so smart, but because the government made a mistake. If they had not published the notice to demolish 88 houses, but demolished one or two every month, slowly slowly, maybe in one or two years they could have demolished the whole village. But to announce they were going to demolish 88 houses for archeological reasons was so grotesque that everyone; politicians, the international media – even the Americans – said this was too extreme, and they put pressure on the government to freeze it. But we know that they can still resume the demolitions in the future, so all the time we have to be very alert."

In June 2010 the Jerusalem municipality approved plans to demolish 22 Palestinians homes in Al-Bustan.

THE JERUSALEM SYNDROME

While I travelled in Israel and Palestine, I always knew that I would return to my home, a safe haven in a country well insulated from war and chaos. That is, or should be, the nature of home, a place of comfort and refuge. For Palestinians it can never be, so as long as house demolitions remain normal policy for the Israeli government.

I asked Meir how ICAHD people measure success in their work. He pauses, looks away, then back at me. "It's very difficult", he says. "The municipality has a long list of houses to be demolished, so when we freeze one, automatically the municipality goes to the next. We may succeed to save the house of Mohammed, but for the municipality it's not a problem because next they go to Ibrahim's house. If we save Ibrahim's house, the municipality says, 'Okay, Yusef is next.' So we can feel happy for five minutes, but no longer because we have to run to another house. We can only say that we have succeeded when we change the policy."

ICAHD estimates that the number of demolition orders in the West Bank and East Jerusalem reaches into the tens of thousands.

"But you know," Meir resumes, "for us this question of success is not so important. We feel that even if there is no chance of success in the immediate future, this is something we must do – not just to get results, but to be human. We know that one day we will succeed, we are sure of that, because there is no other choice. In the Talmud, the rabbis say something like 'Maybe you will not see the results of your work, but you don't have the right to stop working.'"

ICAHD also rebuilds demolished houses, some 200 so far. The most famous is Beit Arabiya, the house of Salim and Arabiya Shawamreh in Anata, near the Shuafat refugee camp where Salim grew up. When the Israeli government refused them a permit to build a house on a small plot of land they'd bought, they built it anyway. In the past eighteen years their house has been demolished four times by the authorities, and rebuilt four times by the Shawamrehs and ICAHD, with Israeli, Palestinian and international volunteers. With the next demolition imminent, under international pressure the government agreed to a compromise: no demolition, but the Shawamreh family couldn't live in the house. To make the best of a terrible situation, the family agreed to turn their house into a peace centre, Beit Arabiya, where Palestinians, Israelis and internationals continue to come for workshops and meetings.

I comment that, like other activists I've met here, Meir seems to have remarkable patience. He smiles. "I try to. You've heard about the Jerusalem syndrome? People that come from abroad, when they come to Jerusalem, suddenly they lose their mind, they feel that God talks to them, they must pray, or bring peace and justice – it happens very much in this city. It may be the that the peace movement is in this syndrome. I'm not sure that we are so healthy, because people say if you still believe in justice and peace in the Middle East, you have to be a little crazy."

AN IMPOSSIBLE MOMENT

In the November 2008 municipal elections, Meir Margalit won a seat on the Jerusalem council.

In the year that followed, Israel launched a massive bombardment and invasion of the prison called Gaza. It followed an ever-tightening siege that some say began in 2005, some in 1948. All Meretz party members in the Knesset voted to support the attack, and public opinion polls consistently showed over 80 per cent public support for the attack among Israelis.

After 22 days of bombardment and ground assault, 1,300–1,400 Palestinians had been killed, including more than 300 children, according to meticulous research by Israeli human rights organization B'Tselem. Thirteen Israelis were killed. Several thousand Palestinians were wounded, and the infrastructure of Gaza was smashed.

A month later, Israeli voters brought to power a coalition of right-wing and religious parties under Prime Minister Binyamin Netanyahu.

The siege of battered Gaza intensified. UN officials called it, repeatedly, a humanitarian disaster.

Across the West Bank and in one East Jerusalem neighbourhood after another, demolition of Palestinian homes continued.

In October 2009 I went to see councillor Meir Margalit at his office, in a warren of small rooms across the street from the honey-coloured stone walls of Jerusalem's old city. When I arrived, he was concluding a meeting with three citizens, a woman and two boys. His office can barely accommodate a desk, a bookcase, and three office chairs. Behind the desk, Meir's wife Sulie looked up briefly from her laptop computer to greet me.

Meir was dressed for work in an open-necked blue shirt, sleeves rolled to the elbow, and dark trousers. His grey beard is more closely trimmed than I remember. When I asked about his new job, first he clarified that although it was a job in the work sense, in the salary sense it was not. In Israel, municipal councillors are volunteers, not paid. "It's a big problem for all of us", said Meir. "Fortunately, part of my work for ICAHD overlaps with I what do in the municipality, so my salary there covers my time for both. I work mostly with the poorest inhabitants of the city. This is my choice, to work on issues concerning justice and discrimination, which is why most of my time I work with Palestinians in East Jerusalem. They are one-third of the population (of about 700,000), but they don't have even one representative on city council, so they come to my party, Meretz, for help."

I asked him how he reads the political climate here. His response is short, and bleak. "Things have become worse", he says. "The new government is more right-wing, more fundamentalist, more extremist. The Foreign Minister, Lieberman, is clearly fascist. So things have become much harder for Palestinians, and for peace-makers. If pressure doesn't come from abroad, things will become even worse in the future."

When his party, Meretz, voted in the Knesset to support the attack on Gaza, was it a difficult moment for him? "An impossible moment", he says. "I participated in the first demonstration the night they started the attack. My friends in the party were not there, and for me that was very difficult to understand. In the next days they started to join protests, but the fact that in the first hours they supported the attack, this is what people remember now. I lost some people who support me, they asked me 'How can you stay in this party?' It is hard to give a good answer, but I still think it's important for people with a clear pacifist approach to stay in Meretz and to work from within. That is my answer. I don't know if it convinced people, but that is why I have stayed."

THE TEN PLAGUES

When I ask him how things are evolving in Jerusalem, he directs me to an article he published recently in the online *Occupation Magazine*, with a biblically inspired title: "Ten Plagues Inflicted on East Jerusalem". The ten plagues: impossibility of legally building a home, the separation fence which severs Palestinian neighbour-hoods and villages from each other and from the city, intensified confiscation of compulsory ID cards by the Interior Ministry, prevention of family unification, escalating settler aggression against Palestinians, home demolitions, the economic crisis that forces more and more families into poverty, contemptuous and violent treatment by the Border Police, archeological digging in disputed areas, and the abysmal lack of municipal services.

He concludes: "Apparently most Israelis prefer not to know what is happening in East Jerusalem, but the city's leaders would do well if they rethink their policies before the huge explosion – of which we've seen just a short 'trailer' in the past few days." The trailer, or preview, refers to ongoing protests at the Al-Aqsa mosque on the Temple Mount.

CITY OF PEACE

Since early morning today, I've heard military helicopters clattering overhead. Would they be related to the protests? Meir nods.

It's not far from his office to the Temple Mount, weaving through ranks of tourist buses into the Jaffa Gate, along paving stones worn smooth by centuries of pilgrimage and conquest, past flocks of the faithful from several continents being herded by their guides into the Church of the Holy Sepulchre and down the Via Dolorosa. Deeper in the old city is the cardo, in Roman times the main street, now a Palestinian market crowded with tiny shops selling sweets, vegetables, holy souvenirs, meat, spices, music, clothes, fabrics, furniture. On a roof in the Christian Quarter I see telltale signs of a Jewish settler outpost – blue and white Israeli flags, a steel fence topped with razor wire, security cameras. From there it's a short walk through a maze of narrow canopy-shaded alleys to the Temple Mount, Haram Al-Sharif to Muslims, Har-ha Bayit to Jews.

Known to ancients as the city of peace, Jerusalem has hardly ever known a moment of it. Fatefully, the devout of three major religions believe this place holds fundamental keys to their faith: for Jews, the rock on which Abraham offered to sacrifice his son and the site of the First and Second Temples, long ago destroyed; for Muslims, the site of the Prophet Muhammad's ascent into heaven, and the home of two venerated mosques, the Al-Aqsa and the Dome of the Rock; and for Christians, places where they believe their Saviour was crucified, buried and resurrected.

All of these sites are in East Jerusalem, some of the most deeply contested ground on earth. This is councillor Meir Margalit's place of work.

When the state of Israel was established in 1948, a UN-brokered agreement created the so-called Green Line, dividing the city into two sectors: West Jerusalem, under Israeli control; East Jerusalem, under Jordanian control. Palestinian residents were not consulted on the arrangement.

In 1967, Israel occupied East Jerusalem, and shortly after imposed Israeli jurisdiction here. To most of the world, even the United States, East Jerusalem is occupied territory. To one Israeli government after another, it is simply Jerusalem, the capital of Israel.

In September 2009, turmoil erupted at the Temple Mount when some Palestinians threw stones at people that Israeli authorities claimed were French tourists, but Palestinians insisted were Jewish religious extremists invading the sacred Al-Aqsa compound. Thousands of Israeli police were deployed to the Temple Mount. Tension mounted further when they limited Muslim access to prayer in the mosque, and arrested a number of Palestinians, including a local leader of the Islamic Movement. Whether or not the particular accusations that sparked the clash were correct, the Palestinian reaction sprang inevitably from the ten plagues.

GREY RACISM

On Meir's desk I noticed the agenda for a conference that he and Sulie will attend next week in Spain. What is the focus? "The same as usual," he replies, "prospects for peace in the Middle East. We could do it in two minutes – no prospects. Thank you, goodbye." I see an ironic grin, but in his eyes, sadness.

Under the circumstances, what he can accomplish as a municipal councillor? He regards me with a steady, intense gaze. After a moment he replies, "We are three leftists in a council with 28 right-wing and religious members, so we can't do as much as we would like. I try to keep good relations with other members. From time to time they need my vote, then we say, 'Okay, I'll support your proposal if you support mine.' If you look at the big picture, there is not much we can do, but on the ground, there are some issues where we can say we have made small gains."

For example? "On the issue of the Jerusalem master plan, I managed to designate more land in East Jerusalem for residential use, so it becomes possible for a few more people to build houses. Also I managed to make the process of getting a building licence a little more simple. There are several families that can say thanks to my pressure their houses have been saved. Of course it is not enough to save one, two, five houses; we need to change policy. Maybe next year things will be better." The old Jewish saying, "Next year in Jerusalem", comes ironically to mind. It has always sounded like a prayer.

I noted Meir's reference to the Jerusalem master plan. A richly detailed 2006 article in the British newspaper the *Guardian* compares policies and practices in apartheid South Africa with parallels in current Israel. In the article Meir Margalit is quoted saying that the Jerusalem urban planning process is driven by "grey racism". I asked him what he means.

"This is not the classical racism that we learn in school," he explains, "when someone hates the other openly and then segregates him. Here it's more like the British empire, when they would discriminate against the natives but without open hate. It comes from the military culture. Senior functionaries in the municipality are mostly from the army. Even after they leave the army, the army doesn't leave them, the culture of militarism is deep in their mind, and they bring it into the civil service. For them, an Arab is an Arab, it doesn't matter if he is from Hezbollah, Nablus or Jerusalem, he is the enemy. It is clear for them that their role is to keep Jewish hegemony in Jerusalem, to keep a formula something like 70:30. So they make life very hard for Palestinians, to convince them to leave the city. If they will not leave, they make it clear to them, You live here only because we let you, so you should be grateful. This is a very colonialist concept, the grey racism that I'm talking about."

Last year we spoke about the Al-Bustan neighbourhood, where plans to demolish 88 homes had been frozen by a vigorous international campaign. In 2009 I asked him for an update. "The municipality has been trying to negotiate with people there", he replied. "They realize that they can't demolish by force, because there is too much international attention. But still they want to demolish the houses, so they are trying to negotiate with the inhabitants that some of them will leave, their houses will be demolished, and they will get a bigger plot of land in another place, with a permit to build a house. The municipality wants to demolish about 15 houses this way."

What does a long-time demolition opponent like him think of this idea? "I don't have the right to tell them what to do", says Meir. "I can understand a family that accepts the demolition of their small house if they can get a bigger plot and house. But if they were to ask me, I would prefer that they refuse, because this is the salami method to destroy the village. They start with 15 houses, then five more, five more, and in a few years all of Bustan will disappear."

Where are the promised new plots located? "The municipality says they are not far, but I don't know. Even the owners don't know."

"That would make me nervous", I remark.

"Yes, of course", says Meir, in a soft, measured tone. He leaves it at that.

GARBAGE POLITICS

We are running out of time, but there is one more thing I want to pursue. On my travels here I've encountered many of the ten plagues, and many attempts to remedy or oppose them, but nearly always it's one at a time. Though I can understand rationally how they connect, from close up it is not so easy to see the big picture, how the whole apparatus of occupation works.

Meir nods. "It's true", he says. "You have to understand the occupation as a matrix of control. I will give you a very symbolic example. In the city of David, Wadi Silwan (see Chapter 8), if you put a garbage container in the village, a standard container such as you see everywhere in West Jerusalem, it is put there to create a sense of who owns this place. You never see this kind of container in East Jerusalem, with the symbol of Jerusalem [the lion of Judah]. When you put it in Wadi Silwan, it's not because the municipality is trying to provide more service there – they are not interested in that." On the contrary, compared to Jewish West Jerusalem, Palestinian East Jerusalem is famously subject to discrimination in municipal services, documented in endless reports. It is the last of the ten plagues on Meir's list.

So if the fancy garbage can isn't a municipal service, what is it? "It is a strategic way to claim the place", says Meir. "The lights in Silwan, the signs, the paving stones – they are the same as you will find in the Jewish Quarter, so it creates the impression that the Jewish quarter and Silwan are part of the same complex. When you bring a tourist to Silwan, and ask them where are you, in a Palestinian or a Jewish place, they say of course it's Jewish, I recognize these stones, the lights, the signs, even the garbage containers. Suddenly you make the Palestinians who live there into foreigners. This is how the municipality works, they create an atmosphere that says, 'This is Israel here, not Palestine.' This is what it looks like, the matrix of control."

This matrix is sharply criticized in a December 2008 confidential report on East Jerusalem from the European Union Heads of Mission, obtained by the *Guardian*. The report accuses the Israeli government of using settlement expansion, house demolitions, discriminatory housing policies and the West Bank barrier as a way of "actively pursuing the illegal annexation" of East Jerusalem. It concludes, "Israel's actions in and around Jerusalem constitute one of the most acute challenges to Israeli-Palestinian peace-making."

LINES IN THE SAND

In May 2009, President Obama of the United States urged the Israeli government to freeze settlement expansion in East Jerusalem. To many Palestinian and Israeli human rights activists it was too little, too late – but still, it was something, coming from the leader of Israel's most generous and unwavering supporter.

Shortly after, Israeli Prime Minister Netanyahu told the press that he would not take orders from anyone on Israeli settlement in East Jerusalem. Settlement expansion continued.

In November, President Obama chided Israel for approving a plan to expand the East Jerusalem settlement of Gilo. He called the plan "dangerous".

That same month, Prime Minister Netanyahu announced a ten-month freeze on new building permits in West Bank settlements. He stressed that construction limits would not apply in East Jerusalem.

In December, the Israeli Construction and Housing Ministry sought bids for the construction of 692 new apartments in three Jewish settlements in East Jerusalem.

It strikes me that every time activists draw a line in the sand here, the sand shifts and the line disappears. By January 2010, the latest line was drawn in the neighbourhood of Sheikh Jarrah, where Palestinian families were being evicted from their homes by force, one by one, making way for settlers to take over the houses. Every Friday the protests grew – on 1 January 2010, more than 2,000 Israelis, Palestinians and internationals – and police reactions became more violent, with more arrests each week. Every Friday, Councillor Margalit was there.

Backed by the Israeli government with its formidable army and police forces, the settlers seem entirely free to set the national agenda. Or perhaps they simply embody it. Either way, it means that people who support human rights and justice are left constantly drawing new lines in the sand, constantly reacting.

"Yes", says Meir. "In most cases we work like fire-fighters. We don't have the capacity or even the time to be proactive, to initiate positive policies. All the time we are trying to solve crises. This is because there are so many crises."

"That must be frustrating", I said.

"Definitely", he replied.

Last year he told me that, despite everything, "One day we will succeed, we are sure of that, because there is no other choice." But what about the times when the crises are too many, and the big picture looks impossibly bleak?

Again he looks at me intently. It feels like a long silence. Then he says, slowly, "There are days, weeks when nothing works. There are days when you cannot sleep because you see so much injustice, so much suffering, and you cannot bring any help. When people come to us with a demolition order, we visit the house, we come to know the wife, the children, we develop close relations. When you fail to save their house, you feel so frustrated you can't sleep. But we do not have the luxury to feel despair for a long time, because always there is more work to be done."

4
Bridge to the World

Ahmad wrote in his Project Hope blog: "My grandfather was working on trucks and my father was a truck driver. They moved in 1948, that means 61 years ago. Then my father married my mother 22 years ago. My whole family is Palestinian and they came to Nablus because the occupation forced them to leave Yafa and come to Nablus." Yafa is an old Palestinian port city, now an extension of Tel Aviv; Israelis call it Jaffa.

From somewhere in the wide world of the internet, Michael (another, not me) responded: "This is very interesting Ahmad. It's very nice to hear about your family. I don't know what you mean by the Occupation. Can you say more about it? Thanks."

Ahmad replied: "The Occupation is army from Israel who killed many people from Palestine and destroyed many houses and put many people in jail. Now they control my country. They put checkpoint between cities so we can't move. Welcome."

FREEDOM

Hazy, crowded Nablus fills a narrow valley between two mountains, rising up the sides of both. The largest city in the Occupied Palestinian Territories, it is home to about 200,000 people, including the residents of three refugee camps.

All traffic in and out of the city, by vehicle or foot, is controlled by Israeli checkpoints at either end of the valley. To get here I caught a passenger van from East Jerusalem to Ramallah, then a bus to Huwara, the southern checkpoint, crossed on foot with other pedestrians to the Palestinian side, then took a taxi into the city. The journey of 55 kilometres, about 35 miles, took half a day.

While I walked through the metal chute, relatively confident with my Canadian passport, several hundred Palestinians waited under hot sun on the other side. They filed slowly through the chute, one by one through the turnstile as the soldiers ordered them, submitting to scrutiny of ID cards, bags and sometimes bodies. Some were refused passage, some detained, some allowed to continue on their way, to the next barrier. How perverse, I thought, that a foreigner can move around here so much more easily than the people of this land.

On the Nablus side I was swept into the scramble for taxis, and settled with three other passengers into an old yellow Mercedes. We had just started moving when Israeli border police with assault rifles barred the way, shouting at the driver to get out. While the rest of the passengers headed off to other taxis, I waited, unsure of protocol, and watched the driver hand over his ID papers, apparently trying to negotiate or plead with the Israelis. When hardly any taxis remained, I grabbed one. As we drove away, I watched police shove the first driver into an armoured vehicle. The second driver didn't look back.

He lives in a village near Nablus, he told me, and has to navigate the barriers every day. "Sometimes it's not bad, sometimes it is, you never know", he said with a shrug, the way I might talk about winter weather in Canada. He worked for a while in Kuwait then in Jordan, before returning to his native Palestine during the 1990s, when movement eased briefly with the Oslo Accords. "Jordan is more beautiful", he said, then added, "Not more beautiful, no. But you can move around there, you can go anywhere you want. You know what I mean?" I offered, "You mean freedom?" He nodded. "Yes. Freedom."

BLOGS

The taxi groans up steep, narrow streets on Mount Jerzim to the airy stone villa that houses Project Hope. It used to be the home of Adel Zu'aiter, lawyer, translator and Palestinian nationalist in the first half of the twentieth century. Today it hums with youthful energy, though at a lower ebb because of Ramadan, the holy month.

The computer room is cool and quiet, with each of nine students focused intently on her screen. This Bridge to the World class happens to be all girls, 12 to 14 years old. They are learning how to create their own blogs, to transcend the walls, physical and political, that entomb Nablus. Project Hope pays for taxis to bring the students here after school and return them home.

The instructor wears an elegant maroon hijab, a fitted headscarf and robe from shoulder to ankle. Wala Shahrori is a computer engineer, a recent graduate of Al-Najah University up the hill from here. During the work day, her two young daughters stay with their grandfather.

I ask her why the Bridge to the World programme was started; why are blogs needed here? "First," she says in a quiet, even voice, "it gives the children practice to improve their English or French. Second, through their blogs they can join with other children outside Palestine, and reflect their ideas to the world. Sometimes they write articles about their situation here, so they can reflect some of our reality. Third, most of them don't have a computer at home, so here they can learn how to use one. The students are selected from our English and French classes in the refugee camps and the old city. Yesterday I had a group from Askar camp, tomorrow one from 'Ein Beit el Ma, and today they are from Balata."

Established in 1950, Balata is the largest refugee camp in the West Bank. On 252 dunums, it houses three generations of refugees, who fled or were driven out of villages and towns in the Yafa area as Jewish forces advanced in 1948. Two hundred and fifty-two dunums, I've learned, is equivalent to 60 acres, the size of the tranquil wooded land I share with my partner in rural Canada. We are two; the residents of Balata, about 30,000.

The three United Nations schools in the camp are so overcrowded, students have to attend in shifts. Health care is rudimentary, social services badly overstretched. Similar conditions prevail at the other camps in Nablus. Not surprisingly, younger residents have been especially active in resisting the occupation.

During the day, Palestinian Authority police patrol Nablus, but night belongs to the Israeli army. A Project Hope volunteer whose family apartment overlooks Balata often sees soldiers come and go after dark in their armoured vehicles. "It's almost normal", she told me. In the morning, a local radio station routinely reports which residents have been killed, injured or taken away. Among them are many children.

This ancient city has become very young, with an estimated 60–70 per cent of its population aged 25 and under. In 2005 the Palestinian Ministry of Health reported that in the five years since the second intifada erupted, 749 children under 18 years of age had been killed by Israeli forces. A little under half of all Palestinians wounded during the same time period were children, more than 9,000 of them.

This is the hard ground in which Project Hope has grown. The conditions that gave rise to its birth were even more traumatic.

In April 2002 the Israeli army and air force launched a massive assault on Nablus and other West Bank cities and towns. The most active phase lasted three weeks here, during which 184 Nablusis were killed and more than three times as many seriously injured. After the invasion, months of curfew were imposed, broken by brief periods of a few hours during which people were allowed to attend to food and health needs and bury their dead.

More than 100 houses in the old city and refugee camps were destroyed by Israeli rockets, tanks and bulldozers. People rebuild as they can afford to, and when they can obtain materials.

SIEGE

Jeremy Wildeman arrived in Nablus midway through the curfew. "I'd never been to a city under seige – it's not a normal experience for a Canadian, right? It was very dangerous in Nablus, a lot of tanks and gunfire. It's shocking to look into the barrel of a tank. I saw a lot of kids shot, usually by rubber bullets, but with live ammunition too. Seeing these boys fighting tanks, it was bizarre. The soldiers weren't much older than them, but of course they had the best western military equipment and the Palestinian kids had stones and the occasional Molotov cocktail. There were still some fighters in Nablus back then, but they were killed off or arrested pretty quickly."

Jeremy was a long way from home, where he grew up in a Saskatchewan village on the Canadian prairies. With an early interest in history, and a university degree in international relations, he taught English for a year to wealthy young people in Saudi Arabia. "It's an interesting country to visit," he says, "but quite an awful place to live, a feudal society mixed with obsessive modern consumption."

In spring 2002 he watched the Israeli invasion of the West Bank on CNN, the BBC and Al-Jazeera English, the news channel based in Qatar. "I was amazed to see what a huge gap there was between what the big American and British networks told their public about what was happening, and what the rest of the world could see on Al-Jazeera."

Jeremy decided to volunteer in the West Bank, where he found his way to Nablus, and to Al-Najah University. There he initiated a video conference programme, which lets students talk with their counterparts in other universities abroad, breaching the barrier of checkpoints and curfews. He also helped start English classes at a medical clinic in the city, which rescued young people who'd been shot by the Israeli soldiers. Jeremy noticed that international volunteers in Nablus had a lot of spare time, so why not teach

English? It would be an asset for the isolated Palestinians, and it wouldn't cost anything. These classes didn't last, but the idea stayed with him.

In the chaos of invasion and siege, Salem Hantoli had also envisioned a more active role for international volunteers. He manages the Al-Yasmeen Hotel in the old city. We talked in his small office beside the lobby.

Born in a village near Nablus in 1973, Salem went to school in the city, then in Morocco, got a scholarship to study in Holland, then another in 2002 for a summer course in the United States. "An official of the American consulate came to Ramallah to meet the Palestinian candidates for scholarships. To get there I used all means of transportation – my feet, donkey, car, bus, and tractor. Because of the siege, just to go from Nablus to Ramallah, which shouldn't take more than an hour by car, it took me a whole day. She was amazed that I got there."

In 2000, Salem was hired to manage the Al-Yasmeen, which is built around a 600-year-old house. It filled up with guests, many of them businesspeople from abroad. Then in September 2000 the second intifada broke out, and the foreign businesspeople went home. Through 2001 the Israeli army systematically isolated West Bank cities, and then in 2002 they invaded.

"From that time until now, it has been very difficult for us", Salem says. "How can you run a hotel and restaurant when people are only thinking about how they can get their own bread?" For two nights at the hotel I was the only guest, though people came in the evening for the meal that breaks the Ramadan fast. The Israeli noose has devastated Nablus, formerly the industrial and commercial centre of the West Bank. According to the United Nations Office for the Coordination of Humanitarian Affairs, because people can't get to jobs and the ability to move goods ranges from difficult to impossible, unemployment increased from 14.2 per cent in 1997 to 60 per cent in 2006, and as high as 80 per cent in the refugee camps and the old city.

In 2002, basic survival was the primary challenge for Nablusis, and international solidarity volunteers played a crucial role. Salem explains, "It became clear to us that when internationals were present, the Israeli soldiers became less violent – they didn't want people to report what they were doing. And during the curfew internationals were the only ones allowed to move around. So we started to ask them to stay in Palestinian homes. In some cases those brave volunteers prevented the Israelis from demolishing houses, although in many cases they were thrown out and the houses destroyed."

During this chaotic period, Salem Hantoli met Jeremy Wildeman. They agreed that international volunteers could be playing a more active role, and English classes would be a good place to start. Salem's motive was outreach.

"The English language is a very important tool", he says. "The Israelis are much better than us at talking to the media, and that is partly because the audience wants to hear people who speak English well. Also, internationals who spend a few months with us will know us better and understand more about our cause. When they return to their homelands, they will have seen with their own eyes and they won't be cheated by all the misleading media. They can tell their neighbours and friends what really happens here. I'm sure in time the western world will understand us more, and the Palestinians will have more solidarity."

At the same time, Jeremy was observing other kinds of need in the devastated city. "This is a society that can't afford anything but the basics – Arabic, maths, religion – but there are other things kids need in growing up, things like art, sport and music. They also need something to do. Throwing stones at soldiers and getting shot isn't much of a life. And meanwhile the girls sit at home – Palestinian society is quite conservative, plus of course the families worry about them being shot. This is no life for kids. So I thought, why not get foreign volunteers to teach these other activities, under the direction of Palestinians?"

PROJECT HOPE

In 2003, Jeremy and Samah Atout, a dynamic young Palestinian woman, set to work recruiting local and foreign volunteers, and building a programme. Jeremy travelled through Canada, the US and Europe, raising awareness and seeking potential partners to provide funding and other support. When I met him on one of these trips a few years later, he still carried his office in a laden backpack half his own height, and on his work travels he still stayed with friends. From the beginning he took no salary, and even now it is minimal.

"When we started we had no money", Jeremy says. "I was only 24 and had no experience. What we did have was a good idea, a few strong local leaders, and trust and commitment on both sides. The big international NGOs [non-governmental organizations] here offer a lot more salary and sometimes even a passport, so to stick with a small organization like ours you have to be a particular kind of person, and very committed." Among the strong local leaders, Salem Hantoli continues to play a key role as treasurer of Project Hope.

In Nablus, Programs Coordinator Tharwa Abu-Zeina talks with me on the curved, columned stone balcony that overlooks Nablus valley. Now and then she is interrupted by phone calls. In a soft, warm September breeze, with muted city sounds floating up from below, it's possible to imagine for a moment what this place might be like if it was free.

Tharwa was born in Kuwait, and came to Nablus in 1992 when her father decided to return home in the relative calm of the early 1990s. At Al-Najah University she got a BA in English Literature and French, then an MA in translation and applied linguistics. "Ever since I was a child I wanted to be a translator", she says. "I love English, it must run in my blood." She laughs brightly, and often. It's a valuable asset in occupied Palestine.

Tharwa joined Project Hope after working several years as a translator and public relations officer at a local health NGO. (Recently she accepted a job in Ramallah, with another organization.) During the invasion, she and her co-workers brought whatever food, water and medicines they could find to wherever it was needed.

Her primary task at Project Hope is to coordinate English classes. "Our local partners provide the space and the students," she says, "and we provide the teachers. We want to make classes available to everyone, from age three to seventy and more. It doesn't cost the students anything, all our classes are free of charge. We focus particularly on the three refugee camps and the old city, because people there are most likely to be denied access to basic life needs. We don't expect them to come to us, we go to them, wherever they live. We try to bring new skills, a new life."

I ask Tharwa how Nablusis regard Project Hope. "I believe it was hard at the start", she replies. "Although people here are very hospitable, they have learned to be cautious of outsiders. They wonder, 'What do you want from us, will you occupy us like the Israelis?' But then during the incursions of 2002, international solidarity volunteers did their best for us, offering themselves as human shields and trying to help the people in most need. Now when people see what Project Hope does and how, giving access to things normally denied to us, they seem to accept it. You can see that the perspective has changed. Technically, Project Hope is a

Canadian NGO, but really it is a Palestinian organization – everyone here knows it as Palestinian-Canadian rather than the other way round. This is how you need to approach people, in a way that they can accept."

THIS IS MY DREAM

Later in the afternoon, Hiba Yousef and Haneen Masri take me on a tour of the old city. They do this as a courtesy to a visitor, but also I have the clear impression that they are proud of their enduring city. In their twenties, they represent the third generation of Palestinians to live and die under Israeli military occupation.

Hiba was born in 1982, to Palestinian refugees living in Dubai. In the 90s, her mother brought Hiba and her siblings to live in Nablus. Their father, who had left Nablus in 1956 to study in Egypt, was not allowed to return. Now he lives in Jordan, as close as he can get to his native land.

A graduate of Al-Quds University in Jerusalem, Hiba is Activity Coordinator at Project Hope. She explains, "If our international volunteers want to teach anything other than English, let's say art or first aid, we ask them to propose it before they come to Nablus, and I will try to find a place for them with one of our partner organizations here."

When a woman in the United States offered to teach classical Indian dance, Hiba negotiated a place for it at the Nablus circus school, where it blended nicely with lessons in *dabkeh*, traditional Arabic dance. A Dutch nurse taught first aid in surrounding villages, which are even more isolated and resource-poor than Nablus.

The presence of international volunteers has an additional benefit here. "One of the goals of the occupation is to make us feel alone, helpless, isolated from each other and from the world", says Hiba. "But now people here can meet volunteers from Canada, the US, Iceland, the UK, France, Holland, Sweden, Norway. It is very important to us to know that these people care enough about Palestine to come here at their own expense."

Haneen Masri volunteers with Project Hope, teaching English in the refugee camps. (Last I heard, she had joined the staff.) She's a native Nablusi, born here in 1985. Graduating from school with top honours, she won a scholarship to study languages in Jordan, where her grandmother lives. After living most of her life in Nablus, Haneen's grandmother went to Amman after her husband died. At 75, she is afraid to return.

To visit her, Haneen has to get through several checkpoints, then the border. Since buses can't cross the checkpoints, she has to change three times. People used to go to Amman for the day, she recalls. "But now, even if everything goes well, if the Israeli soldiers are calm and happy, maybe you can get there in six hours. If the soldiers are bored or in a bad mood, you may have to wait for hours, standing. They don't respect us. All they know in Arabic is "Stay back", "Wait", "Go" – they shout at us. Many of them are younger than me. It's very humiliating."

I ask if she has ever met an Israeli who wasn't a soldier or police. She thinks a moment, then replies, "No. I've seen some on TV, but I have never met one."

At university, Haneen's major language study was Italian. "It's a beautiful language, the language of opera. I would love to go there sometime, to Italy. This is my dream."

Aware by then of the yawning chasm between dream and reality here, I ask if that is possible. "Possible, perhaps," she says, "but very difficult. First, because of the occupation it is not easy to travel out of Palestine. Second, it would be very expensive. And third, even if I could get a scholarship to go there and complete my education, as a Muslim girl I have to live with my parents or my husband. We have our traditions, I couldn't go from place to place alone." I don't hear any complaint in her response, just *this is how it is*.

In 2009 Haneen took on the job of coordinating Project Hope's English as a Second Language programme. She was also selected for a summer exchange in Europe, travelling to Belgium, Germany and Spain. Italy will have to wait.

HIJAB

On our walk through the old city, Haneen and Hiba are the only women on the street; the shops are staffed by men. Any women I see in public wear the hijab (head-covering). By contrast, Hiba wears black jeans and a black T-shirt from the circus school; her black hair, uncovered, falls to the shoulders. Haneen's auburn hair is also free. She wears a long-sleeved country & western plaid shirt with shiny snaps, jeans, and discreet silver earrings.

Since Muslim women's head-coverings have become the focus of such heated debate in Europe and North America, I ask Haneen and Hiba how they feel about it. They share a glance. It's not an easy topic.

Hiba replies, "The number of women in hijab has increased a lot here since the intifada and the invasion. I think for many it is a statement. We hear all the time from the Israelis and the Americans that Islamic people are bad, we are terrorists. They want us to feel ashamed of who we are. But we have no reason to feel ashamed. We are people, good and bad like everyone else. The hijab says I am Muslim and I am proud."

Haneen adds, "I think it makes people feel safe. Under the occupation no one is safe. Who can we trust? Our family. Our traditions. When you don't know what will happen next, you turn to what you do know. The hijab is something we know."

In which case, why does neither of them wear it? Hiba responds, "I don't require it to know who I am." She doesn't sound defiant, just clear. Haneen says quietly, "My mother chooses to wear it, but she has not asked it of me."

We walk deep into the old city, a maze of meandering alleys and arched tunnels built of stone. Despite the heavy heat of late summer, it is shaded and cool in the maze, a practical architecture, with tiny shops set into walls, making and selling wooden furniture, pastries, vegetables, Spiderman backpacks, plastic furniture, modern and traditional Palestinian clothes, CDs, hand-made shoes. A donkey stands biblically in a stone niche, eating grain. Small chickens scratch and peck among the cobble stones. "See how skinny they are", Hiba says with a grin. "They are just pretending to be chickens."

We pass the remains of the Shubi family house – fragments of wall, a dusty tumble of stones, a small faded plaque. An Israeli Caterpillar bulldozer rammed the house, collapsing it. When neighbours dug through the ruins, under fire from soldiers, they found eight members of the family in an inner room, huddled in a circle, dead. Among them were three children, their pregnant mother and 85-year-old grandfather. The plaque outside lists their names, under the heading "Never Forget, Never Forgive".

Now and then I hear the high-pitched whoosh of a fighter jet echo through the valley. Hiba and Haneen don't seem to notice. But suddenly as we turn a corner, a colossal explosion hits us, a sonic punch. I duck. The two young women share a smile. Recovering, I ask, "Didn't you hear it?" "Hear what?" says Haneen. Hiba explains, "It's just the Israeli pilots. They dive their jets to break the sound barrier. They want to frighten us, to remind us of their power. But to us it has become a strange familiar music." Haneen adds, "It's not good, is it, that we have come to accept such things as normal." She shrugs, eloquently.

PEACE BE WITH YOU

Our walk ends at one of the two soap factories still standing after the invasion, perhaps because it is small, and tucked into an obscure alley. Nablusi soap has been famous since the tenth century, exported to Arab countries and Europe. Made by hand from olive oil, water, and a sodium compound, it is prized for its unique unperfumed fragrance and exceptional quality.

Eyes take a moment to adjust to an interior lit only by pale daylight through grime-shrouded windows. We are welcomed by the owner and a younger man, the manager. The owner wears dark glasses, surprising in such dim light. They have no orders for soap at the moment, a direct result of the Israeli siege, so the manager offers to show us around.

We descend into what must be hell when the factory is operating, the furnace room under the vat. At ground level, the soap ingredients are cooked in a huge copper vat sunk into the floor. The mixture is stirred continuously by hand with a large wooden paddle. I can't imagine how hard the work must be, how dangerous, and how hot.

When the solution is ready – experienced soap-makers know by smell – it is carried in wooden barrels up to the next level, and poured into a plank frame on the floor. After it's dried and cut, the individual cakes of soap are taken up another level to an airy open room under the roof, where they are stacked to dry in gorgeous conical towers. This is how it has been done here for more than a millennium.

Haneen asks the owner why he wears sunglasses. He is blind, he replies, made blind by the soda. As we prepare to leave, he tells the manager to give me a cake of the soap they've made. I ask how much. It isn't a graceful question, more a habit of my culture. The owner waves it away. "*Salaam aleikum*", he says. "Peace be with you."

A NORMAL LIFE

On my travels here, I ask Palestinians what they would do if the occupation were to end. Some say they can't imagine it, not in their lifetime.

After thinking a moment, Haneen Masri says: "If the occupation ended, Palestine would be a very beautiful country for living, so of course I would stay. Even with the occupation I would stay – Palestine is my land, my mother, I would not abandon her. I would like to go to other places, but I would come back to help develop this country, to make relations with all of the world, to let them know who we are, how we live, how we think."

Hiba Yousef replies: "When I came here I fell in love with this land, so I don't want to leave it. My father is in Jordan, and before the Israeli invasion I wanted to live there too, but not now. Since the occupation, even though life is harder, it makes me want to stay here. We need people to stay here, to carry hope. This is why I like Project Hope – it helps you to imagine another world, to open new windows."

I asked Salem Hantoli, co-founder of Project Hope, what gives him hope. "For a human being there is no meaning without hope", he said. "I can't think that my kids will live the same life I have lived under occupation. On my travels to different places I've even thought of staying a couple of years to get nationality, just to protect my kids. Many Palestinians think the same way, they want to get their kids different passports – Canadian, American, European – just to protect them from the occupier, to give them the right to move inside their own land." Ironically, at that moment an Israeli fighter jet roared overhead, interrupting him. He waited, then resumed, "It's not a question of leaving. From the Islamic point of view, Palestine is holy land, a land for God, so it's not allowed for anyone to abandon it, or for any leader to negotiate away this holy land."

What kind of future did he wish for his two young children? "I wish they will live in peace and without fear, to have a normal life like any other children."

*   *   *

On her Project Hope student blog, Fatimah wrote: "The city that I dream of is going to be just like Nablus, but with colorful houses, and I want it to be by the sea so I can swim every day. I also don't want it full of houses because I really love nature and I love to see lots of trees everywhere. Of course without occupation, because no one wants to be in a city with occupation."

5
Witness

From the plateau on the Palestinian side, a curtain of dust blurs the Jordanian mountains.

The temperature on this October day is 40 degrees. Daphne Banai tells me it's hotter in the summer.

At its north end the Jordan Valley forms the border between Jordan and Israel, in the south between Jordan and the Palestinian West Bank, occupied by Israel since 1967. The valley is the only link between the West Bank and the outside world.

We descend into the valley, on a road that curls through smoothly rounded hills the colour of pale sand. It's hard for me to imagine how anything could grow here. "Oh," says Daphne, "but by the end of winter it's very, very green, with the most beautiful flowers. Much of the year, though, it's true, the land is difficult. To survive here, you have to know what you're doing and your needs have to be small. As my Palestinian friends here tell me, we don't want more than we have, we're not interested in the things of modern life. We just want to be left alone, to live as we always did."

This is Daphne Banai's MachsomWatch beat.

On another searing day, Neta Efrony and I face a wall of steel, concrete and soldiers. Earlier this morning Neta heard that tension was already building at Kalandia, among the largest of several hundred Israeli military checkpoints across the West Bank. Like many others, it is not located protectively on the border with Israel, but aggressively inside Palestinian territory between the city of Ramallah, the town of Al-Ram, and the Kalandia refugee camp.

Every weekday, thousands of Palestinians must get through it to reach work, school, hospital, relatives, places of worship or markets in the hub of East Jerusalem, only a few kilometres from here. Today, the second Friday in the holy month of Ramadan, more than 100,000 people have come to pray at the Al-Aqsa Mosque, a revered holy site in East Jerusalem. They wait at the barriers, a sea of pilgrims from across the West Bank. Many have been here since dawn.

By 9 a.m. the heat is fierce. I stay close to Neta, who moves purposefully along the barriers. She has witnessed and recorded here for seven years, as the checkpoint grew from a barrier in the road to a fortress. Kalandia is Neta's MachsomWatch beat, as the Jordan Valley is Daphne Banai's.

VERY MUCH A ZIONIST

Born in Wales in 1949, Daphne Banai emigrated to Israel four years later with her parents. After her father died, her mother remarried and moved to France. Still a minor at 16, Daphne went along, but not happily. "I was very much a Zionist, and at 18 I returned here to go to the army. That meant defying my mother, who was strongly against my coming back. There was a big clash, and they wouldn't talk to me, so I was on my own here for two years." After the army she went to make peace with her mother, but soon returned to Israel. "This is my place", she says. "It's who I am."

During the 1970s, Daphne became curious about the Arabs who had remained inside Israel after the 1948 and 1967 wars. "All I knew was that they were the bad guys, we were the good guys, we were forced to fight them, they ran away, end of story. For some reason I developed a strong urge to talk to the bad guys, to hear their stories. But I found that no one among my family, friends, neighbours, co-workers, knew a single Arab."

By chance, at a parent-teacher meeting in the early 1980s, she met an Israeli who hosted monthly meetings in her house, Jews and Arabs together. There Daphne encountered her first Palestinian-Israeli. "To this day she is my best friend", says Daphne. "But the first time I went to visit her home in Tira, I was scared shitless. My husband and children insisted that I call them as soon I got there. This is how we were brought up in this country, to be petrified of Arabs."

In 1948 Jewish military forces expelled her friend's family from Miska, their village. Due to their ties with a local Jewish family, they were allowed to rent a house in nearby Tira, instead of being sent into exile with most of their former neighbours. Later they tried to return to the village, but Israeli bulldozers had flattened it. A few years ago, Daphne and her Palestinian friend placed flowers among the ruins.

After the dialogue group, Daphne immersed herself in Sadaka Reut, a youth movement that builds relationships of equality between Palestinian and Jewish young people. "But all these experiences were inside Israel", she says. "The Occupied Territories were over there, and I had the feeling that issues there would be solved by some two-state political process that didn't have much to do with me."

Late in 2000, the second intifada erupted. Over the next two years, Daphne joined food and medicine convoys to Palestinian villages under siege by the army. "Once you see the gap between the comfort and normality of our lives, and the awful insecurity of the occupied, who don't know when they will be shot, arrested, humiliated, harassed, able to put food on the table – it gets you more and more involved. Eventually it became an obsession."

HOLES IN THE WALL

Neta was born in Jerusalem, "a long time ago", she says with an enigmatic smile. She recalls an earlier wall, the Green Line that cut through Jerusalem for two decades between the 1948 and 1967 wars. "We used to go and peek through holes in the wall. On the other side we saw only ordinary people doing ordinary things, children like us, cars. This was a surprise, because we lived on propaganda and grew up believing the Arabs are monsters."

How did she see them? "I just saw them as people", she replies. "But I didn't go very deeply into what they might want or need. They worked here, we mingled with them – it seemed natural, like some kind of honeymoon. Most people felt that things could go on like this for ever."

The two intifadas ended the honeymoon. By the time of the second, Neta had retired from her job as a documentary-maker at the Israel Broadcasting Authority and was travelling abroad. "When I came back I wanted to be active," she says, "not just to sit and think about what was wrong, but to do something with my legs." In 2002 she joined MachsomWatch.

Machsom translates as "barrier", or the softer official word, "checkpoint". In winter 2001, hearing that Palestinians were being beaten by soldiers at checkpoints, five Israeli women decided to see for themselves. What they saw moved them to form an organization of women with three goals: to monitor the behaviour of the military – at checkpoints and then later at military courts; to monitor and defend Palestinian human and civil rights, and to bear witness by reporting what they witnessed. They decided to limit membership to women, on the assumption that Israeli men were more likely to provoke the soldiers.

At its peak, MachsomWatch had some 400 members, now about 200, ranging in age from their forties to their eighties. Members monitor checkpoints across the West Bank, particularly in the early morning and late afternoon when the most Palestinians are trying to pass through. Occasionally, MachsomWatchers will intervene with soldiers, but mostly they watch, listen and record. The resulting reports, photos and videos are published on the MachsomWatch website. Members talk to the Israeli media whenever they can, and to anyone who'll listen in other countries. "It's important that people know as much as possible what's going on here," says Neta. "What we would really like is to end the occupation. It's a little bit difficult, I should say." Her trace of a smile sharpens the irony.

Daphne Banai's first MachsomWatch shift is burned into her memory. She went with another woman to Abu Dis, a Palestinian village in East Jerusalem where beatings had been reported at the checkpoint. In the village, they were terrified. "We were surrounded by Palestinians," Daphne recalls, "and every one of them I saw as a terrorist who was going to blow himself up or stab me. Most people in Israel are driven by this kind of fear, we're brainwashed with it."

At the checkpoint things were worse than they had heard. "Thousands of people were trying to get through, elderly ones fainting in the heat, livestock dying, soldiers pushing and screaming. There was a woman in labour, they wouldn't let her ambulance through. We called higher officers on the phone, and gradually people started to pass through. But still they wouldn't let the ambulance go. We told the soldiers we wouldn't leave until they let this woman pass. Finally, toward seven or eight, they did. As we walked to our taxi, the ambulance stopped farther down the road, its horn blaring. The doctor got out, he shouted, 'Ladies, ladies, *shukran*, thank you!' We both burst out crying. At that moment we knew this is what we wanted to do."

KALANDIA, 8.45 a.m.

Neta moves slowly around the soldiers, close to the barriers and the Palestinians. She records what she sees with a small video camera, now and then with a still camera.

Women and men are divided into two streams, along with children of the same sex. Women press to the barriers. Many wear black robes, and multi-hued headscarves. They argue and plead with the soldiers, holding out the Israeli-issued ID cards that govern all movement for Palestinians. Soldiers bar their way, either silently or

shouting Arabic words that Neta translates as "Stop", "Get back!"
She adds, "I'm sure this is the only Arabic the soldiers know."

A small girl cries, likely from hunger and thirst after several hours
standing under the sun. A woman – her mother, I assume – drizzles
bottled water over her head. The girl's face lights with a giddy smile.

To our left, rolls of razor-wire merge into a concrete wall two storeys
high, and overlooking it, a guard tower with opaque slit windows.
Neta tells me that this portion of the wall has the comforting official
name, "the Jerusalem envelope". The bland insult of it is interrupted
by defiant graffiti: "This wall will fall, Ctl + Alt + Delete".

After recording here for six years, in 2009 Neta Efrony distilled
her impressions into a one-hour video, *Kalandia*, her second since
she joined MachsomWatch. The first, *To Build a Wall*, documents
how the advancing wall gradually imprisoned Abu Dis. It features
the same qualities that Neta would develop further in *Kalandia*:
quiet, unflinching observation of painful realities, and sparse
personal commentary.

A couple of minutes into the video she tells us – in her own words
but through the less-accented English of a narrator, "My first time at
Kalandia, I wept." On a winter day, her camera watches an elderly
man with a cane gingerly navigate a pile of rubble. When he slips
and falls, her gasp is audible. Other Palestinians help him to his feet.

JORDAN VALLEY, 9 a.m.

Kicking up small dust-storms, Daphne's car bumps over a parched,
rock-strewn field to reach two shepherds she spotted from the
road. At the end of the field, rows of plastic greenhouses and a
barbed-wire fence mark Roi, an Israeli agricultural settlement. We
exchange "*Marhabas*" with the shepherds, weather-burned men in
their thirties. One of them hands her an official-looking document,
which she translates from Hebrew into halting Arabic. She tells me
later that she's learning Arabic.

After we move on, Daphne explains the document: the shepherds
are no longer allowed to cross the road with their sheep, and will be
fined 1,000 shekels if they do. It's an unthinkable sum to people who
live as marginally as these shepherds. "All these rules are completely
arbitrary", says Daphne, her voice tight with anger. "It's nothing
but harassment, anything to make their lives more difficult."

On the road we pass concrete slabs bearing a stark warning in
Arabic, Hebrew and, mysteriously, English: "Danger. Firing zone.
No entry." In late May the army placed one of these next to each

Palestinian dwelling throughout the Jordan Valley. Hundreds of people received demolition orders, and soon after, soldiers arrived in the middle of the night to smash houses, tents, livestock corrals and water tanks. They shot sound bombs into sheep pens, and arrested many young men. All were released without charge after several days.

One day in mid-summer Daphne got a call from a community leader; he had just been informed that the army would be holding manoeuvres on their land, and they had three hours to evacuate. "I started raising hell", she says. "I called the Associated Press, Reuters, human rights organizations, the UN, the British and US embassies, anyone I could think of. By eight in the evening, the army told the people that they didn't have to leave, the manoeuvres had been postponed. After that the American ambassador came here, the assistant to UN Secretary-General Ban Ki-moon, and a few other diplomats, people that Israel fears to offend too much. Then the demolitions stopped. But we know that as soon as the world stops taking notice, they'll be back. It's very simple. They want these people out of the way."

KALANDIA, 10.30 a.m.

The sun climbs, the time of midday prayer approaches, but the soldiers are letting only a trickle of people through the barriers. The rule today is that only men over 50 and women over 45 may proceed to the terminal; the rest are sent away. Tomorrow the rule could be different. But people refused entry don't leave, they've come too far to quit now; instead, they press closer and plead harder. Voices rise. More soldiers gather, some to stand atop concrete barriers with assault rifles ready.

I watch a woman with two young children confront a soldier, brandishing her ID card. She looks proud and fierce. He simply shakes his helmeted head. A few minutes later we notice that the trickle has stopped, now no one gets through. This, Neta tells me, is collective punishment.

Recognizing a senior officer, she walks over to speak with him. The two of them keep glancing toward the barrier. Returning, Neta shrugs. The officer told her he was pleased with the way things were going. But after a few minutes we see him talking to soldiers at the barrier, and the trickle resumes. Under military occupation the exercise of arbitrary control is routine, a reminder of who has power and who does not.

It strikes me that in addition to the devastating impact the occupation has on Palestinians, surely it must also damage young Israeli soldiers. "Yes, of course", says Neta. "I think they are in an awful situation that my country sent them to, and I pity them. On the other hand, when I see soldiers or border police behaving badly because they hate Palestinians, I'm really angry at them. But in general I don't think it's their fault that they're here. I wonder how their mothers can send them to serve."

How much can MachsomWatch women accomplish in situations like this? With hands spread, Neta shrugs eloquently. "We argue often about this in our group. Why should you call the army on the phone and ask them to open another gate? We are not there to improve the occupation. But on the other hand, if you don't do it people suffer more. It's a conflict. In some way we are helping the army. And I think in a way they know it; strangely, they may even appreciate us more than the common public opinion, which calls us traitors."

JORDAN VALLEY, 11 a.m.

We stop at a checkpoint on a remote hill by an army base. Though Daphne's beat now embraces the whole valley, monitoring checkpoints is still the primary task of MachsomWatchers. We apply sunscreen and don our hats.

This is one of three checkpoints that control all passage for Palestinians between the Jordan Valley and the rest of the West Bank. Given its location, miles from Israel, it is clear even to me that it has nothing to do with security, only control. "From 1967," says Daphne, "Israel's plan was to put settlers here, not religious ones but secular ones from kibbutzim, people with some farming background. The object was to annex the whole valley as soon as there were more Israelis than Palestinians. But despite all the special benefits they get, many Israelis left. Life was too hard for them here, too isolated. Religious Jews have been brought in, but not so many as before. Now there are maybe 6-8,000 Israelis in the valley, and about 55,000 Palestinians. So the aim of Israel now is to make the Palestinians leave. That's why they demolish their dwellings, restrict their movement, and don't let them have water."

At the moment there is little traffic at the checkpoint. We watch soldiers stand idle, but still people are kept waiting. Daphne greets Palestinians – "*Salaam aleikum*" – who come through on foot. Most respond in kind; a few stop to chat. A young man laden with plastic shopping bags tells her that yesterday the checkpoint was closed. The soldiers gave no explanation, they hardly ever do. "Come back tomorrow", they say.

In a small yellow taxi-van waiting to go through, Daphne recognizes the driver, a thin man with receding grey hair and a clipped moustache. "He used to call us on his cellphone about abuses he saw at the checkpoint. But somehow the soldiers got onto him, and they beat him up. Now he doesn't call any more." Though we are in plain view, the man looks straight ahead. I think about the many instruments of terror.

While we stand in a small pool of shade, I asked Daphne how her role in MachsomWatch has evolved. "When I first joined, our aim was to help individual Palestinians to cross checkpoints, to prevent harm as much as we could. That's still true – if I'm at a checkpoint and see a problem, of course I'll do what I can to help. But we used to meet with high army officials to see how life could be made easier for the Palestinians. Eventually we decided to stop those meetings. They only enabled the checkpoints to control people better, then the officers could tell the world 'We meet with these women and together we help the Palestinians.' We don't want to provide them with this kind of fig leaf."

KALANDIA, NOON

Neta Efrony greets other MachsomWatchers as they circulate, take photos, talk to soldiers. One says to me in English, "It turns my stomach that we who went through all we did can now stop other people from worshipping at their holy place."

When another member moves in close to take photos, the Palestinian woman who confronted the soldier – she still hasn't got through – speaks sharply and waves her hand at the photo-taker, "Go away!" A MachsomWatcher translates: "She says, 'All you do is click-click-click, and what does it do for us?'" Neta nods. "It's true. A woman just asked me, 'Please help me to get through, I only want to cross today, only today, only to pray.' We're Israeli so to them we must be powerful. But what can we do?"

While we watched two young soldiers turn away an elderly woman, a MachsomWatch member said to me, "Nothing will change here until the US and Europe put enough pressure on Israel to make it change."

Here is the MachsomWatch dilemma, the dilemma of the witness. It's familiar to me as a writer, having the power to observe, to organize and convey impressions, and sometimes even to amplify muted voices from "the other side" – but beyond that, hardly any power at all.

Small groups of men slung with cameras gather on the near side of the barriers. "International press", says Neta. "They're waiting for the big show." She points at adolescent boys hovering on the edge of the restless throng. As frustration builds, some of them may start throwing stones at the soldiers, and the soldiers will shoot. Several boys have been killed here in the past few years. This is the big show.

The number of soldiers has doubled now, on the ground and on the concrete blocks. Others uncover crates of what we assume to be tear-gas canisters – even the bold Neta is wary of going close enough to see.

Shortly after noon, the midday call to prayer rings out from loudspeakers in Al-Ram. Time is running out for people at the barrier. A tall man with a long greying beard, dark robe and white skull-cap climbs onto a boulder, and in a strong voice begins to recite passages from the Qur'an.

The journalists spring into action, honing in on the attentive crowd he gathers. Soon he descends from the rock, and leads a small crowd of men and a few women in prayer, kneeling on the stony ground. Photographers scramble in so close, they nearly fall over their subjects. Neta keeps a nervous eye on the restless boys hovering at the margins.

Here and there in her video, she inserts an introspective comment over a stark image. In one sequence, young soldiers argue over the papers of an elderly man in a suit and robe. Neta says, "Palestinians keep asking me, 'What do we get out of this, what are you doing for us?' What am I doing indeed, clearing my own conscience?" But then she says that other Palestinians insist, "Film this. Film this so people can see."

Surely this is why she does it, so that people will see, and something will come of it? "I hope so", says Neta. "But I'm not sure. I heard from another film director that there's no chance for this film to be seen because Israelis are tired, the world is tired, nobody wants to hear about this any more. So I don't know if my film will have any influence, or even if it will be shown."

JORDAN VALLEY, 2.30 p.m.

As a murky sun slides down the wide sky, we pass two men sitting on a mound of earth beside their tractor, near a closed gate that seems to lead nowhere. Daphne backs up the car. "I want to talk to them", she says. "That gate should be open by now."

There is no wall or fence here; the gate is a steel bar on a hinge between two concrete blocks. Beyond it a rough track winds away into the hills. The men tell Daphne in Arabic that they're waiting for the gate to be opened so they can go visit their kids, who stay with relatives in the village in order to attend school there. She explains to me, "The army is supposed to open this gate three times a week, for an hour in the morning and an hour in the afternoon, so people can get to Tamun for supplies, school or to visit relatives."

The naïve Canadian asks: since there's nobody here, why don't they just go round? Daphne leads me to a ditch left of the gate. It's filled with coils of razor-wire. "These ditches run parallel to the roads all along here, so that no one can cross except through the gates. One day I came here and found that not only had the army neglected to open the gate, they had also forgotten to lock it. It was winter, quite cold, so I said to the people waiting, 'Go through, I'll take responsibility.' They said, 'No, no, we can't.' They were right, I should never have said that. Just over there is a guard tower; you can't see it from here, but they see everything. If anyone sneaks through, it's very likely he will be caught. And while they wouldn't do much to me, the consequences for a Palestinian would be very bad. Finally I called the army, I said, 'Look, if you don't come and open the gate I will!' They came in ten minutes."

At this point she resorts to a similar call. Her manner on the phone is calm, matter of fact, not aggressive. In less than ten minutes an army jeep arrives. Ignoring Daphne, the soldiers unlock the gate and swing it open. Then, taking their time, they inspect the tractor. Under her breath, Daphne says, "I know this officer. He's a brute." Eventually they let the two men go, and depart in their jeep. We watch the tractor until it disappears in slow motion over the brow of the hill.

KALANDIA, 1 p.m.

At the barrier, people continue to argue and plead, the soldiers turn them away with shouts and gestures. They could be herding cows.

An older woman who gets through the outer barrier raises her hands to the sky in praise, her face bursting with relief to get this far.

On our drive to Kalandia, I commented to Neta about the mysterious accidents of birth by which I happen to be born in Canada, she in Israel, and the people on the other side of the barrier in Palestine. "In Buddhism there are no accidents", she replied, with a smile.

At about the same time she joined MachsomWatch, Neta attended a talk by a Tibetan Buddhist nun. It was transformative. "All that this woman said sounded so logical, so right to me, I fell immediately in love with these ideas. What was logical? That if there is no God, then we are responsible for what we do. Then, that everything in life is cause and effect. Then, that nothing in the world is by itself, everything is connected. And of course the psychological aspect of how to deal with anger, happiness, your emotions – all of it makes so much sense."

The prayer concludes, the religious man stands and turns away from the barrier. The people he gathered follow him. Few Palestinians remain now at the barrier. Either they've got through, or they've given up and left. There are two more Fridays in Ramadan; they may try again. We watch half a dozen boys gesture and shout at the soldiers. Eventually, they too wander away. As soon as it's clear there will be no big show today, the international journalists vanish. Neta and I stay for another hour – she wants to keep an eye on things.

Soldiers remove the steel barriers and a huge front-end loader bullies the concrete barriers aside. I comment to Neta that with these giant machines you can re-make reality any way you like. "Just like that", she says, with a snap of her fingers.

The daily grind resumes. Men unload racks of bread and rolls from a van, and carry them by hand into the terminal. There they will be examined and passed through the metal detector. If the bread passes, other men with Jerusalem permits will load it onto other vans for delivery on the other side.

JORDAN VALLEY, 3.30 p.m.

Beside the settlement of Roi, with its ranks of plastic greenhouses ringed by razor-wire, we visit a shepherd family that Daphne knows. They live in a tent, really a tattered patchwork of old grain sacks and plastic sheet held aloft by a few poles. It has to be portable; since 2002 they have been evicted four times by the army, most recently because the settlers said they might hack into water pipes that irrigate the greenhouses. In fact, the father asked to buy water, but the settlers refused.

Today being Thursday, the gate to Tubas village will be open for an hour, so the father has gone to visit three of his children there;

they stay in a rented apartment with his other wife in order to attend school in the village.

We drink sweet, spicy sage tea with the younger wife and the children. They chat with Daphne and watch me, wide-eyed. One son has just returned from buying water in the village, three hours' drive each way on the tractor. They have to do this twice a day. Daphne tells me that the youngest daughter, now three, was born on one of the nights when soldiers destroyed their dwelling. They named her Sumud, which means "endurance", or "holding your ground".

Suddenly a grey-white rocket with stubby wings whooshes overhead and disappears down the valley. I'm the only one who looks up. Another follows a few minutes later, then another. This is the first time I've seen remote-controlled drones, the pilotless aircraft that the Israelis and Americans use for surveillance and bombing.

An older son reports that when he was tending the sheep on the other side of the settlement a month ago, settlers came with soldiers and beat him. "Then, just for fun," Daphne translates, "they surrounded the sheep, making smaller and smaller circles with their jeeps until they ran over three of the sheep." She adds, "For people who have so little, three sheep could be their income for a whole year."

Two of the girls bring us a pair of goat kids, born that morning, their eyes not yet open. Daphne and I hold them in our laps, small, woolly bodies with bony legs. Watching us, the children grin with delight. Except for Sumud, she just watches with a steady gaze.

Later, driving west into a livid dusk, I ask Daphne what being an Israeli means to her. She is silent for awhile, negotiating a corner where a flash flood washed out half the road last winter. Back on solid ground, she replies, "I'm a citizen, I live here. This is my culture, my way of life. But I have to say, I'm becoming more alienated all the time. The Gaza attack was a big crack in my sense of belonging. The atmosphere in Israel during that attack – rejoicing that more and more Palestinians were killed and hurt – that was intolerable to me. I have friends in Gaza, they called me when they were under attack, terrified. But many people in Israel wanted more victims. These are my people." She's quiet awhile, driving, then she adds, "Perhaps if I were younger I might decide to leave. But now, I don't know."

She sounds so torn, I'm moved to say, "It seems to me that when people leave here, it's because they want to be comfortable, to live in a place like Canada where it's even easier to ignore the suffering of others. But you stay, you're willing to be uncomfortable, which means you must have strong feelings for the place."

"Yes", Daphne replies, "I have very strong feelings for Israel, but also about where it's going – to a terrible, terrible place. There might come a time when I have to say this is not my place any more, I don't belong here. Even now my work is abroad. (She books holiday apartments for Israelis on vacation.) But I don't see any other place where I would feel at home. If I'm abroad, I would be an Israeli abroad. I don't know exactly what it means, but this is who I am."

In July 2010, demolitions of Palestinian homes, encampments, water tanks and animal pens escalated sharply in the Jordan Valley. In each case the army offered the same standard excuse: the area was "a closed military zone". In 2001, following his first term as Prime Minister of Israel, Binyamin Netanyahu promised that if he regained office he would turn the entire Jordan Valley into a closed military zone.

Before she dropped me off at the train station in Tel Aviv, I asked Daphne Banai how she feels about the movement to boycott Israel. She sighs. "I really don't like that kind of action", she says. "It brings a lot of pain, and I'm not even sure it will work. But life is so comfortable in Israel, and if people don't care what harm they do to others, then we need more drastic action to make them realize that being occupiers also damages their own lives. That includes me; I have no doubt my business abroad will be hurt. But we can't go on like this. I don't see Israelis having the motivation to make real change unless something interferes with this good life we have. So I would say that, with very mixed feelings, I'm for it. I really can't see that we have any other choice."

COMPASSION

Neta Efrony's fears that no one will see her video turn out to be unwarranted. She has been invited to show the video at film festivals and solidarity events both in Israel and abroad. At some of these she is harangued by Zionists, which she finds wearing, but other people tell her *Kalandia* moved them to tears, and to action.

The video ends on a regular weekday, business as usual at the fortress-checkpoint. By dawn on a February morning, men seeking work on the other side are already packed into the outer hall, collateral damage from the occupation and a strangled economy. With hardly any movement through the chutes, there is time to talk.

"Look what they're doing to people", a grey-haired man says quietly to Neta's camera. "Animals pass with more dignity."

Some younger men clamber up the metal bars to balance precariously beside gleaming curls of razor-wire. Up there, at least they can see what's happening. One of them waves at Neta to come up. Camera running, she scales the wall. Hands reach down to help. From above we see the entire hall, crammed with Palestinians, waiting.

In her voice-over, Neta takes us for a moment along her Buddhist path, "... a path that acknowledges no chosen people, no better or worse people. A path of compassion. Compassion is what we could be feeling towards one another. Compassion means that all sentient beings may live in bliss. Compassion means not just the self, but the other as well. I know compassion exists for us in Judaism too. But where is it? Where has it gone?"

6
There is a Law

Secret Israeli database reveals full extent of illegal settlement.
(*Haaretz*, English edition, 1 February 2009)

Readers of the Israeli newspaper may have wondered, since when is illegal settlement news? Only four years before, Prime Minister Ariel Sharon, who had urged settlers to occupy every hilltop in the West Bank, commissioned a report on the results. Headed by Talia Sasson, former head of the State Prosecution Criminal Department, the report concluded that for years, Israeli state bodies had been discreetly diverting millions of shekels in cash and services to build West Bank settlements and outposts, knowing they were illegal under Israel's own laws.

To Dror Etkes, the leaked database wasn't news, but it was pure gold.

In 2005, embarrassed too often by journalists' questions that peace and human rights activists could answer better than the army, Israel's military establishment asked Baruch Spiegel, a Brigadier General in the army reserves, to build a comprehensive database on the status of all Israeli settlements and outposts in the occupied West Bank.

A year later, Dror Etkes requested a copy from the Minister of Defence, through the 1998 Freedom of Information law. The minister's office acknowledged the request, but did nothing further. Eventually Dror took the minister to court. Government lawyers argued that the database contained sensitive security information, and also its release could harm Israel's foreign relations – two factors that allow the state to withhold information. But how could the database be so sensitive, Dror's lawyer asked, when it only talks about settlements, supposedly a matter of public record? The court reserved its judgment.

Late in 2008, investigative journalist Uri Blau invited Dror Etkes to look at something he had just acquired. "He opened the computer and showed me this document," says Dror, "about 250 pages, all the settlements in alphabetical ordered, each one with a list of related information. Uri got it from one of his sources – I don't know who, and you don't ask. I told him this was what I had been after for three years, the Spiegel report. I read the whole thing that night." Eight months later, a trace of excitement still lingers in Dror's voice.

Ironically, a month after *Haaretz* published Uri Blau's article and the database, the court ruled that it was too sensitive to be released. The irony deepens; nothing "sensitive" is published, Dror explains, without prior approval by Israeli military censors.

But why was this particular document such a prize? Didn't Dror already know most of its contents from his research with Peace Now and Yesh Din? "Not most," he replies, "but part. From the report we learned a lot about master plans for the settlements, permits, the land status of some settlements – many things we didn't know before. Most important, the report lists in detail which construction is illegal in which settlement. So finally we had an official document in black and white, which the government had done everything it could to hide, confirming what we have been saying for years about the Israeli state's illegal land grab in the West Bank, contradicting even its own laws. This report exposed the whole crap that's going on there."

SETTLEMENT WATCH

I met Dror Etkes at the home of a mutual friend who grew up in the same Jerusalem neighbourhood as he did, French Hill, built soon after the Israeli army captured East and North Jerusalem in the 1967 war. Dror was born a year after the war. His name means "freedom". On a fiercely hot September day, he arrived at my friend's house in shorts, a T-shirt and sandals.

I asked him what influences had shaped him as a child. They were mixed, he says. "At home, my parents held – and my father still holds – rather leftish, dovish Zionist positions. In the Israeli context this means we should look for an agreement with the Palestinians which includes some kind of a territorial component. At the same time, I went to a conservative religious school where many of the teachers were settlers, and quite a few of the kids went to live in settlements. Also the youth movement I belonged to until I was 15, Akiva, believes strongly in the settler ideology. So there was a sharp dissonance between what I learned at home and at school."

After completing his army service in 1989, Dror travelled for seven years in the United States, Central America and Europe. "I was exposed to many other realities and ways of seeing conflict and political issues", he says. "In Central America I witnessed much conflict, and I came to see US policy – and by the way, Israeli companies operating as an auxiliary to the US patron there – from a very critical perspective. When I came back, you could say I was a few steps farther to the left."

Then in 2000 the second intifada erupted. "There was so much bloodshed", says Dror. "I was a young father by then, with a daughter just born, so suddenly I was responsible for another soul. For the first time I experienced fear. Here in Jerusalem, you never knew when a bus you were on could explode. At the same time I could still see the broader issue of the occupation, and feel solidarity with a big part of the Palestinian people. It brought me to think about what could be done to reduce the influence of crazy fanatic murderers on both sides."

In 2001, the long-established Peace Now organization asked Dror Etkes to coordinate its Settlement Watch project. Founded in 1978 during Israeli-Egyptian peace talks, Peace Now defines itself as the country's oldest peace movement, and the largest extra-parliamentary movement in Israel. Settlement Watch would gather precise concrete data on settlement construction and all related infrastructure in the occupied West Bank.

How was the information gathered? "Two main tools", Dror replies. "I spent 50–70 per cent of my time on the ground in the West Bank, so I came to know the area quite well. We're talking about approximately 5,500 square kilometres. The second tool was to fly over the West Bank taking photos, World War I technique, just by looking down. Then in 2004 we took a big jump when we hired professional aerial photographers to cover parts of the West Bank where we thought settlement and outpost action were taking place. Every three months this gave us an aerial survey, on a GIS [geographic information system] programme so that we could easily see what had changed. This increased very dramatically both our data and our ability to analyse it."

How did they use the data? "Every quarter year we published a report", says Dror. "The local media would often pick it up; sometimes a US paper. Our primary goal was to improve Israeli discourse about the settlements, to inject an essential element that is often missing – facts. Most Israelis don't have a clue what is going on over there, and the Israeli government lies without hesitation about these issues. As long as there was no independent civilian voice to challenge the government, the official information was a mockery. They would say they dismantled an outpost, but now we could prove with a photo that they did not. If we accomplished one thing, I would say we forced them to put out less misinformation about their deeds."

In 2008, Peace Now identified 120 settlements and 99 outposts throughout the West Bank, not including East Jerusalem. Outposts are settlements-in-waiting. Together the settlements and outposts housed some 289,600 Israelis; an additional 190,000 lived in East Jerusalem settlements. All these settlements and outposts are considered illegal by international law, which prohibits occupying powers from transferring their own population into occupied territory. But for those who hold that God promised this land to the Jews, no further legal justification is needed.

A LAND WITHOUT PEOPLE

No other issue illustrates so starkly the dilemma of the Zionist enterprise, and the growing obstacle it poses to any chance for a just peace in this broken land.

Anyone familiar with an authentic history of North America will recognize the settlement pattern. Europeans arrived on the Atlantic coast armed with advanced weapons, a hunger for land, the convenient myth that the "new world" was empty of inhabitants, and a belief that their god had promised them this land. As they spread deeper into it, they constructed settlements, fortresses to defend the settlements, and armies to put down resistance from the original inhabitants, who according to the founding myth weren't supposed to be there. They also created an array of legal arguments and a heroic historical account to justify and celebrate the national project. By "they" I mean my ancestors, the people who founded Canada, my country.

In mainstream western media, if we hear of Israeli settlements at all, we tend to hear only that their founders are often at odds with the government, and that any attempt to remove them for the sake of a viable peace agreement would lead inevitably to conflict, even civil war, and therefore it is impossible. As the settlements grow, it becomes more impossible.

From Israelis who challenge this argument I learned that, far from being seen as a threat by the government, the settlers are actually Zionism's pioneers, who have counted on state support from one government after another since Israel was born. Though the cost of this support is a closely-guarded state secret, a careful reading between the budget lines by experienced analysts in 2003 revealed that even then, costs of the settlement enterprise to Israeli taxpayers already exceeded US$2.5 billion each year. This estimate included tax incentives and other subsidies to settlers, schools and industry, land acquisition, and a massive infrastructure – special roads, electricity, water and sewage systems. It did not include army and police costs, which could easily double the estimate. As the settlements grow, so do the costs.

The estimate also excluded the cost to Palestinians. For them, the settlement enterprise has been a catastrophe that keeps getting worse. Despite all the two-state rhetoric, it makes a viable Palestinian state less and less possible, at the same time making life less and less liveable. Under these conditions, what chance can there be for a just peace?

CLEAN HANDS

In 2007, Dror Etkes moved from the venerable Peace Now to head the Settlement Policy Judicial Advocacy Project at Yesh Din, a human rights organization formed two years before "to oppose the continuing violation of Palestinian human rights in the Occupied Palestinian Territory". Its board includes many former Israeli government officials and senior military officers.

I asked Dror why he made the move. "I felt I had exhausted my ability to do anything new at Peace Now", he replied. "Publicizing information is a good way to slow things down, maybe even to enforce the laws better, but you can't force the government to dismantle anything, not even something totally illegal. If you want to pressure the state more effectively, you need to raise more sharply the contradictions between the ethos which it claims for itself – a nation of law, the only democracy in the Middle East et cetera – and what it actually does on the ground. This brings you to a very sensitive question: who is running Israeli affairs in the West Bank: the army and bodies which represent the state, or some kind of paramilitary groups equipped and empowered by the state – in other words, the settlers? Which then brings you to the deeper question that I consider most vital for Israeli society to face: what is the nature of this country? Is it a mature, responsible state, or is it still a national liberation movement, not committed to the codes of behaviour that should govern a state?"

Although these questions that Dror poses are huge and abstract, in fact the Yesh Din lands project is firmly grounded in a very practical objective: to recover for its registered Palestinian owners land that was stolen from them to build Israeli settlements. Land being essential to life, this goal fits well within the scope of Yesh Din's current focus on settler violence in the West Bank.

The first step in a very long process is to identify particularly glaring examples of illegal building on stolen land. The second, absolutely crucial step is to find the Palestinians who hold title to the land, and then to convince them to grant power of attorney to the lawyers that work with the project.

At this point in history, I find it hard to imagine that many Palestinians would trust an Israeli with power of attorney, one of the last threads of legal connection they have to their land. I asked Dror how he and the lawyers persuade Palestinians to trust them. "It's not easy", he replied. "Obviously the issue is extremely sensitive, and for a Palestinian to hand over registered documents and their ID, or maybe inheritance documents issued in a sharia court after the death of their father, this is not at all simple. Basically we have to convince them that we come with clean hands. It's a matter of how we represent the project, and reflect enough optimism to justify locating the documents. You don't just find them in a kitchen drawer, sometimes we have to go to the Civil Administration or the courts. But on other hand, we don't want to fool anyone by saying, 'If you do this, next week you'll have your land back.'"

When I saw Dror again a year later, I asked him how the clean-hands approach was going. "It becomes better with time. I can see a change in the way we're addressed. Also we have help from Palestinians who know us, who can act as intermediaries. That's crucial. We are known. But I have to say, until now we have not been able to bring one centimetre of land back to Palestinians. I think in the next year we will be successful." To the sceptical ear there could be an undertone of next year in Jerusalem. But the way he says it, the hope sounds authentic, even grounded.

Where they hope to find success is in an intricate battle with a very powerful opponent not famous for compromise. Once Dror and the lawyers identify a potentially winnable case, persuade the legal owner to cooperate, and locate the necessary documents, they write to the appropriate government authorities and demand in the name of the titled owners that the illegal occupants, the settlers, get off the land. "Of course, the authorities won't comply", Dror explained. "So then we go to the High Court, which is supposed to help individuals harmed by state actions. Although we organize and pay for the petitions, we go to court not as ourselves, but representing the individual who has title to this land. Once it starts, such a case could run for several years. Legally speaking, we are asking for something very simple, but politically, it's extremely complicated."

Why is it so complicated? Given the circumstances, it seems rather a silly question. But to understand exactly how the process works, it has to be asked. With an equivalent investment in being understood, Dror is patient and meticulous in his response. "What we are demanding is that the state of Israel carry out destruction orders which have been issued by itself, by the government body responsible for civil administration in the occupied West Bank. They have an inspection department which is supposed to inspect all construction in Area C, where the settlements are, and to issue destruction orders for houses and other buildings that are constructed illegally. This department actually does what it's supposed to do, they do check and they've issued literally thousands of destruction orders – we have the entire list of them, after a long legal fight through Freedom of Information. So the civil administration issues these destruction orders, to uproot or dismantle illegal settlements and outposts, but then nobody ever carries them out. This is exactly the crack in the system that we're trying to open. We say to the High Court that according to your law, this is illegal. This is not about my ideas of how people should live together; it's not about apartheid or anything like that: it is entirely about your law. It is you, the state, who issued the destruction orders, so already you admit that these buildings are illegal."

I assume that this brings us back full-circle to the leaked Spiegel report, and why obtaining it was such a crucial breakthrough. "Exactly", said Dror. "Now, in every petition we make to the court, we quote the relevant sections of this report. For example, where construction has been done on what we know to be private Palestinian property, we will quote that fact from Spiegel, which matches our information. Since the government can't refute what is in their own report, this pushes them into a corner. Of course, they can delay; they can give the court affidavits from this or that general saying how much law enforcement activity there is in the West Bank. The state's game is to give the court an excuse not to intervene. But we try to undercut this tactic by showing that the state systematically avoids doing what it is required to do by law."

THE CASE OF OFRA

A bit lost by now in the tangle of detail, I asked Dror for a more graphic illustration of what he does. Earlier I would have accompanied him through a checkpoint, past the separation wall into the occupied West Bank, where he would photograph illegal construction on the ground, until he was chased out by settlers or their private security forces. Now, in a striking gesture of change, Dror Etkes flips open his laptop on our mutual friend's dining room table. "Let's go to Ofra", he says, and with a few clicks, we're there.

In a flat grey aerial photo, Ofra looks unremarkable, houses, streets, trees; basically a suburb. But Dror calls it "the Mayflower of settlements". Northeast of Ramallah in the West Bank, it was founded in the 1970s by settler activists quite similar to the young people who now put trailers on Palestinian hilltops and call them Israeli outposts. Ofra is home to some 3,000 Israelis, including a number of well-known political figures and entertainers. According to Dror, the majority of it is constructed on private Palestinian property. The Spiegel report confirms, "A majority of the construction in the community is on registered private lands without any legal basis whatsoever and no possibility of converting the land to non-private use."

Dror clicks through a series of aerial photos. On one of them he points to a pale slash, a bypass road built to serve the settlement. Click, and we're looking at Ofra in 1990. Fewer houses, no bypass road. "The land here was still cultivated by the nearby Palestinian village, Ein Yabrud", says Dror. Click. Ofra again, but now with a blue line around it. Here landownership data from the Civil Administration is superimposed onto the latest aerial photograph of the settlement. "The blue line indicates the official area of the settlement. You can see that just about everything lies on private Palestinian property."

At this point he turns from the screen. "I have to tell you," he says, with an almost childlike air of excitement, "to be able to work like this with GIS and computer imaging, it's a total revolution in what we can do, even from four, three years ago. This is all official information. Not only can you see what the legal status is, you can also go back in history – [click] – to see what was here in 1990, and what has happened – [click] – since then. When you put these things together, you get a very good idea of what is legally vulnerable, and what is not."

Ofra is legally vulnerable. In October 2009, Dror and human rights lawyer Michael Sfard went to a High Court hearing on the first petition to be launched by the Yesh Din lands project. Initiated in June 2008, it focused on nine houses in the Ofra settlement. Dror explains, "After we caught them building these nine new houses on private Palestinian land in the middle of the settlement, we raised a petition against it, but the judge refused to issue an injunction forbidding them to inhabit the houses. Actually the settlers worked very hard to finish the construction, they even worked on Shabbat [the Sabbath], when according to Jewish religious law you are absolutely not allowed to work. It showed how this law, like any other law, reflects human and cultural priorities. Anyway, after settlers had already moved into these houses, the High Court ruled that because the houses were illegal, nobody could use them. But the Minister of Justice, who is a very clever lawyer, interpreted 'nobody' to mean only the four officials named in our petition: the Minister of Defence, the military chief of the West Bank, the chief of police, and the head of the civil administration – it is only these four who are not allowed to use these houses, but everybody else can. *Scandalous.*" He emits the last word with restrained fury.

Since the Israeli government was determined to keep the settlers in the nine houses, their next tactic was the usual one, to delay. In due course the state confirmed that yes, the houses were illegal, and demolition orders had been issued. And then nothing happened. Finally, under pressure from the court, which was under pressure from Yesh Din's lawyer, in mid 2009 the Minister of Defence told the court flatly that the houses would not be demolished.

"This is breaking the rules of the game", says Dror, with a sardonic smile. "They're supposed to say yes, we will demolish, but then delay and delay, telling the court every few months why it has not yet been done. But this time they said, 'No, we won't demolish.' So here the state comes to a constitutional point of crisis. They will try to use nice words and disguise it, but the question on the table is really quite simple: is the High Court going to allow the government to protect robbers, to say it will not enforce its own laws? Legally speaking, this is a simple question, but politically speaking, it is quite explosive."

NO CLEAR ANSWERS

In 2008, I read in *Haaretz* that Dror Etkes was "the person most hated in the settlements".

To the settlers, who are not accustomed to being thwarted, the Ofra case wasn't his first offence. In 2006, Dror's research led to court petitions that forced the government to demolish several houses in the illegal outpost of Amona, sparking a violent confrontation between settlers and soldiers. In the ongoing case of Migron, he helped prepare a petition which resulted in a court order that the government, which had invested heavily in the illegal settlement, must evacuate the occupants, 50 settler families. Three years later, they are still there; the government keeps assuring the court that it is negotiating with them.

I asked Dror how he felt about being so famous. "You mean infamous", he says, with a smile in which I read – though I don't know him well enough to say for sure – an element of mischief. "I take it as a compliment."

He said this so lightly, I laughed. "No, really", he insisted. "It means that you are accomplishing something. They understand very well that once you focus not on the question of principle, but on the actual practice of settlements and compare it with Israeli law, it is much more effective, and so it is much more of a threat. You eliminate endless *kvetch*, as we say in Yiddish. Good, bad, occupied, not occupied, greater Israel, smaller Israel, Zionist, not Zionist, apartheid, not apartheid – it's endless, but there is nothing new that Israelis can say about it. Once I left all that aside, and talked only about this illegal house and the law, you reach the conclusion that if the state follows its own laws, it has to act against the settlers. What they are used to is the state always with them, not against them. Now we have about 20 petitions in process. This is not personal, it doesn't give me any joy. But unfortunately it's a historical truth that if you harm the system, you will also harm people who benefit from it. In the case of the settlers, they will never move until they have to. So I feel at peace with being infamous. Absolutely."

An Israeli human rights lawyer told me that when an individual client's needs clash with a larger opportunity to force a change in policy, it can pose a serious ethical dilemma. Given the nature of the Yesh Din lands project, I imagine that similar dilemmas might arise for them. "Yes", Dror replied without hesitation. "I can give you an example. Half a year ago we raised a petition against a water purification system built for the Ofra settlement on private Palestinian property. Twenty-five years ago the land was confiscated to build a sewage plant. After a few years, the settlement expanded and then the houses were too close to the sewage plant, so they stopped using it. For years the sewage went down into the valley, poisoning the water for Palestinians. About two years ago, Ofra started to build a new water purification system, in which the state invested almost 8 million shekels. Everything was illegal – no construction licence, and it was built on land that doesn't belong to them. For a year I wondered if we should raise a petition or not.

Eventually we decided to do it. In this case we succeeded, and now the state is not allowed to finish construction. Of course, they may find a trick to retroactively legalize it, but for now, the sewage is still going down into the valley where Palestinians live."

He adds, "This is a classic dilemma. Which way do you go: do you continue on principle, causing ecological damage and harm, or do you give up the case? We faced the same situation in another place, and decided the opposite, we didn't push for a petition. In that case I spoke with Palestinians in the area, and they said they would prefer to leave it alone. They have a right to a say. So there you have two situations, and it went both ways. I have no clear answers."

Neither, apparently, has the High Court. In June 2010, ruling on the latest Yesh Din petition concerning the Ofra water treatment plant, the court demanded to know why the government had failed to shut it down as previously ordered by the court. When a government official implied that the state might legalize the installation retroactively by confiscating the privately-owned Palestinian land, Supreme Court President Dorit Beinish commented that the state regularly employs similar tactics.

THE LAND OF ISRAEL

In September 2009, the state prosecutor's office suggested to the press that it might be time for a new tactic. Instead of responding to the court on illegal housing petitions in the usual way, avoiding the issue of legality but agreeing to issue stop-work orders, settlements in the West Bank might simply be legalized retroactively. This startling proposal, a trial balloon, emerged in response to yet another Yesh Din petition seeking the demolition of twelve mobile homes built on Palestinian land in the settlement of Kokhav Yaakov.

In October, the Israeli press reported that the defence and interior ministers would form a task force to facilitate construction in the West Bank, by removing "bureaucratic obstacles".

In November, to placate Washington, Prime Minister Netanyahu announced a ten-month freeze on new building permits in West Bank settlements. He stressed that construction limits would not apply in East Jerusalem, where construction proceeds rapidly.

In December, Peace Now reported that construction was continuing on more than 3,000 housing units in West Bank settlements, at a rate higher than construction currently approved and taking place inside Israel. After receiving calls from soldiers and even settlers reporting new construction in some settlements, Peace Now announced that it would commission a series of aerial photographs of all settlements and outposts, to identify new construction.

In July 2010, while President Obama commended Prime Minister Netanyahu for his "restraint", the Israeli human rights organization B'Tselem published a major report on the settlement enterprise. Despite Netanyahu's "moratorium", said B'Tselem, by a variety of tactics Israel had appropriated more than 42 per cent of the West Bank for settlement expansion.

None of this is news to Dror; in fact, it's old history. "This pattern was shaped in the 1920s and 1930s as part of the Zionist ethos, the idea that every new farm had a role in shaping and defending the territory of the future state of Israel. There is a distinction you have to understand between the state of Israel and the land of Israel. The land of Israel is a biblical concept; romantic, even mythic. On the other hand, the state of Israel is a modern entity with borders and laws. The settlements sit on the land of Israel, religiously speaking, but they do not sit in the state of Israel, politically speaking. Our inability to understand this distinction amounts to a public sickness in this country. This is the issue we are facing."

*   *   *

The light is fading, it's late in the afternoon. Dror closes his computer, and heads home to a small community outside the city. Today is his daughter's birthday, a party is planned.

Later tonight he will start work on a new petition to the court.

7
This is My Homeland

"At my high school, one of my favourite teachers was Shakeeb Jahshan, who taught us Arabic. Do you know this name, Shakeeb Jahshan? He was a poet, a famous Palestinian poet here in Nazareth. I appreciated this man very much, he was a role model for me. He would teach us not just the language, but how to love your land, your people, how to serve your community. However, we could not learn his poetry in school. This is a strange situation – you have direct contact with a famous poet but you can't study his poems. So I and other students organized that we would meet with Shakeeb Jahshan once a week after school. He did this voluntarily, and people who cared about Arabic language and poetry would join us to study his poetry."

We are talking in Dr Yousef Jabareen's office, by a busy street in central Nazareth, the largest city in the Galilee region. Widely known as the "Arab capital of Israel", Nazareth is also believed by Christians to be the birthplace of Jesus. Tour buses speed past, carrying the faithful to churches, monasteries and souvenir shops in the old city.

With short dark hair greying at the temples and a close-trimmed beard, Yousef is dressed for a hot October day in a short-sleeved blue shirt and black trousers. I have only an hour with him before he has to drive to Tel Aviv University, to give a lecture on minority rights and the law.

He lives with his family in Umm Al-Fahm, a smaller city about 30 minutes' drive from here in the "triangle" area, adjacent to the West Bank. He was born there in 1972. I ask him how his identity as an Arab or Palestinian in Israel evolved. He replies, "For me, a very important source of information and awareness about the larger picture was *Al-Ittihad*, the only daily Arabic newspaper in Israel. My family had a subscription to it. Though it was published by the Communist Party, it was not just about communism, but also the cause of Palestinians in general, and the Palestinian community inside Israel in particular."

Al-Ittihad (The Union) was founded in 1944, banned several times by the British colonial authorities and later several times by the Israeli government. From 1948 to 1966, Palestinians who remained in the new state lived under Israeli military rule. "If you read *Al-Ittihad* it had to be in secret", says Yousef. "People who had in their possession any materials with Palestinian content were targeted as communists or nationalists. Arabs were also forced to fly the Israeli flag, which is a flag of the Jewish religion and Zionism, over every school. I know that this generation went through a very hard period, but they survived. Now we continue the struggle that they started."

In addition to reading about the larger picture, the young Yousef also discovered the immediate world for himself. Moving to a school in Nazareth at the age of 13, he would travel on the regular bus from Umm Al-Fahm. It passed through the Jewish town of Afula, founded in 1925 by American Zionists. "Every day I would see nice roads, new buildings, many trees in Afula, but in Umm Al-Fahm and Nazareth, nothing like that. Afula had a central bus station, but in Umm Al-Fahm the bus would only stop on the edge of the town, a long way from where I lived – in Jewish municipalities the government provided public transport, but in Arab municipalities, nothing. So instead of 40 minutes, often it took two hours to get home from school. My eyes couldn't miss these gaps, it looked like two different worlds."

At school, Shakeeb Jahshan's poetry wasn't the only gap. Yousef explains, "The Israeli education system didn't then, and still doesn't, recognize the unique identity of Arab citizens as Palestinians. The curriculum is dictated by the government, and we have to adhere to it because when we finish high school everyone has to take the same standardized national exams to qualify for college or university. There is nothing in this curriculum about our history, 1948 or since; nothing about our Palestinian heritage, our leadership, our culture. Sometimes you would think our history ended in 1948, and after that it's a blank."

Clearly the future leadership would include Yousef Jabareen. At 14 he was elected head of the students' council at his school, then the same again in high school. When the first intifada broke out in 1987, he invited guest speakers to explain what was happening in the West Bank and Gaza, how the occupation worked, and why Palestinians needed an independent state. At Hebrew University, once again he was elected head of the Arab student committee.

CIVIL RIGHTS

Among the file boxes and Arabic and Hebrew titles on his crowded bookshelves, I see *The History of Human Rights*; *American Indian Law: Cases and Materials*, *We Won't Go Back* and *Access Denied*.

Often I've heard Palestinians equate education with liberation. In Yousef Jabareen's case the equation also included the law. "I wanted to be lawyer since I was 14 or 15", he says. "I would read about civil rights lawyers, both Jewish and Arab within Israel, and people like Nelson Mandela, also a lawyer. Seeing how these people struggled against injustice in their own contexts combined with my feeling of injustice as a Palestinian to create this decision to study law."

While he studied, he also worked with the Association for Civil Rights in Israel (ACRI), on issues arising from the military occupation, mostly trying to negotiate permits for Palestinians to move, study or work. For a 20-year-old who learned in his classes that the law is a neutral instrument, work on the ground was a shock. "I remember the first time I went with a Jewish lawyer to a military court in Ramallah, and I saw that the judge had the same military uniform as the prosecutor. This was against everything I believed a judge should be, neutral and objective – at law school I studied one thing, but on the ground I saw something completely different."

There were brief satisfactions, a permit granted here, a bit of compensation won there. But the bad news, he says, was that the occupation continued. He began to learn the limits of individual law.

After graduating in the mid 1990s, Yousef won a New Israel Fund scholarship to study for a Master's degree in civil rights and international law at American University in Washington, DC. Why did he choose the US? "Because that's where the scholarship was," he replies, "but also because Israeli law is very influenced by American legal tradition, and many Israeli lawyers and judges have their education in the US, so if you bring an argument from the US system, often it is seen as convincing here. When you go to the US, you go to the source of the influence."

Yousef's Jewish-American academic supervisor supported his decision to intern with the Arab-American Anti-Discrimination Committee. "That was a good experience for me", he says. "Though our experience as Palestinians here is quite unique, it also has some common characteristics with Arab-Americans. We both face racial profiling, stereotypes, racism, and employment discrimination." Every time Yousef responded to an ad for an apartment to rent in Washington, as soon as he spoke his name the landlord would hang up.

Back in Israel, he worked as legal adviser to ACRI in Haifa, heading their project on equality for Arab citizens in Israel. "This is what I wanted to do," says Yousef, "to represent the cause of equal rights for our community. I thought the Israeli courts would be more friendly to civil rights issues than the military courts in the West Bank. There you lose all the time, but here you should have some chance to succeed."

In one famous case, an Arab family had tried to buy a building lot in a new Jewish settlement called Katzir, but were rejected because they were Arabs. With Yousef Jabareen and ACRI, they petitioned the High Court. Five years later it ruled that the rejection was illegal because the land in question was state-owned, and the state couldn't legally discriminate on the basis of ethnicity. It was an important, hard-won victory. But then the Jewish Agency, which adminsters state land, refused to implement it. Only now, says Yousef, 15 years after the case was filed in 1995, finally the family has a permit to build.

Though gratified by the outcome, Yousef Jabareen had serious questions about the context. "To think that such a simple case would take all these years, it raises a question mark about the ability of the legal system to change, even in an individual case. But then too, even if we do have a good case like this, it will have only very limited impact on one or two families. It won't address general issues that affect the whole community."

Other cases confirmed his impression: as long as Arab citizens of Israel were unable to influence policy, they would be stuck fighting one costly case after another while the system remained intact and immovable.

In 2000, Yousef Jabareen went back to the US on another scholarship, this time to work on a PhD in law, policy and minority rights at Georgetown University in Washington. For his thesis he wrote a comparative study on the civil rights of African-Americans and Palestinians in Israel. He explains, "Both are not full citizens. I found many issues to be similar, especially the role of whiteness or white supremacy in the US, which is similar to the role of Jewishness or Jewish supremacy in Israel. Of course, I could also see differences. But in general the US experience gave me some hope. After so many years of slavery and then segregation, with a very oppressive regime to enforce it, now 50 years later the segregation laws are gone – that's a big change, at least in the legal system. And in 2008

an African-American was elected president. In historical terms this
is a relatively short period. I'm not saying that an African-American
president will change the situation, but still, 50 years ago nobody
would have believed this could happen in the US. Today nobody
believes real change is possible in Israel. So who knows, maybe the
US experience is a source for hope."

DIRASAT

Returning to Israel in 2003, Dr Yousef Jabareen taught several
university and college courses on minority rights and the Arab
community. He also began to build the practical foundations for a
dream that had come to him in the US: a think-tank for Palestinian
Israelis, or "a think-and-do-tank", as he puts it.

As detailed in a recent Dirasat study, the disparities between Arab
and Jewish Israelis are shocking: significantly lower life expectancy
for both females and males, more than double the infant mortality,
more than double the poverty rate. While Arab citizens comprise
18 per cent of the country's population, they own only 3.5 per cent
of the land. In 2005, 94.5 per cent of civil service employees were
Jewish, 5 per cent Arab. The drop-out rate for Arab high school
students is double the rate for Jewish students. And so on. All the
figures are taken from Israeli government sources, which tend to
be lower than figures gathered by NGOs.

"We don't lack knowledge of these disparities", says Yousef. "The
challenge is to determine what can be done about them. If we could
bring together Arab experts in these fields not only to analyse the
situation but to recommend actual policy changes, this could make a
major contribution to our community. It wouldn't be limited to the
law or academic writings, but much broader, trying to see the entire
picture from a variety of perspectives, out of which we could then
make practical recommendations – first to our own leaders, so they
could better understand what they should be asking for, but also to
present our findings to decision-making people in the government."

Yousef consulted widely with Arab community leaders, academics,
and NGOs, both Arab and Jewish. Most supported the initiative
enthusiastically. To get more grassroots input, he and his colleagues
organized community sessions to brainstorm which issues were in
most urgent need of attention. "It was an endless list," he says,
"for which we would need millions of dollars. We decided to focus
on three critical issues: education, local government, and better
research on our community, so that we can make more effective

demands. Luckily, we got support not just from our own community but also from funding sources such as the Ford Foundation, the New Israel Fund and the European Union. So things are moving." Yousef Jabareen became founding director of Dirasat, the Arab Centre for Law and Policy.

Number one on the issues list is education. In a July 2009 article for the Israeli newspaper *Haaretz*, Yousef wrote that from 2006 to 2008, the rate of Arab high school students who passed their final exams fell by almost 20 per cent. He points out that while the Israeli state invests US$1,000 per Jewish pupil annually, for Arab pupils it invests only US$200, and concludes that the continued deterioration of the education system will "perpetuate social injustices, alienation and exclusion, and could lead to civil unrest".

Within the vast field of education, Dirasat working groups are concentrating on two vital elements: teacher training, and the structure of the education system – who makes decisions and how – with a particular emphasis on curriculum. But I'm still having difficulty translating these large, abstract concepts into real-life issues, so I ask Yousef for an example.

"One of our colleagues has looked into the psychometric exam, the mandatory exam that determines who will enter university. This researcher found that in the last 20 years, there is a constant gap of at least 100 points out of 800 in the scores between Jews and Arabs. We argue that when this gap is so consistent, it indicates that something is wrong, and ultimately that the exam process itself is discriminatory. We choose to believe that those responsible for creating these exams at the ministry don't intend to prejudice Arab candidates. So we hope that by bringing our findings and conclusions to them, it will help convince them to do something about this problem. A small example: why should Arab students have to take this exam only at the Jewish universities; why can't they take it at one of the private colleges here in Nazareth? They would feel more comfortable within their own communities, and they wouldn't have to travel at 6 a.m. to Jerusalem or sleep over in Tel Aviv the night before. So our recommendations are on two levels, short and long term. Overall policies are hard to change, but maybe at least some small improvements can be made in the short term."

I comment that, sadly, government shelves everywhere are filled with good reports on issues of urgent concern. What pressures can Dirasat bring to bear: first to get heard, then to get results? Yousef nods. "You're right", he says. "That is where these things often go. In our case, we are still in the early stages – gathering knowledge, analysing it, and shaping policy recommendations – but certainly the next step will be strategic, how do we reach the government. It may be an advantage that many of us teach at Israeli universities and colleges, so we have good connections with Jewish scholars who are involved in these issues. In Israel many policies are influenced by academics and researchers. Not all of them are right-wing; not all of them produce problematic results out of intentional prejudice. In some cases it comes from not fully understanding the situation. We think that if we bring convincing materials, we will have them on our side to help change the situation."

He smiles. I must be looking sceptical. "Yes, I know", he says. "This is the more hopeful scenario. If the decision-makers really are racist and have no intention of changing the situation, well, that's another scenario."

Earlier today, Yousef told me that his determination to study law had caused tension between him and his father. As he described it, a warm smile lit his face. "A typical Arab dad, he wanted me to be – what do you think? – a physician. That was his dream for me, he started to call me doctor even when I was 15, 17, and he could see that my grades were high enough to go to medical school. But my mind went in a different direction. I solved the problem by telling him 'I promise that you will continue to call me "doctor", but it will be in law. I'll be a doctor, but not a physician.' Today I think I made the right decision. It gave me a good background and skills to deal with issues that disturbed me when I was young. If you can, it's good to do what you like to do. It's a prescription for happiness."

THE POLITICS OF HOPE

When we spoke earlier about curriculum gaps, Yousef Jabareen said, "Now the new right-wing government is even trying to silence one word in the curriculum, just one word, '*Nakba*' [the 1948 catastrophe when more than 700,000 Palestinians lost their homes and their land], that small word that tells you Palestinians had this experience. Even this, the new minister decided to delete. He announced yesterday that they will collect all the text books, and re-edit them to delete this word."

The 2009 election of the Netanyahu-Lieberman government doesn't bode well for equality in Israel. In its first year the new regime introduced a variety of legislation that will make life even more difficult on many fronts for Palestinian Israelis. How do Yousef and his colleagues navigate through these increasingly turbulent times? "Instead of starting from zero, we try to build on what's already been done", Yousef replies. "For example, a report was prepared for the previous Minister of Education, and approved by the professional level at the ministry. We think it has some good recommendations, so now we are advocating that it be implemented. Yes, it's a tough regime, and I understand that things will be more difficult. But we always say we want to do politics of hope, not politics of blame or despair. If we didn't have hope, why would we have bothered to establish a public policy group like Dirasat?"

Yousef's two children are powerful incentives for hope. His son is eight, his daughter five. "When they were born," he says, "it was a new feeling for me, a new sense of future. You want your kids to live a better life – if not an optimal one then at least a better one than we had. My life is better than my father's, and their lives should be better than mine. This is why we continue to work for change."

THIS IS MY HOMELAND

On my travels I found that people in the West Bank and Gaza identify themselves without hesitation as Palestinian, proudly, even defiantly. For Palestinians within the state of Israel, identity is more complicated. Officially they are called Arab citizens of Israel. Most Israelis – even some progressives – refer to them from habit as Arab-Israelis. As in the time of Yousef's parents when reading *Al-Ittihad* was considered subversive, in the current climate, assertions of Palestinian-ness tend to be regarded as suspicious.

In 2009, Foreign Minister Avigdor Lieberman's Yisrael Beiteinu party, which has become Israel's third largest political party, proposed legislation requiring all citizens to swear a loyalty oath "to the state of Israel as a Jewish, Zionist and democratic state". Those who refused would not be issued a national identity card, which would essentially revoke their citizenship. The proposal was rejected by the cabinet, but other such measures are in the works. Clearly, for Arab citizens of Israel, the writing is on the wall.

Under the circumstances, I hesitate to ask Dr Yousef Jabareen how he defines his nationality. But then it occurs to me that if anyone would know the boundaries of safety, surely it would be a lawyer. So I ask him, "How do you define your nationality?"

He regards me steadily. After a moment he asks, "What do you mean, 'nationality'?"

"If you asked me the same question, I'd say Canadian, by birth and citizenship. What would you say?"

Again he pauses. I understand that for him, unlike me, there are implications. Then he says, "I would say I'm an Arab-Palestinian, a citizen of Israel. As a citizen of Israel, with an Israeli passport, I am struggling to achieve full rights and equality. A major aspect of my identity that gives me a lot of strength is the fact that I feel indigenous. I have roots in this land, through my father, my grandfather. This is my homeland. That helps form my attititude to any political institution around me, in this case the state of Israel. I expect that it should treat me as no less than anybody else, because nobody else has a better claim to belong here. I say this to my Jewish colleagues – we are both here, I'm part of a family that has been living here for generations, and I don't accept to live in a situation where you have a higher status, or any kind of special privilege over me."

But isn't this exactly the situation in which he lives? "True", he says. "If this really was my state, a state for the benefit of everybody, I would be in a different place by now. I might be a high-ranked official, even a minister, or the dean of a law school. Instead of having always to ask for resources as a minority, I would be in a position to allocate resources, fairly for all. So I live with the sense that this state is not allowing me, or my community in general, the possibility to fulfil ourselves according to our skills and our dreams."

He looks at his watch, our time is running out. I'm moved to comment, "From what I've seen of high-ranked officials, maybe it's better for your community that you continue to do what you're doing."

He looks puzzled, then bursts into laughter. "Yeah", he says. "I won't say I could be a high official and still be happy, but at least I want to be allowed the choice. Who knows, maybe if I was a high official, I might have to resign so I could work in a civil society organization like Dirasat."

And who knows, maybe one day the poetry of Shakeeb Jahshan will be studied here during regular school hours.

8
Facts Under the Ground

On the surface, Silwan is a crowded Palestinian neighbourhood on a steep slope in East Jerusalem. It runs from the walled Old City, down the Wadi Al-Hilweh – Kidron Valley to the Israelis – between the Mount of Olives and Mount Zion.

Densely stacked up both sides of the valley, houses glow in honey-coloured afternoon light. On flat rooftops I see satellite dishes, water tanks, shade canopies, laundry flapping, children playing. A brisk breeze up from the valley moderates the September heat. In the midst of Ramadan Islamic holy days, the streets are unusually quiet.

Standing in a loose arc on the main City of David viewing platform, we are 22 people, most under the age of 40; a few Israelis, the rest of us from abroad. Some wear blue vests marked "World Council of Churches". We are taking the alternative archaeological tour of Silwan, to be conducted in English today.

Our guide is Yonathan Mizrachi, a casually dressed Israeli archeologist with lively dark eyes behind glasses, and a pony-tail greying at the edges. Rocking from foot to foot like a boxer, he talks fast – not surprising, given that he plans to introduce us to several eventful millennia and a highly embattled present, all before supper.

He tells us he has an agenda. "In a place like this you depend on your guide to explain what you see. If you went on a tour run by Elad you would get a different agenda, and different information. Remember that every archeologist has his own methods and interests, so all of it has to be questioned – does it make sense, is it logical?" This habit of inquiry, it turns out, is crucial to Yonathan's life and work.

Normally the City of David tourist complex would be thronged. The Elad organization leads over 400,000 visitors a year through the site, but on this eve of the Jewish Shabbat we have the place to ourselves – almost. A security guard in black T-shirt and khakis hovers nearby, talking quietly into a radio phone. Our presence here is legal, but it would not sit well with Elad, which operates the site and employs the guard.

Though a powerful presence here, Elad is a relatively recent arrival. In the nineteenth and twentieth centuries, European and American archeological digs turned up evidence of human habitation here dating back 40–50 centuries. In 1967 the Israeli military occupied the Old City and the arc of Palestinian villages around it; the region and its population were annexed to Jerusalem, and became known officially as East Jerusalem. The Palestinians were not granted citizenship, only "residence".

Soon Israeli archeologists began to dig into their neighbourhoods, and eventually the Wadi Al-Hilweh site, called the City of David, became part of a chain of national parks surrounding the Old City. "Elad" is an acronym for *el ir David*, the City of David. Founded in 1986 by a former commander of an elite Israeli military unit, the private settler foundation began to acquire property here by a variety of means. Though difficult to trace, their abundant funding appears to come primarily from foreign sources, most likely in the United States.

Through government connections, Elad quickly won approval to construct settlers' housing on sites believed to be archeologically signficant – despite objections from the Israel Antiquities Authority, which is responsible for protecting such sites and their contents.

In the early 1990s, when the Oslo Accords briefly raised hopes for a political settlement that could return East Jerusalem to Palestinian sovereignty, the Nature and National Parks Authority took preventative action, awarding Elad a contract to manage – essentially to control – the archeological park in Silwan. In an ironic twist, the private foundation then hired its former nemesis, the public Israeli Antiquities Authority, to dig for it.

Our tour begins over an excavation. From an elaborate array of platforms, stairs and walkways we look down into a large pit with partially exposed walls of beige stone blocks, stabilized by sandbags and mortar, and beside them a mobile conveyor belt, presumably to remove rubble. The whole scene strikes me as somewhat arranged, a stage set.

Yonathan Mizrachi tells us this is, or was, a real dig. Apparently it unearthed intentional construction from periods up to 3,000–4,000 years ago, the remains of houses on a scale that suggests rich people lived here, high on the slope. "Archeology is a very long process", says our guide. "First you excavate, then you interpret what you have found, you try to understand what it means. That takes time."

By contrast, the Israeli archeologist who directed the dig announced immediately and emphatically that she had found a large building from the tenth century BCE, which she took to be part of a palace; because it is assumed that King David lived in the tenth century, it must have been his.

Not so fast, says our guide. "Other archeologists believe it may be wrong to conclude that this building belongs to the tenth century. Why? The piece of wall you see here has been used for hundreds or even thousands of years, by many different cultures. The Canaanites, Judeans, Romans, Byzantines and Muslims may all have used some part of it, so it becomes very hard to tell exactly who built what, and when. In the end you have to question how much or how little archeologists can really understand the past. That's just one of the problems here."

PEOPLE OF THE WALL

Who is our guide, and what is he doing here? Born in 1971, Yonathan Mizrachi describes his childhood as normal and average – he grew up in Jerusalem; joined the army at 18; wondered what to do next; began, then abandoned, a range of studies at university. Finally he settled on archeology. Why? "All my life I was interested more in history, but when I started archeology, it felt like history with an added factor. I wanted to do something that related to people. In history you stay inside, you look at documents. But in archeology you do excavations out in the field, and in most places where you do that, you meet the people who live there. Often these are people of different experience and different cultures from yours. This is what I wanted."

He sought work where many Israeli archeologists do, at the Antiquities Authority. His first jobs were disappointing, just digs, lacking the contact with current inhabitants that he craved. He took a rest from archeology, worked with teenagers, taught school. Then, in 2002, work began on the Jerusalem sections of the separation wall, and Yonathan was assigned the task of checking the route as it advanced, to ensure that no antiquities would be destroyed.

As the bulldozers ploughed through Palestinian neighbourhoods and villages, they also endangered sites of longest habitation in the Jerusalem area, and thus the largest concentrations of antiquities. Here Yonathan would also meet the present, in the form of Palestinians unlucky enough to live in the path of the advancing wall. As these encounters intensified, he began to write his impressions, later gathering them into a book, *People of the Wall*.

By the time Yonathan published the book, his position with the Israeli Antiquities Authority had become untenable. First, he could not publish without the Authority's permission, but more important for him, the archeological work still lacked the vital element – respectful engagement with current inhabitants. Often as he worked, he was accompanied by Israeli security guards. Clearly, this was archeology from above.

Still searching for a more egalitarian approach, he identified two potential options: community archeology and Silwan.

In community archeology, archeologists cooperate with local residents to look more deeply into the long-term story of the place where they live. Yonathan joined Professor Rafael Greenberg, an archeologist from Tel Aviv University, to work on a project in the West Jerusalem working-class neighbourhood of Ir Ganim-Qiryat Menahem. Excavations there have turned up intentional constructions from the Iron Age II (around 1000–600 BCE), also the later Persian and Roman periods.

Since the project is sponsored by the community rather than the academy, priorities are set by consensus, skills and findings are shared; residents and academics assemble the story together. To Yonathan, this would provide more of the lively engagement that he had been craving.

THE BIBLE SAYS

On our tour, we go deeper into the earth under Silwan. From up on the surface I hear church bells tolling and a call to prayer from the mosque, evocative aural postcards from the Holy City, but also reminders that this continues to be one of the most bitterly contested places on the planet.

When a British explorer came looking for the temple of Solomon in nineteenth-century Jerusalem, he ended up unearthing a vertical shaft just below the platform where we are standing. He assumed that it must belong to the water system of the old city. Because the Bible says ancient Jerusalem was the city of King David, Christian explorers – latter-day Crusaders armed with shovels – concluded that it must be so, and so it has been called ever since.

However, in many decades of intensive searching, archeologists from France, Britain, the US and Israel have failed to turn up any convincing evidence that King David lived here. In fact, some archeologists argue that since there is a marked gap in archeological evidence here from the tenth century BCE, and it is generally agreed that this is when King David lived, it is logical to conclude that he didn't live here.

This argument misses the point, says our guide. "If you believe in the Bible, you will continue to believe that he lived here no matter how much excavation you do. If you don't believe in the Bible, you will continue not to believe he lived here, no matter what happens in archeology. We try to suggest something else, that proving whether King David did or didn't live here is not what archeology should be doing. We say our purpose should be to learn about cultures, not historical figures – that's the job of historians. In archeology we should be learning how people lived, what they believed, what was the relationship between rich and poor, how did these things change from one period to another. By learning these things about cultures in the past, it helps us to understand better our own culture and the cultures around us today."

How did Jonathan find his way to the beleaguered streets of Silwan? His salvage work with the Israeli Antiquities Authority raised his interest in the area, and he wanted to return, but this time with a different agenda. He and a few other Israeli archeologists had begun to suspect that their vocation was being abused in Silwan, though they were not yet clear how or to what degree. "It took us a while to get to know the local people better", says Yonathan. "They have learned to be quite suspicious toward Israelis. When we come here, they ask themselves, 'What's your real purpose, who do you work for?' It took years."

In 2005 their sense of urgency increased dramatically when the municipal government announced plans to destroy 88 homes in Al-Bustan, an Arab neighbourhood at the lower end of Silwan, and to replace them with a park. Elad had lobbied for the project. "According to people who believe the Bible," says Yonathan, "that was the border of the City of David. It doesn't matter that it was actually a Canaanite city." Some Israeli archeologists believe there had once been a garden there – "bustan" is Arabic for "garden" or "orchard" – perhaps a royal garden. Municipal authorities claimed the houses were illegal because they were built without permits – permits which are virtually impossible for Palestinians to obtain from the Israeli authorities. Though a court petition by Palestinian and Israeli activists halted the demolitions, all sides knew the stay of execution would be temporary.

In June 2010, Jerusalem municipal authorities announced that 22 Palestinian homes would be demolished. Further demolitions are expected.

For Yonathan and his colleagues, the ongoing struggle confirmed their sense that archeology was being used here not as a tool of discovery but as a weapon; in this case serving a larger, hidden agenda: to isolate the whole slope from adjacent Arab neighbourhoods, ultimately rendering impossible the formation of a viable Palestinian state with East Jerusalem as its capital. Suddenly the need sharpened for community-based archeology in Silwan.

To foster it, Yonathan and others launched a new organization – Emek Shaveh, "the valley of Shaveh". "Shaveh" is Hebrew for "equal", he says, and valley of Shaveh represents a place of compromise. Emek Shaveh is "a non-profit association of archaeologists, local residents and human rights activists working to change the role of archaeology in the Israeli-Palestinian conflict. We believe that archaeology can be used as a bridge between peoples and cultures, and that it has the power to influence the dynamic of the Israeli-Palestinian conflict in a way that can benefit the future of all the peoples in this region."

Though it is gaining support from scholars abroad, the group is built around a few determined Israeli archeologists and Palestinian community activists. Other Israeli archeologists have expressed support privately, but their academic world is small enough that those who take public stands critical of the power structure can easily become targets.

What moved the group to action? "We felt that the settlers are using archeology to enlarge Jewish settlement here," Yonathan replies, "and that this will have a huge impact on the Palestinian residents. We knew from the beginning that we would be dealing not just with the Elad organization, but also with all levels of government that support them. If you think of it from the human point of view, the Palestinians live in this place that other people want, and there is something bad, something wrong being done here. That's why I want to help."

Though the group focuses on Silwan, the issues it raises are common to the settlement project throughout East Jerusalem and the West Bank. More than 200,000 Israeli Jews already live in growing settlements across the area called East Jerusalem. Settlements on occupied land are considered illegal under international law. The government of Israel claims that East Jerusalem is not technically occupied, because it was captured in the 1967 war and then annexed to Jerusalem – a territorial acquisition which has so far failed to win legal recognition by any country, even Israel's most faithful ally, the United States.

NOBODY OWNS THE PAST

We descend to a deeper platform, and peer down at shadowy stone walls that run in parallel. They were likely built at different periods, says our guide, from the Iron Age to the Byzantine. He draws our attention to one section, partially collapsed. "This is the most important wall," says Yonathan, "the one that the archeologist who led the dig says is from King David in the tenth century BCE. Other archeologists believe it originated much earlier, probably in the thirteenth century BCE. That's the most we can say with confidence."

Here among the stones under Silwan, sharply drawn, are two fundamentally different visions of how archeology should work. For the people who started Emek Shaveh, the goals are clear. From their website:

We believe that archaeology can and should be used to promote understanding, not conflict.

We do not assign different values to different cultures: all strata contribute to an understanding of Jerusalem's history on equal terms.

Since archaeology provides an independent view of human and social origins, it is inherently critical of all historical narratives.

Since archaeologists appropriate public property, the use they make of this property must be justified, particularly to the public whose property was appropriated.

For the Elad organization, the driving purpose of archeology is quite different. From their website:

The Ir David Foundation is committed to continuing King David's legacy and strengthening Israel's current and historic connection to Jerusalem through four key initiatives: archaeological excavation, tourism development, residential revitalization and educational programming.

Moving deeper into the warren of excavations, we come closer to the heart of the archeological conflict here. Yonathan indicates several shallow pits hewn into the rock. It's likely that some were used to store water, he explains, and some may have been used by Jews of the Second Temple period for their ritual baths before prayer.

One of the people on the tour asks him what we might be hearing at this point on the Elad tour. "You'd hear about King David," he replies, "how he conquered Jerusalem, where he lived, all according to the Bible. You'd hear about the Second Temple. What you would hear is all about Jewish Jerusalem. You're supposed to feel this is a Jewish site, we can't give it up, we can't even share it, it belongs to the Jewish nation. What we try to suggest instead is that nobody owns the past. Even if tomorrow you were to find an inscription here, 'Welcome to King David's Palace', it doesn't mean the Jewish people own this site. If you found evidence of a church here, or a mosque, that doesn't mean it belongs to the Vatican or to Muslims. We say the past belongs to everyone, especially in a place like this with such a rich, varied past, and everyone has a right to learn from it, it doesn't matter who you are."

In contrast to our questioning walk with Yonathan, the Elad tour includes glossy brochures and a sumptuous 3D movie that confirms with dramatic computer-generated simulations what faithful pilgrims want to believe about the past. The website does the same: "A tour through the City of David brings visitors face to face with the personalities and places of the Bible. As such, this is the only place on earth where the only guidebook needed is the Bible itself."

Back on the surface, we continue our descent into the valley, down a steep, narrow street past shuttered houses and shops no wider than the spread of my arms. We pass a larger house behind a wall, a settler house, identifiable by its tall communications aerial and Israeli flags on the roof. On the flat top of another settler house, a security guard in the standard black T-shirt and khakis watches us from inside a small guard house. Yonathan tells us that there are now an estimated 30–50 settler houses in Silwan: about 300 settlers. The government pays for the guards. I notice a settler family out for a walk in what looks like a private path, walled on both sides. An adult male, presumably the father, wears a bulletproof vest and carries an assault rifle.

Next stop on our tour is a broad green canvas-covered structure, surrounded by barbed wire. Elad owns this piece of land, and last year decided to excavate. As usual, the Israeli Antiquities Authority would do the work. "The problem we have here," says our guide, "is that if you excavate in the middle of a village, people should feel it has some connection to them. But as you can see, here you can't get in, and you don't know what's being done. The residents fear that this land has just been taken away from them. We think there should be another kind of relationship with the residents – they should feel the site belongs to their community, and they should feel that the work will have some benefit for them."

Apparently the Silwanis' fears turned out to be justified: Elad and the Antiquities Authority have begun to excavate a tunnel under cover of the tent, part of a grand plan to turn an ancient drainage tunnel into an underground walkway from the Wailing Wall in the Old City to the Shiloah pool to the south. Tourists would be able to walk the whole route without ever having to see, let alone meet, any of the people who live on the surface. Silwan would become invisible and irrelevant.

When cracks began to appear in the walls of Palestinian homes over the excavation, residents filed a petition with the Israel Supreme Court to end the digging. That night, police raided several homes in Silwan and arrested five residents. As it often happens in these cases, the charges were eventually dropped, but the point was made. At the same time, the court granted an injunction against further digging. All concerned knew it would be temporary.

Yonathan told me later that the residents had lost again. The Supreme Court ruled that Elad and the Israel Antiquities Authority could continue to excavate because the site is so important to the Jewish heritage.

In winter 2009, the floor in a local school collapsed into a gaping hole, injuring three students. A year later, one of Silwan's main streets collapsed, swallowing the front end of a municipal bus.

JAWAD SIYAM

At this point in the tour, Yonathan introduces us to Jawad Siyam, a founder of the Silwan Residents' Committee. "Welcome to Silwan", he says, a quiet assertion of both hospitality and homeland. We sit together on a wide circle of plastic chairs under a canvas canopy – the protest tent. A banner flapping over the entrance proclaims in Arabic and English, "To Dig a Tunnel Means to Kill a Village". Next to the tent a few recently planted olive saplings hold on in the dry heat. At the edge of the dusty lot a white horse stands in a little stable tucked in under the edge of a house. As Jawad tells us about his village, the horse wanders out to graze on the few blades of grass it can find here and there.

Jawad looks about 40, in T-shirt and tracksuit trousers, sunglasses perched atop his balding head. He has lived here since 1968 when he was born in what was then still a village, his family still raising vegetables, chickens and sheep, harvesting olives and lemons from their trees. Educated in Turkey (American studies) and Germany (communications and social work), Jawad is married to a Bosnian Serb, with two young children. Since he initiated the petition to the Supreme Court, he is harassed frequently by the Israeli municipal police and Shabak, the secret police.

"By the way," Jawad warns us with a trace of smile, "you are on camera here. They want to know everyone who comes to the tent. They have cameras everywhere; we are watched all the time. Elad has a huge camera over the village; it sees everything. We call it 'the Guantanamo camera'."

Nothing Palestinian is secure here. Elad wants to turn the lot where we are sitting into a parking lot, for the convenience of tourists that flock to the City of David complex. "We said, 'Why a parking lot when we don't have schools, sport clubs, or a community centre?' The owner of this land said he would give me licence to build three floors here, a school or whatever, and he would keep the first floor for parking. The municipal authorities refused permission. So we went to court. We won – for now. But then the police come, like today; it's a Saturday, it's Ramadan and very quiet here, but still they come to harass people. Every day they arrest someone. But when the settlers take our olives and we call the police, nothing happens."

Jawad covers a lot of ground in the short time he has our attention. While Elad can afford to operate tours daily all year except Sabbaths and holidays, the alternative tours occur only when one of the volunteer Emek Shaveh archeologists can find time to lead it.

"We used to sell little things to tourists", says Jawad. "This is how I paid for my education, but they don't allow that any more. We can't even sell our own vegetables in the shops here. It's a very bad situation economically for us." Before the Israeli occupation, Silwan was largely self-sufficient, one of the wealthiest villages in the area. Now it has become one of the poorest neighbourhoods in East Jerusalem.

Every house here is under threat. On the way here, Yonathan pointed out one with a grey door. It belongs to Jawad's family. Twice the settlers have tried to take the house, says Jawad, and both times the documents they used have been proved in court to have been faked. "But no one was punished," says Jawad, "and the settlers still occupy the house. That's how it is here." His voice cracks a little, he sounds weary.

A few weeks before our tour, the Jerusalem municipality announced that the Arabic names of the main streets in Silwan would be replaced by Hebrew names appropriate to the City of David enterprise. "This street is called Wadi Hilweh," says Jawad. "It means 'valley of Hilweh'. It is named after the aunt of my mother, who was killed during the time of the British occupation. Now they change it to 'City of David Heights'. They say there is another street called Wadi Hilweh in another place, but in that place there is no valley, so it makes no sense." Elsewhere this might only be a bureaucratic irritant, but here it's another step toward erasure and oblivion.

Jawad Siyam continues to organize for the survival of his village, inch by inch, past and present, above and below the surface. Yonathan tells us that he was instrumental in launching elections for a local citizens' committee, a first for Silwan, and with co-workers he overcame innumerable obstacles to start a small community centre. It offers classes in art, music, English and Hebrew, a library, a summer day camp, and simply a place to meet and talk in relative safety.

The afternoon is fading, and the tour near its end. Our guide concludes, "Many nations, cultures, religions and rulers have come to this place, they built and destroyed, but through all of that, life continued. This is why we feel archeology isn't just about what was built in the past, it's about how the past connects to the present, and this is why we feel the people who live here belong to the place, and the place belongs to them."

As if on cue, bells start tolling far up the slope, at one of the churches in the Old City.

In an attempt to limit the harm being done here in the name of their profession, Yonathan and his colleagues launched an online petition to remove control of archaeology in Silwan from the hands of Elad. So far, it carries the signatures of concerned scholars in Israel, the United States, Canada, Germany, England, Scotland, France, Switzerland, Austria, the Netherlands, Morocco, Australia, Spain, Finland and Argentina.

In the protest tent I watched Jawad and Yonathan sitting side by side, introducing us to their connected worlds above and below the surface of Silwan. I saw an Israeli and a Palestinian who have become allies. Under different circumstances, this is how things could be here. Under different circumstances, why not?

Then Jawad's parting comment reminded me of how different the circumstances would have to be, here and throughout this land. He said, "The problem for us in Silwan is that someone is coming here not to be my neighbour, but to replace me."

9
A Drop in the Sea

Early Saturday morning, Shabbat (Sabbath), we sail along the smooth dark ribbon of Highway 6, now named the Yitzak Rabin highway after the former prime minister. He was murdered in 1995 by an Israeli orthodox Jew, enraged that Rabin had entertained the idea of peace with the Palestinians. A right-wing campaign has been gathering support for the killer's release from prison.

I'm the first passenger, and the white van the only vehicle on the road. The young driver wears cool wraparound sunglasses. The van belongs to him, he says, and he gets hired either by westerners – usually the press – or today by Physicians for Human Rights (PHR) for their mobile clinic in Tulkarem. I ask him if it's hard to work a full day while fasting from dawn to dusk through the Ramadan holy month. Forgoing food and water doesn't bother him, he says. The hard part is doing without a smoke.

In the town of Taybeh we pick up PHR personnel, and medical supplies in stacks of clear plastic bins. Brilliant cerise bougainvillea spills over stone walls of elegant old houses. Their arched windows are shuttered against the rising heat.

Then from a rural kibbutz, Yad Hannah, we pick up a short, sturdy woman with grey hair in a braid, a loose shirt and brightly-patterned balloon trousers. PHR mobile clinic manager Salah Haj Yihyeh suggests that she sit beside me, probably because she's fluent in English. Her name is Pnina Feiler. A retired nurse, she has volunteered for years on these mobile clinics, every Saturday.

MY ANTI-WAR SCHOOL

Born in Poland in 1926, Pnina Feiler came to Palestine in 1938 with her mother. Try it out for a year, her father said, and if you like it I'll join you. Then the Germans invaded Poland, and they never saw him again.

In 1945 Pnina went to the American University in Beirut, heading for a scholarship to study medicine. Three years later, with war looming in Palestine, she returned home to work as a nurse in a Tel Aviv hospital.

"That was my anti-war school", she says in a gravelled voice. "I saw what happens when people get wounded, or blind, or whatever, and I learned that this is the worst thing you can do. War gives you a habit to kill; in fact, you are a hero when you do. It makes people aggressive, then they come home and beat their wives, their children. It's very difficult to maintain the border between this you may do, and this you may not."

This insight of hers had earlier roots. Shortly after she arrived in Palestine, her brother introduced her to the Communist Youth, an illegal organization under the British colonial regime. "It appealed to me as a very humane ideology, about human beings and distributing the wealth of the nation, not just about what I can buy and sell. I left the party a long time ago, but still to this day I consider myself a communist."

At this point the van has to stop at a checkpoint. "This road is only for the settlers", says Pnina. "It makes everything very complicated. From my kibbutz we used to walk over the fields to Tulkarem: it was a five-minute walk. Now look how far we have to go, thanks to the occupation."

WE ARE PALESTINIANS

Salah Haj Yihyeh goes out to negotiate with the soldiers. Clearly there won't be time to talk with him today, but we meet later at the PHR office in Jaffa. Amiram Gil, then director of advocacy for the Occupied Palestinian Territory Department, translates Salah's Hebrew – his second language, learned in childhood – to English.

Born in the year of the Six Day War, 1967, Salah grew up in Taybeh, his grandparents and parents refugees there since 1948. "Every year on Nakba day – for Israelis the day of independence, but for us the day we lost our land – we go to what was my grandmother's house in a village that is now Kibbutz Yakum near Netanya. All the village land was confiscated in 1948 by the state of Israel. My family still have the documents that prove they own this land, but it means nothing. The houses of my grandparents on both my mother's and father's side are still there, at the entrance to the kibbutz. Once when we came visiting there, we found migrant workers living in those houses. Probably they worked in agriculture on the kibbutz."

Salah is a citizen of Israel. I asked him how he defines his national identity. "I'm Palestinian", he replies, in a quiet, even voice that I imagine to be well-suited to negotiating with soldiers. "Ever since I was born, I've seen myself as Palestinian, and it is very important for me that my children grow up with this national identity. We are Palestinians who live in Israel, but still, we are Palestinians. This will continue."

After high school, Salah studied journalism in Tel Aviv. As a fledgling journalist he covered the eruption of the first intifada in 1987. Within a year he met Israeli doctors who had just launched Physicians for Human Rights, based at the time in the home of founder and current president, Dr Ruchama Marton. Salah volunteered for two years with PHR, then moved into the job he still does today, managing the mobile clinics.

At checkpoints it is Salah who must deal with the soldiers, face to face. I asked him what arguments he uses. "Sometimes you have to be creative", he says. "For example, last week we had a medical day in the village of Qabatiya, near Jenin. This is considered Area A (nominally controlled by the Palestinian Authority), in which Israeli civilians are not allowed, so at the checkpoint near Nablus, when they asked where we were headed, I told them Sebastia, in Area C (under direct Israeli control), which we can access. In many cases to get to Area C you have to go through Area A, which causes many of the checkpoint problems. We have been stopped for three, four, five hours, but always we insist on eventually going to that village, even if only for an hour to show solidarity, to emphasize the right of patients to treatment, and our right as health care providers to attend to patients."

Whatever Salah said to the soldiers, today it works – he reboards the van, and we pass through the checkpoint. "He has to be quite a diplomat", I comment. "Oh," Pnina replies, "he has to be many things."

She described herself earlier as a communist. What does that mean today? "Look," she says, "in Israel there is a huge gap between the top 1 per cent or even one-tenth of 1 per cent who have so much money, and huge numbers at the bottom that have very little. Those top ones don't know what to do with all their money, and the bottom ones don't know what to do without it. This doesn't make sense, does it? But look," she says, pointing out the window, "now we are approaching our destination, the refugee camp, Nur Al-Shams. It means 'the light of the sun', a very romantic name."

THE CLINIC

The camp is located inside Tulkarem city. Our van twists and jolts through narrow, dusty streets crowded with small homes and shops. In front of one, a cow is tethered. Nur Al-Shams houses more than 8,000 Palestinians on one-fifth of a square kilometre of land. Only 15 kilometres from the Mediterranean, the city and camp are cut off from the sea, Israel and the West Bank by the wall and other barriers. As in many other parts of the Occcupied Territories, the intrusion of the wall destroyed, confiscated or cut off access to a large swathe of the most fertile land in the district, including fields, orchards, greenhouses and wells.

"Tulkarem used to be an important centre", says Pnina. "People would come here from the surrounding villages for all kinds of things, including medical treatment." In 2002, the Israeli invasion of the West Bank smashed hundreds of homes, schools and medical facilities here. Periodic military attacks continue.

Today's clinic is at the women's centre and girls' school, in the densely packed interior of the refugee camp. The corridor is already thronged with people waiting for medical treatment. Salah Haj Yihyeh distributes charts and supplies for the various clinics.

I asked him how the clinics work. "We have local Palestinian partners in West Bank municipalities and in the Medical Relief organization. We discuss with them where the mobile clinic should go; for example, where checkpoints or barriers block people's access to health care, or where medical services in their own community can't provide for particular needs like diabetes, asthma or heart disease. Under the occupation, the medical system in the West Bank and Gaza is very weak."

Though health care is the core of PHR's work, the context is solidarity. "We want to demonstrate our identification with Palestinians in the Occupied Territories, and our support for ending the occupation, for freedom, and for building an independent state. It is important for us to see with our own eyes what is happening on the ground in terms of human rights violations, especially the denial of the right to health, then to report what we see to the Israeli media and the international community."

ONLY ONE CHAIR

I sit in a small classroom with Pnina Feiler and Dr Eldad Kisch, a retired endocrinologist and volunteer with PHR. "So you're writing a book", he says, with a wry smile. "Is it about the good guys?" I want to ask which "good guys" he means, but the first patients enter and the clinic begins.

First in are a man wearing a long-sleeved shirt and trousers, a woman in hijab and two small children. The woman does most of the talking, in Arabic, which Pnina translates into Hebrew for the doctor. He checks the boy's throat glands, explaining in English for my benefit, "This boy didn't grow much for two years, then he started. She's concerned that he may be short for his age, which is six."

While the parents and the nurse discuss the matter, Eldad Kisch comments to me, "Something here doesn't fit – the medical record seems to predate the boy's birth. It's a problem when you have to go through so many channels, I don't always get the answers I want. It's my fault, I should have learned Arabic."

A young man, one of several doing traffic control in the corridor, taps at the classroom window. Pnina waves at him to wait a little. From her ample bag she fishes out a brightly coloured transfer tattoo for the boy, whose expression suddenly transforms from wide-eyed fear to shy delight. Pnina assures the parents that his height is normal. When they look unconvinced, she stands and demonstrates with hand gestures that she is even shorter than the boy's mother, that's how it is, there is no problem. Finally the mother smiles, relieved.

Next to enter are a woman walking with a cane, and a girl in her early teens. While Pnina gives the girl an injection, Dr Kisch explains to me, "A lot of what we see here is diabetes. It's very difficult at Ramadan because of the effect that fasting has on the blood sugar. On top of that, the daughter here doesn't understand the consequences of drinking Coke and eating whatever she wants." While Pnina delivers a diabetes pep talk to the girl, and the mother nods in parental solidarity, I ask the doctor about his background.

He grew up in Holland, and emigrated to Israel in 1962 with two of his three brothers. I asked why he came. "I'm a Jew," he replies, "born before the Second World War, so you can do your own guesswork. I come from a very Zionist family, and we will not be dependent on the good will of somebody else for our survival. I strongly believe that Israel is our country. After saying that, it doesn't mean we have to suppress another nation or people. It's very difficult, because we have together only one chair, and we must share it in some humane way. The terrible contradiction is that we sit on the land of the Bible and all that stuff, but for many generations it was not ours. I can understand that not every Arab is happy with the claims that we Jews have on this land, but my background tells me very strongly that I need an independent country. How we are going to solve the problem I don't know. I'm not very optimistic."

I reply, "But still, here you are in Tulkarem." He replies, "I find it intolerable that ten kilometres from my home there are people living with medicine that is 30 years antiquated. That is not our fault. We do a lot of harm, but it's not right to say everything is our fault." Pnina adds, quietly, "No. But a lot of it is."

The door opens, and several people try to squeeze past the traffic director. Holding her hand up, Pnina says in Arabic, "One at a time, one at a time." The sense of urgency is visceral here, at a clinic that will end in a few hours and not return for several weeks.

A KIND OF BRIDGE

The mobile clinic is one of several programmes run in Israel and the Occupied Territories by PHR. To get a sense of what drives the organization, I met Ran Yaron at the PHR office in Jaffa. Ran is director of the Occupied Palestinian Territory (OPT) Department.

The city bus from downtown Tel Aviv curves between hotel towers and the glittering Mediterranean into Jaffa, and remnants of old Palestine – arches and filigrees of Arabic architecture, domes and minarets. Commerce hums on Allenby Street, named after the British general who led the conquest of Palestine and Syria in 1917–18, preparing the ground on which Israel would later flourish. On the streets I see people of East African origin – Ethiopian Jews? – and Asian construction workers rebuilding the broad palm-columned median of Jerusalem Boulevard. On upper floors above the streets, laundry hangs limp on shuttered balconies. With no breeze today, the humid heat is brutal.

Ran Yaron looks a lot cooler and fresher than I feel. We sit amid stacks of cartons – the PHR archives, he explains, which they haven't had time to stow since their move from Tel Aviv, after their former landlord refused to renew their lease. "For political reasons?" I ask. He nods.

Born in 1979, Ran grew up in Jerusalem, and graduated from Hebrew University with two degrees in Arabic language and literature. Why did he decide to study Arabic? "Jerusalem is a bi-national city", he replies. "We lived in a neighbourhood near the border of '67, so Palestinians were our neighbours, and I had Palestinian friends. As a Jerusalem resident, at least before the separation barrier was built, it was difficult not to be in touch with Palestinians. You would buy from them, visit their places, so it made sense to learn their language. I'm talking for myself; unfortunately this is not the case for many Israelis. I see it as a kind of bridge. For Palestinians it's unusual to encounter Israelis who speak Arabic, so it can help to create understanding."

His first job at PHR was as a caseworker, handling on average 70 phone calls a day from Palestinians in the West Bank and Gaza who needed medical care. "Often we are their last option," he says, "so you have to do everything you can for each person." His mobile phone has already vibrated several times since I arrived. "You've only been here half an hour, and you see how many phone calls I get. This is normal here."

Why did he choose PHR? "Since I finished my army service, working in intelligence, and since my second or third year of university, where I also studied political science, I wanted to work in a place where I could combine my Arabic skills with a political or social way of thinking. Physicians for Human Rights is an excellent combination for me. Here I can speak Arabic, and I also like the combination of helping people, actually doing something for individuals, but at the same time opposing the occupation, which we consider a violation of human rights, specifically the right to health."

PHR maintains five departments, each dealing with right to health in a particular sector. In addition to the OPT project, another serves asylum-seekers, refugees with no status and thus no legal access to health care; another works with Bedouin villagers in the Negev desert who are denied access to necessities like clean water and electricity, essential to health; another serves Israeli citizens whose health care is limited by poverty; another campaigns for adequate health care in Israeli prisons.

PHR also holds open clinics at the back of the building, providing health care to local people who lack it for a variety of reasons. "Since we moved to Jaffa," says Ran, "there has been a change in the kind of patients that come to our open clinics. Here we see more Palestinians, who have no social rights in Israel. Some have collaborated with the Israeli military, and they fear that if they go back to Palestine they will be killed, so they stay here and live underground. People are damaged and corrupted in so many ways by the occupation."

When I told Ran that I was writing about grassroots peace/justice activists in Israel–Palestine, he said, "I have to clarify that I'm not a peace activist. We are human rights activists here." What's the difference? "The main difference is our goal," he replies, "which is not to bring peace between the Israeli people and the Palestinians, but to support the basic human right to health. We are an Israeli organization, we cooperate with the Israeli authorities, and we try to demand accountability from them. With its direct occupation in the West Bank and effective control over Gaza, we think that Israel holds complete responsibility for health among Palestinians. This has many roots, including 40 years of occupation and the siege of Gaza, but it has created a situation where many fields of health care are not available to Palestinians."

NO OTHER OPTION

The OPT project accepts individual requests for forms of health care that can't be obtained in the Occupied Territories. Formal applications are prepared, with assessments from Israeli medical personnel, and these are submitted to the Civil Administration, the military apparatus that controls the Occupied Territories. PHR's goal is to help patients obtain permits to pass through checkpoints and get the health care they need.

Over the past two years the success rate in Gaza has dropped sharply. "Before the election of Hamas," says Ran, "90 per cent of the Palestinians who applied got permits, we appealed on behalf of the remaining 10 per cent, and, of those, about 75 per cent got approved. Today we hardly get 25 per cent of our applications approved. Now we have to tell patients we did all we could and the final answer is no. For many, this means staying in Gaza to die. They have no other option."

According to Amiram Gil, then director of advocacy at the OPT Department, pressure is brought to bear on Israel whenever possible through international embassies, consulates, and NGOs. Still, for residents of Gaza the situation continues to deteriorate. In summer 2009, the army flatly refused to process any further applications from human rights organizations.

Salah says the same applies to mobile clinics. Even after Israel tightened the noose around Gaza early in 2008, PHR still managed to negotiate entry for 14 medical teams. "Since the war, we have only been able to get in twice; the last time six months ago. Then the army completely stopped approving our applications, without giving any official reason. This happened soon after PHR and the Palestinian Medical Relief Society sponsored a fact-finding mission of international experts into Gaza, which issued a critical report on human rights violations by the Israeli forces – especially the right to health. We suspect that these two facts are connected. But still we try to get entry permits to go into Gaza – just this week we renewed our application – but so far it hasn't worked."

The mobile clinic to the West Bank is the longest-running PHR project. But given the worsening political climate in Israel, I asked Ran Yaron how long he thought the clinic could retain its hard-earned mobility. "Salah has been doing this from the beginning, so he's very experienced", says Ran. "Fortunately, our activities are quite known, even by the Israeli army, so when we arrive at a checkpoint, usually they let us cross. In general, we don't ask for permits for our doctors and nurses to enter the West Bank, because that would acknowledge the legitimacy of the occupation. If there is a problem, we try to negotiate by phone with the army, or enter from another place."

SOCIALLY COLOURED MEDICINE

At the clinic in Nur Al-Shams, next in line are a man in a dark suit and a woman covered in black from head to toe, hands in black gloves; only her eyes show. The man hands over a sheaf of medical records and does most of the talking. While Pnina questions them, Dr Kisch comments quietly to me, "It's understandable that the Europeans don't like this kind of dress. I don't either."

It transpires that the woman had an operation in Jordan, in which part of the thyroid was removed. Her veil is pulled back for a moment so the doctor can check the glands in her throat. The doctor explains, "Apparently there was both an operation and a biopsy. She wants to know, 'Do I need another operation?' If these were well-organized people and there was a biopsy every two years, the answer would be no. But since she lives close by and they can bring in their records, in this case we don't have to do guesswork."

Now and then I hear frustration in his questions and comments. Pnina continues to translate calmly back and forth. She is assertive in her exchanges with him, but at one point she asks him gruffly, "Well, what do you want to do here?" After all, he is the doctor and there is a hierarchy. From Pnina I see an expressive gesture now and then, hands spread wide, eyes closed – *what can you do?*

From the street outside, the loudspeaker calls Muslims to prayer. Time is passing, and many anxious faces still hover at the window.

Next in is an elderly man hobbling with a crutch, short of breath and in obvious pain. He hasn't been sleeping. "This man is ten years younger than Pnina", says Dr Kisch. "They age quickly here. Drugs are so expensive, sometimes people will take only half of what they should. Medicine is socially coloured here."

Pnina tells the man he must eat and drink for the sake of his blood sugar. The doctor comments to me, "What you're seeing here is a health issue jeopardized by religious practice. Jews can be exempted from fasting by their rabbis for health reasons. We should have a meeting about this with the religious leaders here."

A middle-aged woman in hijab worries that she's losing her hair. Pnina advises her to change her head-covering from nylon or polyester, neither of which breathes, to cotton.

From the intensity of the exchanges, it strikes me that each person attending this clinic is hungry to be understood – not just across language or medical issues, but more fundamentally: "Do you understand who we are, and what we contend with?" At the same time, the PHR personnel are determined to impart as much practical health advice as they can in an impossibly short time.

Approaching 2 p.m., the noise level in the corridor rises, tension mounting as clinic time runs out.

VITAL SIGNS

Since the February 2009 election of a more overtly right-wing government in Israel, human rights initiatives have become increasingly vulnerable.

In June, Dr Eldad Kisch posted this comment to the PHR website: "We have been allowed across the Green Line on a regular basis for many years, even in the absence of official blessing, with some hitches occurring from time to time. Now, very recently, the rules seem to have been sharpened and tightened (is that the heavy hand of our new government again?), and we have been warned that legal steps will be taken against the Jewish-Israelis in our group if we are caught again 'sneaking' across the Green Line." He makes his own position clear: "PHR is a group of mixed Jewish-Arab medical and paramedical professionals; that is the beauty of it, and we will not let this cooperation be cut in two."

I asked Salah Haj Yihyeh how he experienced the change. "It's true, this kind of thing has been happening more and more. When Eldad Kisch wrote that, we were on our way back from a village. We were stopped at the checkpoint and forced to stay there until night time. They claimed we were at Area A without a permit. When we apply for permits they are often denied, and when we go, we may be held for many hours at checkpoints. On the other side, we know that because of what patients have to go through to reach a hospital in the West Bank, many give up even trying to get treatment."

In July 2009, PHR released a position paper, *Torture in Israel and Physicians' Involvement in Torture*. It reported testimony from torture victims that Israeli doctors had examined them before, during and after interrogations, but failed to report cases of torture that were revealed in these examinations. The paper concluded, "Such participation in torture stands in stark opposition to international conventions to which Israel is a signatory and to the rules of medical ethics that apply to physicians, and may make physicians who participate in torture legally accountable."

That same month, Israeli media reported that the government had launched an initiative to cut off international funding to several prominent Israeli human rights organizations, including PHR.

In 2010, after the Goldstone report concluded that Israel may have committed war crimes in its 2008–09 assault on Gaza, a new bill was introduced in the Knesset to shut down any Israeli NGO "suspected of provision of information or involvement in law suits against Israeli officials or commanders for breaches of International Humanitarian Law, or war crimes". Among the targets is PHR.

A DROP IN THE SEA

At Nur Al-Shams the last patient departs, and the clinic concludes. The nurse hands the doctor a packaged disinfectant hand-wipe, retrieved from the depths of her capacious bag. This being a classroom, there is no running water. "I got them from a restaurant that went bankrupt", says Pnina.

Normally the clinic would conclude with a dinner put on by the hosts, a gesture of hospitality and solidarity. But today, in the midst of the Ramadan fast, the meal is skipped. Perhaps it's just as well, since a new tension is now evident among the PHR personnel: how will it go at the checkpoint? Though military control applies in all directions here, getting into the Occupied Territories tends to be a lot easier than getting back into Israel.

Packing up his doctor kit, Eldad Kisch asks me, "What do you think, are we bringing peace on earth?"

Caught off guard – usually I'm the one asking questions – all I manage is a vague attempt to encapsulate the vast tangle of thoughts and impressions I'm gathering here, which will take at least a book to convey. "Patiently, perhaps. Who can tell?"

"But at least we do no harm," says Dr Kisch, "which is already something. You know what I like best? It's when they bring their kids, because they never see any normal Israelis, only soldiers. I don't think peace will be made on this level, with these people and me. It's politicians who must do that work. But it's important that on the level of normal people there be no enmity from the ground up, and that's where I think I give something." He repeats, "Something."

Settling herself into the van for the journey home, Pnina Feiler takes up the same theme. "I'm aware – I think all of us aware – that what we do is a drop in the sea. I don't know how much it helps, but I do know that if you do nothing it doesn't help at all. It's very important to show solidarity with the people who are under occupation. Usually we have a small meeting before we start work, to tell about our organization, and to hear from our hosts about their town, the camp, problems they face. We always stress that we are against the occupation, and we hope for a time when we can live together in peace."

I reply, "If it happens, it will be people like you who built the foundation for it."

Pnina says, "Oh, but it's a shaky one."

"But surely better than none?"

"That's what I say. As long as you see only the enemy, all of them one big group of terrible people, it's very difficult to see anything else."

In Jaffa I asked Ran Yaron if he could imagine the conflict ending in his lifetime. "I'm not optimistic", he replies. "I'm sorry to be pessimistic, but this is the reality I see. I also don't believe that the work I do will solve the conflict, or end the occupation. In a strange way that makes it easier to do the work. The motive becomes simpler – you do it because it needs to be done."

I asked Salah Haj Yihyeh if he could see the occupation ending in his lifetime. He shakes his head. "It won't end as long as Israel continues to deceive the international community into believing that it is the Palestinians who oppose peace, even though when you look at what happens on the ground, you see that it is Israel, whether governed by the left or the right, which continues the occupation and gives no sign of any willingness to give up the

Occupied Territories in order to achieve peace. Even when you have an international court decision that the separation barrier is illegal, even then nothing happens – quite the contrary; Israel continues to build whatever it wants in the Occupied Territories. The Obama administration has failed to achieve any progress. And even if tomorrow international pressure pushed Israel into a corner, I fear that Israel would engage in some sort of provocation, maybe start a third intifada; for example, over the holy places in Jerusalem, to divert attention from everything it is doing to maintain the occupation. This is why I am pessimistic."

Yet he continues to work as if change were possible. What sustains him? "I believe the work PHR does can still provide some solidarity, some sort of comfort that we are able to work together in this very depressing situation. This is one of the few things we can still do to show Palestinians that a bridge to peace is still possible, even though it is small, narrow and weak."

On the street in Tulkarem, the cow we passed this morning now hangs in pieces, freshly butchered. Pnina asks our driver to stop, so she and others in the van can buy some. When she returns with paper-wrapped bundles, she tells me, "The prices are very good here, and you can't get any fresher." As we pull away, the cow's suspended head regards us with wide dark eyes.

Approaching the checkpoint, word comes back from Salah to fasten our seatbelts. Eldad Kisch explains, "The soldiers here are recruited locally, some of them settlers, and they have short shrift for Palestinians and fellow-travellers like us. They like to catch you on things like seatbelts. Sometimes we have to wait for hours – they can do body searches, anything they want."

Today we are lucky. After our papers are scrutinized, we pass.

The highway climbs into a broad vista of hazy hills and valleys, fading away to an invisible horizon.

10
Dreams Have Their Uses

In Jafar Farah's early teens, a cousin invited him to join the Communist Youth movement in Haifa. "It was the only place in our neighbourhood where a young person could go, it was either there or the street", says Jafar. "They had a library, ping-pong, and this football game, you know, that you play with your hands? These things were very important in Wadi Nisnas. Daily life was tough here. On summer nights my brother and I would stand outside the cinema and sell sabras [prickly pears]. For us the cinema was not a place where you watched movies, it was a place to get money so you could pay for such things as school uniforms and medicine. Of course it was illegal, and the city inspectors would run after you."

Jafar Farah continued to have an ambiguous relationship with official power.

When the top Israeli general publicly denounced Palestinians as "crocodiles", Jafar organized a protest at Haifa University. At 18, he had just been elected to the Arab student committee. Shortly after, his parents received a visit from the Shin Bet, the Israeli secret police.

"They wouldn't talk to my mother, a woman, but they told my father he must force me to leave the Communist Party. My father said, 'I have no influence on him, not since he left home.' They said, 'Then who does have influence?' 'His mother', my father said. That was true; it still is. So they told my mother that if I didn't leave the Communist Party they would throw me out of the university and arrest me. My mother told them, 'Look, this is the only club in our neighbourhood. You offer nothing to our kids, you push them to become drug users, losers. I don't want that for my son. If you arrest him for being a drug user I would be ashamed. But if you arrest him for being politically active, I would be more proud of him.'"

They did, and she was.

WADI NISNAS

The taxi from the Haifa port groans up the lower slope of the Carmel Ridge, turning here, turning there. In the mirror the driver looks lost. From the Star of David hanging off the mirror, I assume that he's Jewish. Deeper in the Arab neighbourhood the streets narrow and he looks increasingly nervous. Pedestrians are plentiful here, why doesn't he ask one of them for directions? Instead he calls someone on his mobile phone. A few more turns and we arrive at the Mossawa Centre. The car door is hardly closed when he guns the engine and disappears.

Set in spacious grounds behind gates, the Mossawa building is faded but still imposing. Before 1948 it housed the British consulate and the Iraqi Petroleum Company, jointly owned by several of the world's largest oil companies. "When we bought the building it had been closed for 20 years", says Jafar. "It was headquarters for drug dealers in this neighbourhood, and every two weeks the police would raid. Now, finally, we can say with some pride that it belongs to our community."

In a white shirt and pressed black trousers, Jafar Farah leads me up to his office on the second floor, chatting with several people en route. He is director of the Mossawa Centre. He has a warm smile, curly black hair and a moustache. As I tell him what I'm doing, his eyes narrow – an inquiring mind, checking the story. Then he nods, and we begin.

HOLOCAUST LESSONS

Jafar Farah grew up in Kababir, higher up the Carmel Ridge, a mixed neighbourhood of Arabs and Jews. "We were one of a few Arab Christian families in that neighbourhood. I studied in a Muslim school, with the Qur'an as part of my education. Some Christian families didn't like that, so they took their kids out of the Islamic classes, but my mother insisted that I continue with the Qur'an, pray in the mosque, practise everything related to Islam, and understand that this is part of our identity as Palestinians."

When they moved to a house next to religious Jews, Jafar learned to speak fluent Hebrew. "I remember Sabbath days when the Jews weren't allowed to turn on their lights, so they would ask us Arab kids to do it for them. The mentality of isolation that defines life so much in Israel was not part of my childhood."

After his father became disabled, the family moved down to Wadi Nisnas. Jafar was nine. Life, as he said, was tough – the poorest neighbourhood in Haifa, a decaying house, domestic violence, charity food from the local church. Jafar's mother returned for awhile to her family, and Jafar was placed in a Christian boarding school. "At this school I discovered Christianity in a very deep way; I even thought about becoming a priest. But after I was elected to the Arab students' committee, I started to have confrontations with the priests and the principal. It wasn't easy to survive in such a school. Of 15 students supported by the Haifa welfare services, I was the only one who graduated."

By then Jafar had joined the Communist Youth movement. Aside from offering a refuge from the streets, it also represents another strand in his formation. From the 1920s to the 1940s, his great-uncle was a trade union leader in Palestine, author of several books, and in the 1920s one of the first Palestinians to visit the Soviet Union. He was also a prominent nationalist. His foresight, says Jafar, helped save the family from the 1948 exodus. "In the war, unlike many others, he understood why the Jewish military pressured Palestinians to leave Haifa, supposedly for their own safety. Those who did leave, thinking it would only be for a few days, found that a few days became 63 years, and they could only dream of coming back to their home."

At 19 Jafar went to Germany on a student exchange. The event that left the most enduring impact on him was a visit to a Nazi concentration camp. "People said to me 'Why are you going, you're an Arab?'", he recalls. "In fact, I came to believe that every Arab youth should go to such a place, in order to understand how cruel human beings can be. This is also related to our conflict here – we Palestinians are paying the price of what was done to the Jews in the Holocaust, not by us but by Europeans, while the international community remained silent. This is part of my identity. I feel that no one can claim that history protects them from becoming fascist."

MY WELCOME PARTY

By then Jafar was in second year at Haifa University, had been elected leader of the Arab students' committee, and was earning his university fees by working as a facilitator of Jewish-Arab dialogue groups. He had already been hauled before the university court four times for organizing demonstrations, arrested (after the Shin Bet failed to bully his mother) and expelled for half a year.

By 1989 he headed the national union of Arab students. After organizing another demonstration he was arrested again, charged with illegal demonstration and affiliation with the Palestine Liberation Organization (PLO), at the time still designated a terrorist organization by the Israeli government. He was held for nine days and interrogated by the secret police. "It was horrible", he says, and leaves it at that. Court hearings would grind on for the next three years. During that period, Jafar's brother was imprisoned for several months because he raised a Palestinian flag in Haifa.

Widely covered in the media, Jafar's arrest finished his job as dialogue facilitator. I was moved to comment, "So much for dialogue." Jafar chuckled. "Most of these groups were only dialogue for the sake of dialogue. They had no intention to transform reality between the two communities."

While Jafar searched for a new job, a Jewish fellow-student who had covered his case for the newspaper *Haaretz* told Jafar that her editor wanted to see him. "I told this editor I had no experience in journalism," says Jafar, "but he said, 'Fine, most people here don't have any. There is no school for journalism here, and anyway most graduates of journalism school are no good as journalists.' He sent me to meet the news coordinator, who said to me, 'I know who you are, there is nothing for you here.' But the editor told him, 'I decide who works here, not you.' So the news coordinator said, 'Okay, but I won't give him anything to work on, he'll have to find his own stories.' This was my welcome party."

For the next seven years Jafar Farah wrote feature stories in Hebrew for the newspaper and its weekend magazine. Though he refused to be limited to "Arab" topics, as a Palestinian he was able to bring a unique perspective to Jewish readers; for example, in a series of articles on young Fatah fighters and their families under siege in the Jenin refugee camp.

In the mid 1990s Jafar accompanied a group of Jewish journalists to the Haifa jail. "I began to ask tough questions about how they treat prisoners, how they do body searches, and so forth. Of course, they denied that such things happened, but I said, 'Excuse me, but I've experienced these things myself, I know this jail from the inside, I know where you do these things.' The other journalists were quite shocked. I said, 'If such things don't happen, why not let us speak to the prisoners?' The commander of the prison didn't like that, she jumped up and down. It was very embarrassing for them."

While building a career as an investigative journalist, Jafar Farah also launched CEGAS, the Committee for Educational Guidance for Arab Students. It still shares the Mossawa building in Wadi Nisnas. "This centre was a dream of mine since I graduated in 1991", he says. "When we asked Haifa University to open residences to Arab students, they refused. So we rented the building ourselves, we renovated it, and we created the first residence for Arab students, girls and boys, so they could get higher education. We paid out almost half a million dollars. When we came to Jewish and Palestinian funders, they didn't believe in the project, so we lost that money, but now hundreds of people have got higher education, and they are out working around the country."

A thriving career in journalism, an innovative community initiative – Jafar describes these as "dreams of a normal life". When PLO Chairman Yasser Arafat and Israeli Prime Minister Yitzak Rabin signed the Olso Accords in 1993, suddenly for many Palestinians such dreams moved into the realm of possibility. "By then the court hearings against me had been going on for three years, but now after Oslo the newspaper asked the Minister of Justice to dismiss the case. They said yes, they would do it as part of the peace agreement. Suddenly here was our chance for a normal life. I could be a normal journalist with a normal career. My wife and I even took the decision to have kids, because finally life would be normal. Of course it was an illusion, but it was an illusion that we wanted to believe."

This may be the truest and saddest summary of Oslo that I've heard.

EQUALITY

For different people the illusion collapsed at different rates; in Jafar's case it didn't take long. "Immediately after the signing of Oslo," he says, "the right-wing agenda was to ensure that there would be no majority in Israel for any peace agreement. To prevent Arab-Israelis from becoming part of such a majority, we had to be disqualified from the political scene, from the media and from the economy. At the same time, Israeli Jews had to be incited to regard us as a fifth column. As early as '94, you could see an escalating campaign to accomplish this."

In the latter half of the decade, attacks increased against Palestinians, both in the Occupied Territories and inside Israel. In 1997, Israeli police demolished three houses in an Arab village near Haifa, to make way for the expansion of an adjacent Jewish village. "Because you could live much cheaper there than in Haifa, my editor happened to live in that Jewish village", says Jafar. "When people in the Arab village decided to rebuild their houses, the police came to demolish them again, and a confrontation started. I went there with my camera. I asked the editor to come, to see what was happening, the beatings, the tear gas. He didn't come. Still smelling of tear gas, I went to him in the morning with my photos, I told him, 'I have the story.' He said, 'Someone else will write it, you are too involved.' After working here seven years, now suddenly when there is a confrontation between Jews and Arabs I have to prove my credibility as an Arab journalist? I submitted my resignation. He was shocked; they offered to let me write for the network of *Haaretz* papers, and so forth, but I refused. To continue as a journalist in this kind of atmosphere would be impossible."

This was the atmosphere in which the Mossawa Centre was born. Mossawa means equality. A poster in the lobby shows the snout of an assault rifle. The bullet emerging from it is a pencil.

People in a range of NGOs had recognized that if Arab-Israelis were to thrive, they would have to achieve equality as citizens. To do this, they would have to find more effective ways to deal with the national government, but first they would need a clearer understanding of how it operates, and how they might influence policy. "We had never been part of the government process", Jafar explains. "For example, although we are 20 per cent of the population, only six per cent of government workers are Arab, and most of them work only at the lowest levels. To change policy, you need to influence decision-makers at higher levels. This is the basis for what we proposed to do."

The birth was rough. The Mossawa Centre started as a joint project of Arab NGOs and Shatil, the New Israel Fund (NIF), whose stated goal is "to promote democracy, tolerance, and social justice in Israel". At the end of Mossawa's first year, NIF officials said they had only agreed to host the project for a year, and henceforth it would be up to the Arab NGOs. The union of Arab NGOs failed to fund-raise, says Jafar, and instead decided to terminate the project. He organized an emergency meeting of colleagues, and argued that since the Mossawa Centre was an essential community resource, they should keep it alive on a voluntary basis until funds could be found. For nine months they worked without salaries.

The next hurdle was the same government that they hoped eventually to influence. In Israel, all NGOs have be approved by the Ministry of Internal Affairs. When the Mossawa Centre applied to register as an NGO, the minister turned them down. They went to court, the judge ruled that the minister had no grounds for rejecting their application, and finally in May 2000 the centre won its registration. This three-year struggle was a taste of the challenges ahead.

TO PROTECT YOUR COMMUNITY

According to its website, the Mossawa Centre's mission is "to achieve equal rights for the 1.3 million Arab citizens of Israel … while preserving their national and cultural rights as Palestinians". Under the circumstances, it's a daunting mission, to say the least. I ask Jafar for some examples that illustrate how they do it.

He leans back in his chair. It's a complicated question, in a large field. He begins with the subject of violence against Arab-Israelis. "After the October 2000 demonstrations [in Israel, as the second intifada erupted], when 13 Arab-Israeli citizens were killed by Israeli police, I said that we should pursue both civil and criminal charges against the killers. The Arab leadership made a serious mistake at the time in cooperating with what was later called the Or Commission (of inquiry), which ended with a fine report, but it made no charges, which left the police feeling protected to use more violence against Arab citizens. By now, 44 Arab-Israelis have been killed, hundreds injured and many more harassed by Israeli police and by Jewish civilians, their neighbours. This led us to start doing our own investigations, forcing the authorities to take the killers to court. In a few cases we succeeded, in others we failed."

He shows me a full-page story from last weekend's edition of *Yedioth Ahronoth*, Israel's most widely read newspaper. In Hebrew, the story includes photos of two men, one of them in uniform. "He is a police officer," says Jafar, "and this is the Arab-Israeli that he killed. Finally, after working for four years with the family of the victim, we managed to get the police officer convicted and sent to jail for 15 months. The case is now going to the Supreme Court on appeals. But to even get to this point, you have to fight a whole system that justifies violence against Arab citizens. When you sit in the court and see the faces of the killer and his police officer friends, you can see how confident they are. He is backed up by his chief, by the national commander of the police, by the government, even by the court. In another case where we got a conviction, the police officer went to jail for half a year. Normally the minimum sentence for such a charge, the *minimum*, is three to five years. But not when the victim is Arab and the killer is a police officer."

What do the Mossawa Centre and its allies, which include Israeli Jews, hope to achieve by pursuing these cases? "Of course, we can't bring the victim back to life", Jafar replies. "And even though you know it is such a low level of punishment, still you have to do what you can to protect your community. Our aim isn't only punishment, it is also to create second thoughts in the police. When they meet Arab citizens, the police are civil servants who should provide service, not use violence automatically. We want them to know there is a price for that."

Earlier this morning, Jafar Farah faced an arm of the system – in this case, a lobby group for police officers – at a press conference outside the Knesset, the Israeli parliament in Jerusalem. A member of the Knesset, formerly a deputy commmander of the police, told the press to be cautious with Arabs. Jafar says, "He told them, 'They are preparing honey for us.' He used the word 'honey', meaning 'Watch out, they want to trap the Jews.' In front of the media I said to him, 'How can you talk this kind of racism, you are supported by our tax money? And why are you protecting this person who was convicted by the court?' This is the system we face. Three weeks ago a Jewish police commander shot his neighbour in an argument. Because the victim was Jewish, the killer was arrested immediately and charged with murder. When the victim is Arab, the killer is released, and in court the victim's family has to look at him, still in his uniform, and his police friends sitting there with their guns. And outside the court you see a demonstration in support of the killer. How can this happen? How can this hatred, this fascism develop?"

He leans forward, both hands flat on the table, and his eyes hold mine. I have no useful response to offer. In his voice, low and constricted, I hear the cost of opposing such a powerful, tightly woven system.

DREAMS HAVE THEIR USES

Though no less a challenge to the status quo, another strand of Mossawa's work is much lower-profile, almost invisible: the seeking of social and economic justice for Arab-Israelis. Arab citizens comprise 20 per cent of the Israeli population but have access to less than 5 per cent of national budget resources. This gap has an impact in every sphere of life – employment, health, child poverty, schools, road safety, water and sewage systems, culture. The Israeli National Insurance Institute reports that the poverty rate among Arab families is 3.28 times that of Jewish families.

Mossawa's social-economic justice unit monitors the national budget year by year, department by department, building databases to compare funding allocations with the actual needs of Arab-Israeli communities. As neo-liberalism tightens its stranglehold on Israel, public resources shrink in virtually every realm except the military. In their analysis of the 2009–10 budget, Mossawa staff note sharp cuts in nearly every ministry, many of them specifically targeting or at least destructive to Arab communities. The report also documents numerous cases of a more devious form of cuts, where existing budget allocations to Arab areas are not implemented.

As in the challenge to state-sanctioned violence, the goal of attaining economic justice – especially under increasingly right-wing governments – strikes me as a rather elusive dream. "Ah," says Jafar, with the air of someone who recognizes a familiar argument, "but the good thing about dreams is that they allow you to move outside the limits imposed on you as a Palestinian. Police violence and economic injustice are not inevitable. As a result of our advocacy we have seen schools and sewage systems built, and we've seen an increase of 1 per cent in the hiring of Arabs to government jobs. One per cent doesn't seem like anything, but it equals about 500 additional workers. I meet people who say, 'I was employed on this program to build a bridge', but they don't know that it was due to Mossawa's advocacy. So you see," says Jafar with a wry smile, "dreams have their uses."

THE LUXURY OF DESPAIR

His third example of Mossawa's work delves into an even larger and more obscure realm.

Israel has no written constitution to guide its affairs and define the rights of its citizens. Israeli historians ascribe this situation to an impasse between Jewish founders who wanted a modern civil constitution, and others who wanted the new state to be governed by ancient Judaic religious texts. Instead of either, from 1958 to 2001 a succession of Knessets would enact eleven "Basic Laws" to define the nature of the Israeli state. Together with evolving legislation and interpretation by the High Court, these would serve the functions of a more formal constitution.

But neither the founding tensions nor the desire for a formal made-in-Israel constitution have disappeared. In the last decade, a major campaign has given the process new urgency, both inside and outside the Knesset.

For Jafar Farah and others, the campaign conceals a grave threat. It hinges on an apparently innocuous idea, the constitutional guarantee that Israel is a Jewish state. This is not a new idea. In the 1948 Declaration of the Establishment of the State of Israel, the country is described as both a Jewish state and a democracy with equal rights for all citizens. But many, both Palestinians and Jews, argue that the two are contradictory, and Israel cannot be both.

Jafar explains, "If you changed the American constitution to say that the United States is a white state, can you imagine what this would mean to African-Americans? What would it matter then if you said it's a democracy? This is what we told Members of Congress when we went to the US in April: in Israel it would have the same effect if you said in the constitution that this is a Jewish state. It would guarantee two classes of citizens: the first class Jewish, the second class those who are not. In practice this may already be the case, but in all our efforts to change it, we would now also have to work against the constitution and the courts that would interpret it."

In confronting the threat, once again Mossawa would take on powerful Israeli interests. "It was very important for us to not face this alone as the Arab community", says Jafar. "That is what the right-wing wanted, the Arabs against the Jews. Instead we built a coalition with Jewish women's organizations, the lawyers bar, trade unions, and others who support the separation of authorities, including people not involved in the human rights movement but committed to the sovereignty of the Supreme Court. Our message was that a constitution without equality will hurt many people – not just the Arab community, but women, workers, homos and lesbians – so we have to stand together against the right-wing and tell them no constitution without equality."

The coalition prevailed – for the moment. But then the campaign to entrench the Jewish state moved up a level, out of reach in the diplomatic realm. "Suddenly they took this question of the Jewish state into negotiations with Abu Mazen [then President of the Palestinian National Authority]. For the first time, recognition of Israel as a Jewish state became a new precondition in peace negotiations, put in three years ago by Tzipi Livni and Olmert [then Foreign Minister and Prime Minister of Israel, respectively]. Now Bibi Netanyahu [current Prime Minister of Israel] uses it as a precondition because he's not interested in serious negotiations. If this gets international approval, it will be a huge disaster. We are now in talks with leaders in the US and Europe, trying to convince them that what they should be doing is protecting the right of all citizens of Israel to be equals."

YOU KEEP TRYING

For Jafar Farah the struggle continues, on many fronts. I asked him, "Given the array of forces you've described, how much real pressure can you exert in trying to change policy?" Again he leaned back in his chair. His eyes dark, he looked tired.

"Look," he said, "obviously it's not enough pressure, or else why would the Arab community still get only 5 per cent in the budget? But you keep trying. Even a general strike would not be enough, it wouldn't be covered in the media unless you go and block the Knesset and the prime minister's office. When they cut the allowance for children and single mothers in 2003, Jewish women made a big demonstration, they almost closed Jerusalem. We brought twelve buses of Arab people that suffer from the same issue to march in solidarity with the Jewish mothers. The voice of the poor will never be heard unless we have this kind of solidarity between groups. So you go to workers, to leaders, you organize conferences and media campaigns, you go to the Americans, the Europeans, the OECD [the Paris-based Organization for Economic Cooperation and Development]; you tell them that if Israel wants to be part of the club, they should ask what the government is doing to ensure that poverty in the Arab community is treated in a professional, not a racist way. This is what you do. Very often you don't succeed. But you keep trying."

Due to effective campaigning by organizations like Mossawa, Israel's admittance to the powerful OECD had been stalled by the embarrassing fact that its poverty rates were higher than those of any OECD member state, 50 per cent among Arab Israelis; gaps between rich and poor in Israel were also among the highest. However, intense pressure from Israel and its allies seems to have worked. In May 2010, the OECD welcomed Israel as a new member. None of the realities on the ground had changed. On the contrary, in July 2010 new laws introduced in the Knesset would further restrict Arab Israelis' access to civil service jobs.

As Jafar said, you keep trying.

ONLY SILENCE

During Israel's 2006 assault on Lebanon, Jafar Farah was arrested at a non-violent protest in the Carmel neighbourhood, where he used to turn on the lights for his orthodox Jewish neighbours. Before the 2009 elections he was arrested again.

"I am not a criminal", he says calmly. "I sit with the Minister of Finance to discuss the state budget, I sit at a round table with members of the European Parliament. But I don't have any illusion that I am protected. In every crisis here you risk to be arrested or killed. At any time, a police officer can feel he's a hero if he arrests a human rights defender, without thinking twice. Irresponsible people are leading this country to disaster after disaster. They keep telling the international community they're protecting the Jewish people. What security have they brought? Zero. Israel is less secure today than it was in the '50s, '60s and '70s. This leadership cannot achieve security for the Jews, and their failure will destroy us all."

Given what I've heard from him today, I have to ask, does he experience despair? He looks at me for a long moment, steadily, before he replies. "There are days when you feel frustrated and sad, you even cry – in the Gaza war, to see 90 per cent of the Jewish population wanting more and more victims, I felt 'How can I live with these people, how can I find the energy to continue talking to my Jewish colleagues?' Yesterday in Gaza, the day before in Lebanon, the next day in the West Bank, maybe in a few days Haifa – we are going from catastrophe to catastrophe. I keep hoping that other countries won't be silent when human life and dignity are demolished like this, but from what I see there is only silence toward these crimes. How can we protect human dignity? It gets lost so easily."

A heavy silence hangs in the room. I don't know what to say. Perhaps something about people I know, ordinary people who don't have much power but who exercise what little they do have by refusing to be silent. People like him. But Jafar speaks first. "Yes, I experience despair. Some days I want to forget it, leave this place – there are other things I want to do. But then you think of your responsibilities to your children [he and his wife have three], and to Mossawa. The development of Palestinian civil society in Israel is something new. After '48 the Israelis closed everything except the churches. So to build an NGO culture here, and sustain an organization like this is pioneering work, especially when the government doesn't like what you do. You can't just wake up in the morning and say I'm going to do something else. In our reality, despair and doing what you want, these are luxuries."

Luxury or not, I'm curious: what else does he want to do? He smiles. It makes him look less tired, younger. "I would like to start a university. I see Mossawa as a place where people can think, dream, do community research, plan. But still we need a university. A university should be about research, freedom of thought, a platform for building democracy. We don't have this. Since 1981 the Israeli government has refused every application for an Arab university. This is one of my dreams."

"Dreams have their uses", I quoted back to him. He laughed. "And I would like to start a TV station. I think having our own TV station could help our community a lot."

11
Civil-izing Israel

On 26 April 2009, Israeli police raided the homes of New Profile members in four communities. They detained six Israeli citizens and seized their home computers, along with those of partners and children.

While the six detainees were interrogated by police, lawyers were not allowed to be present. When the New Profile members were released on bail, they were forbidden to contact any other member for 30 days.

Ten more members were later summoned for interrogation.

Why are the Israeli authorities so afraid of these people?

RUTH HILLER

On a hot September day in Tel Aviv, I met Ruth Hiller, a founder of New Profile. We borrowed a small room at the Zochrot centre (see Chapter 14). Seated squarely on an office chair, this middle-aged woman with greying hair doesn't look dangerous to me, but she does look determined.

New Profile emerged from the questions of women. By the end of its first half-century, Israel had fought several wars, developed a huge military apparatus, and still occupied southern Lebanon, Gaza and the West Bank, but didn't seem any more secure for it. Ruth met other women questioning their part in this destructive but apparently immovable state of affairs. In October 1998, they called for a public day of discussion on the military state and conscience.

A hundred and fifty people showed up, and two weeks later New Profile was born. The Israeli military uses a system of profiles to classify each recruit's fitness for combat or other roles, but so far there isn't one to embrace pacifists and people who refuse. Also, the founders of the new organization intend to change the profile of Israel itself, from a military state to a civil society.

Born in California in 1954, Ruth Hiller came to Israel at the age of 17. She lives on a small kibbutz, Ha'ogen, near Netanya on the Mediterranean coast. "I fell in love with the romance of being a settler and creating a nation. Everything seemed so young then, so full of potential and promise." Also American-born, her partner-to-be Gary visited the kibbutz; they met, married, and produced six children.

How did her awareness of Palestinians evolve? "I know now that there was a lot of not seeing things back then," she replies, "but I had six kids and I was very absorbed with raising them." A significant shift occurred in 1987 with the first intifada. "That was the first time I learned that the Zionist story wasn't complete. By then some of the romantic euphoria was fading, the kibbutz was going into privatization – a lot of dreams were breaking down. I started going to Friday demonstrations with Women in Black, protesting army violence and human rights abuses. I also had questions about the occupation, but at the time I wasn't brave enough to go any farther. Living on a kibbutz, there's a lot of pressure to stay within accepted norms. To be more progressive I would have to hide, be a closet leftist. In the kibbutz, you walk a line."

When Ruth's eldest son Yinnon refused to serve in the army, Ruth crossed the line.

In Israel most men must serve in the military for three years, and women for two, starting at 18. "The induction process actually starts when you're sixteen," Ruth explains, "when your name – your identity really – moves from the Ministry of the Interior to the Ministry of Defence. At that point your child is not your child any more, but the state's."

After long discussions with her son, Ruth told him she would support his decision fully, but on two conditions. "First we had to do everything we could to keep him out of jail, because jail is a really bad place for kids. Second, he would walk this path with me, we would consult together and make decisions together. He agreed. It took longer this way to get him out of the military, but in the long run others have benefited."

Unable to identify sources on refusal in Israel, Ruth sought advice from war resisters in the United States, who directed her back to a few activists they knew in Israel, including the founders of Yesh Gvul. Established in 1982 during the first Israeli invasion of Lebanon, it supports "soldiers who refuse duties of a repressive or aggressive nature". As its motto says, "There are things that decent people don't do."

When military police tried to induct Yinnon by force, he and Ruth took the army to court. "It took us three years", Ruth says. "Finally they let him go as 'unsuitable for military service', exactly what he said when he was 16, a pacifist and therefore not suitable. But it was a good case, it set precedents. And each step of the way we acquired more experience and more information that you can't get from the military or the state. Now we want to make sure this information is available to the public."

The vehicle would be New Profile. One of its principal functions is to provide a range of supports to people considering refusal, going through the process, or in jail for refusing. The military state can be terrifying, and no one should have to face it alone. It was in this context that Haggai Matar encountered New Profile.

PURITY OF ARMS

Haggai's apartment is one of several on a small courtyard in a modest Tel Aviv neighbourhood. I wait for a while at the gate before he arrives on his bicycle. Someone had tried to pick the lock that morning. This is not the first time, says Haggai. Last time they succeeded, but stole only his computer – on the same day that computers were stolen from the homes of several other activists.

Haggai is slim, with a light-brown beard and longish hair. His T-shirt proclaims "No more walls!" Someone sent it anonymously to New Profile. We sink into comfortable chairs in a tiny living room. A cat whines for food, but soon settles purring on Haggai's lap.

Born Israeli in 1984, Haggai Matar grew up in a suburb of Tel Aviv. Along the way he picked up some quite varied images of Palestinians. "From the mainstream we learned that Arabs are the enemy, people who blow themselves up, and you with them", he says. "The basic notion was that Israel always reaches out for peace, but nobody listens. At the same time, I grew up in a fairly left-wing house; especially my mother, who would sign petitions and attend demonstrations. I knew that I shouldn't be racist, I shouldn't see Arabs as only enemies. It only added to my confusion that I didn't know any actual Palestinians. Since the first intifada, a main function of the military regime in the Occupied Territories is to separate us from them."

From the age of twelve, when Prime Minister Yitzak Rabin was assassinated by a Jewish zealot, Haggai began to ask serious questions. In 1999 he joined other Israeli, Jordanian and Palestinian youth at a summer camp – the first time he met Palestinians face to face. He also took up a correspondence that his mother had initiated, with one of many hundreds of Palestinians held by Israel in administrative detention, without charge or trial. Like many prisoners, he had learned to speak and write the jailers' language, Hebrew. "It was hard for me to understand how this man could be a threat," says Haggai, "when all I got from him was friendship and solidarity."

In 2000, the first year of the second intifada, Haggai joined a solidarity convoy taking food and water to Kfar Yassuf, a West Bank village beseiged by the army. "I actually went there with a real fear for my life", he says. "I had heard about street fighting in refugee camps between our soldiers and Palestinians, and going into the village, through the narrow streets with Arabs all around, I kept thinking, 'What if one of them tries to shoot me?' But we were very warmly welcomed. Then while we were unloading the trucks together, the Israeli Border Police attacked us, confiscated the trucks and destroyed the food. Suddenly I saw that it's not Israelis versus Palestinians here, as we are always told, but here Israelis are working with Palestinians and the army of Israel is attacking us."

By then Haggai was 16, the age when army induction begins. Among other things, inductees learn the mission and values of the Israeli Defence Forces (IDF). The sixth value provides the famous mantra, Purity of Arms: "IDF soldiers will not use their weapons and force to harm human beings who are not combatants or prisoners of war, and will do all in their power to avoid causing harm to their lives, bodies, dignity and property."

Haggai had seen otherwise: home demolitions, ambulances blocked at checkpoints, destruction of water tanks and electricity supplies, violent repression of non-violent protests, and assaults on unarmed Palestinians. "I realized that I could not join the army, and instead of getting out via some personal issue, quietly, with no fuss, I would have to refuse, and make a point of why I refused: the issue isn't me; it's you, the army, what you are doing is wrong."

Along with four friends, Haggai refused to serve in the IDF. In October 2002, Adam Maor, Matan Kaminer and Haggai Matar went to prison. (See Chapter 12.)

In September 2004, he went free. Shortly after, he joined an organization which had provided crucial support through his prison term – New Profile.

DIANA DOLEV

On my second trip to gather material for this book, Diana Dolev offered to accommodate me at her house in Binyamina, a 30-minute train ride from Tel Aviv. She and her husband Ariel were delightful hosts, generous with their hospitality, their time and their stories.

When I arrived at their house, they had just returned from a performance by their daughter Yaara and her partner Amit, who run a contemporary dance company. A massage therapist by profession, Ariel was massaging the weary calves and feet of the two dancers. With their two young children, they were all preparing to go for a family dinner at a favourite restaurant in a Palestinian village not far from here. They would celebrate one of the children's birthdays, and the news that Yaara's sister Sharon had been confirmed as Greenpeace anti-nuclear and disarmament campaigner in Israel.

Diana Dolev was born in Tel Aviv three years before the state of Israel. Her great-grandparents emigrated to Palestine in the 1880s from the Ukraine and Rumania.

Diana grew up in Haifa, she and her parents living with her grandfather, who ran a thriving business there. She had little contact with Palestinians either in Haifa or in Binyamina, where the family moved in 1951. Were there no Palestinian villages nearby? "They were wiped out", Diana replies. "We didn't learn anything about that at school, nothing about the Nakba or the ethnic cleansing. When I started teaching about the Nakba, suddenly it occurred to me to ask my mother what happened to the villages. She said, 'Oh, that was further inland, we didn't see anything.' Even in those days they must have had tactics to hush it up so people wouldn't realize what was going on."

Diana has particularly poignant memories of Tantura, an empty village on what she calls the most beautiful beach between Binyamina and Haifa, where her parents converted a demolished house near the water into a cottage. "Later I learned the real story of Tantura – the Palestinians were driven out of the village in 1948, but the houses stayed there until after '67. When refugees went there to visit their former homes, Israelis from the kibbutz and the moshav saw them, and they bulldozed what was left of the houses."

OLIVE BRANCHES IN GAZA

Soon after Yaara was born, the young family moved to Arad, a new Israeli town north of the Dead Sea. Over time, Diana Dolev began to ask questions. "After the '67 war," she says, "some politicians said 'Now we have something to bargain with, we'll return the Occupied Territories and they'll accept our terms for peace.' I thought this was a good idea, but as time went by, nobody talked any more about land for peace, and the Palestinians still lived under occupation."

Her first venture into activism wasn't aimed at the occupation, but the lack of medical services for children in Arad. "One day in the kitchen, I remember thinking 'Why the hell doesn't somebody do something about it?' Then it dawned on me, who is this somebody if it's not me?"

Soon Diana immersed herself in education for peace, giving workshops in schools across Israel. She also joined peace vigils with Women in Black, set up a local branch of the Association for Civil Rights, quitting when it disowned any activity in the Occupied Territories. At the end of the 1980s she helped found the Gaza team.

Sparked by an encounter with an Israeli lawyer who worked with Palestinian prisoners, the team gathered personal accounts of human rights violations by Israeli occupying forces in the Gaza Strip, since 1967 one of the most densely packed open-air prisons on earth. They also helped people as well as they could to get work permits, or compensation for injuries, or in attempts to bring perpetrators to justice.

"The things we learned were overwhelming", Diana said. "I remember a story that someone told us: during the curfew, soldiers were walking in an alley, and one of them threw a smoke grenade into a garden. The family told us their baby had died, suffocated by the smoke. We sent letters, and the army said they checked, nobody knows of such an occurrence, therefore it didn't happen. Years later when the group Breaking the Silence started publishing the stories of individual soldiers, one told of walking with his unit in Gaza, a soldier threw a grenade into a garden, and an old man came out with a dead baby in his arms."

What became of all the testimonies? "It was very frustrating", says Diana. "With very few exceptions, the media simply wasn't interested." In 1992 she sent a detailed report on the team's findings to the prime minister, ministers of government, members of the Knesset, and the Israeli media. Not a single response came back, nor did any item appear in the media.

That same year, Diana went to London for her PhD in art history. Her supervisor told her that she would have to choose: continue to spend the bulk of her time at vigils and demonstrations, or work on her thesis. She chose to complete her PhD thesis, on how the architectural master plans for Hebrew University in Jerusalem embody the militaristic ideology of Israel.

Then in 1998 she heard that some women were preparing to grapple with the military state and conscience. Diana couldn't resist. She attended the meeting that launched New Profile.

DOROTHY NAOR

Diana described fellow New Profiler Dorothy Naor affectionately as "the only person I know who can be in more than one place at the same time". But at 78, even Dorothy has limits. "In the beginning," she tells me, "Israel [her husband] and I ran round to every demonstration, but you burn out quickly that way, so I finally decided I had to cut back." She still gives public talks when she travels abroad, and continues to take people like me to occupied villages in the West Bank (see Chapter 1). She is also the person primarily responsible for the New Profile listserv.

In a media-saturated world, it becomes increasingly difficult to sift through the blizzard of noise and image to kernels of human truth. On this elusive quest I've found the New Profile listserv to be an invaluable aid, a digest of informative articles from a huge range of sources, Israeli, Palestinian and international. Others contribute content, but mostly the listserv is compiled by Dorothy. With more than 2,000 subscribers, it has a wide reach, and many of them forward it to their lists. After Dorothy dropped me off at the train station following our trek to the West Bank, she headed home to work on it.

Today's dispatches in my inbox included an update on Egyptian police assaults on the Viva Palestina emergency convoy as it tried to reach Gaza; an article on a new campaign in the West Bank to boycott goods produced in illegal Israeli settlements; and a newspaper report that senior Israeli army officers had cancelled a trip to Britain, fearing that they might face arrest for war crimes in Gaza.

Almost always Dorothy writes a pungent introduction to the dispatches. She explains, "From teaching experience, I know it's not so effective if you just hand out something without comment. If it's something you feel is important, you should say so."

GUNS AND SOLDIERS EVERYWHERE

New Profile is a registered non-profit organization with about 45 members, women and men, aged 16–80. It's charter begins, "We, a group of feminist women and men ...." I ask Ruth Hiller how feminism shapes the organization. "It's central to everything we do", she replies. "We have no hierarchy, no board, and no office, we work out of our homes. Though sometimes people get small fees for particular projects, most of our work is done on a volunteer basis. Working in teams helps a lot with isolation, and it allows us to learn from each other, since we believe that sharing knowledge is a better approach than holding onto it for your own advantage. By doing that we share power. Aside from policy decisions, which we make together, day-to-day decisions are all made by the working groups."

In Binyamina I ask Diana Dolev how this admirable approach works in practice. "It's not easy", she replies. "Because we don't believe in hierarchy, everybody does everything, and you can't fire anybody because we're all volunteers. And we have to discuss everything until we're exhausted and fed up." She laughs, but with evident tenderness for her non-hierarchical fellow-volunteers.

She also expresses ready affection for what Dorothy Naor calls New Profile's younger set. "They are so smart, so informed", Diana says. "We look at them in awe, we who grew up in Israeli society without asking questions, but they are full of questions, critical and aware where we were in darkness."

The desire to ask questions moved Diana and a colleague to see if a local school principal would introduce New Profile's ideas to her staff, parents, and perhaps even the students. "She was a bit reluctant," says Diana, "but we'll see. She's worried that we'll incite her students not to serve in the army, which we assured her is something we do not do, but she didn't seem to believe us."

What do they hope to accomplish in the school? "We want to encourage anyone – teachers, parents, pupils – to ask questions", Diana replied. "We live in a very nationalistic society, where the agents for promoting the status quo feed you what they call facts, axioms, which they teach you not to question. We're trying to deconstruct these axioms. Is serving in the army the only way you can serve society? Is the term 'to serve the state' even appropriate; doesn't it have a fascistic connotation? Does the state need people to serve it, or should the state serve its citizens? How does it affect our society to put the army on a pedestal and revere it? How does this affect our concept of democracy? These are the kinds of questions we would ask."

Travelling in Israel, I was often shocked by the pervasiveness of armed soldiers and even armed civilians – settlers, I was told – on streets, buses, trains, everywhere, with assault rifles hanging as casually off the shoulder as the ubiquitous backpack in North

America. New Profile's subtitle is "movement for the civil-ization of Israeli society". I ask Ruth Hiller what it means.

"What you saw here, guns and soldiers everywhere," she replies, "we don't see at all. I have to retrain myself to see these things. Civil society isn't just about having schools, a fire brigade and such things, it's also about how we behave as neighbours, it's about respectful coexistence, and no obvious hierarchy between the military and civil spheres. Do you want a country with a military or a military with a country? Who makes a better prime minister, a general or a civilian? How does the military prepare you for a civilian job? Creating a civil society means creating something egalitarian, rather than having a male elite run everything, with qualifications entirely defined by your military background. But we don't ask such questions here, we're too afraid – we're people of the book who don't know how to question."

I'm beginning to understand why the Israeli authorities might fear these people. They ask so many questions.

A TRUE ISRAELI

Haggai Matar coordinates the organization's youth groups across Israel, mostly in the larger centres. "The point is to have a framework where they can talk about things openly", he explains. "What interests them, what troubles them, especially but not only concerning military service? At school they have no one to talk to about these things. Soldiers actually serve in schools here; they guide young people in how to find the army unit that best suits them and how to go through the induction process, but they provide nothing on what the law says about not serving. School staff are oriented that way too. So you need a place where you can raise these questions, and get alternative information." (In 2009 another refuser took over this job. See chapter 12.)

Haggai also volunteers with the New Profile counselling network. "This is for people who have already decided not to go to the army", he said. "We can tell them about legal ways to do that, and then we can escort them all the way through to getting their release. But group leaders can't talk about the draft, and especially not tell anyone how to avoid it. In Israel, counselling people not to go to the army is severely punished under the law. So if someone in a youth group says 'I'm not going to the army', I will send them to consult with someone else. We don't do this only for legal reasons;

it is actually closer to our values not to pressure people, but to talk openly about options."

In November 2009, the Israeli media reported army data indicating that, in addition to the relative few who refuse to serve on principle, more than a quarter of eligible males and almost half of all eligible females use a variety of exemptions to avoid enlisting. Orthodox Jewish males studying in religious schools are automatically exempt.

The authorities are quick to blame falling enlistment on New Profile, but Haggai Matar ascribes it to fundamental changes in Israel. He explains, "As so many normal state functions get privatized, it breaks down the historic collectivist belief that Israel was built on the idea that everybody goes to the army to protect everybody. Once you lose that, why would you go to the army? If you belong to the upper or upper-middle class, it used to be that you had to do it to be accepted, to get a good job. But now you can buy an education and get a job anywhere, so why waste two or three years of your life in the army? If you're part of the other group, the ones at the bottom who get less and less from the state, why would you choose to serve such a state?"

In reaction to the drop in enlistment, a multi-media campaign was launched in 2008 by a well-funded organization, the Israeli Forum for the Promotion of Equal Share in the Burden. Suddenly their ads appeared everywhere with the stirring slogan, "A True Israeli Does Not Dodge".

The Minister of Education announced in 2009 that some 300 additional army officers would work with teachers to promote conscription. The minister also announced that conscription rates at each school in Israel would be published. Henceforth Israeli schools would be judged not by their academic standards, but by their military recruitment rates.

In response to the "A True Israeli Does Not Dodge" campaign, New Profile launched its own: "A True Israeli Does Not Dodge The Truth". Haggai said, "As usual, we want to encourage people to think and ask questions. Of course, we can't begin to match the other campaign's resources, but we do try to get in the news somehow, even if it's only a short message about the need to question – then our website is flooded with inquiries. We do what we can."

I WON'T BE SILENCED

Before the raids on New Profile members' homes, the organization had already been a right-wing target. In 2008 the Forum for the

Promotion of Equal Share petitioned the High Court to cancel New Profile's non-profit status, which would have limited their access to funding.

In November 2009, the government's criminal investigation against New Profile collapsed for lack of evidence. The non-profit status case remained before the court.

In December, the Minister of Education forbade Israeli high schools to host any speakers from New Profile. As a result, New Profile was barred from participating in a series of high school events on human rights and civic freedoms. The entire series, organized by the respected Association for Civil Rights in Israel, was then cancelled altogether.

I asked Ruth Hiller how she felt about the escalating attacks. "I won't be silenced", she said. "If you won't listen to me, I'll go over here where somebody else will. Eventually the circle will widen. In New Profile we talk a lot about the many roles of women, including the mother. We talk about Sarah, the mother of Isaac in the bible. Why didn't she protest when Abraham took her child up to be sacrificed? We need to hear her voice, questioning, protecting the children."

I know from experience that a primary qualification for grassroots work is patience. Ruth nods. "Sometimes you just want to get on a roof and scream, have a big demonstration", she says. "That may bring a moment of satisfaction, the feeling that at least you're doing something, but it doesn't bring real change. Real change of the kind we seek is painfully slow. I can see it in the ten years since we started. I see it in the calls to our counselling network, which you can call if have questions about conscription, and you'll be paired up with a mentor. The woman in charge of that says we get about 60 applicants a month. When we started it was one to four. That's change."

SOMETHING TO BUILD ON

By now I've stopped asking people whether they experience despair, but instead how do they deal with it, what keeps them going?

After a long pause, Diana Dolev replies, "I think I'm a very stubborn person. When someone tries to hand me a picture that's not complete, that actually conceals quite a lot, it annoys me very much, so I'm always trying to discover more. In fact, I find hidden agendas more interesting than conspicuous ones. The hidden agenda provides you with more points of view, a richer, more intricate picture, sometimes one that is full of paradoxes."

Her research on the Hebrew University master plans led to a widening inquiry into the ways that a military mindset shapes public buildings, and how this affects people who use the buildings. "I have nothing to lose," she says, "not like the young who are looking for a career in academia. I know I won't be head of a department or a member of a research team in a big university. I teach in a college, and don't get funded for research, so I don't depend on anyone for that, I just go along."

When I ask Ruth Hiller what keeps her going, she replies, "I keep thinking things can't get worse here, but they do. My son got his first call-up notice from the army last Sunday. This is the fourth child, and I'm going through it again. Even though I know what to do by now, I still feel helpless. So I have to gather my energies, and persevere. It helps me not to throw myself into everything, but to stay focused on what we're doing in New Profile. When we get overwhelmed, we come together and support one another. That's what teamwork does, you are never alone."

And Dorothy Naor? "Looking ahead, I can see only more bloodshed. I don't see any leaders in Israel or the western world that will improve things here. The only way to make real change here is through the international grassroots, through boycott, divestment and sanctions, in the hope that eventually it can put enough pressure on banks and governments, as it did in South Africa. I just want to stop the bloodshed, for the sake of my children, my grandchildren, for future generations."

In 2010, a new law was introduced in the Knesset to criminalize support for any boycott of Israel. In one of her listserv messages, Dorothy commented that if the law passed, as expected, she would continue her work from prison.

In addition to his New Profile work, Haggai Matar attends university, writes for a local paper, and is active in several justice and human rights campaigns, including Anarchists Against the Wall. Formed in 2003–04, it grew as the separation barrier advanced from village to village, and Palestinians invited Israelis and internationals to join their non-violent struggles against it.

On his first trip to the West Bank, Haggai feared for his life from Palestinians. Does he now fear the soldiers? "Constantly", he replies. "But you know, our solidarity with Palestinians doesn't end with the protests. We also support legal struggles against the fence. We want to be partners in life, to resist the separation of people by the growing apartheid regime. Usually we can't stop the fence from being built, but living and working together, that's our goal."

What keeps him going? "We don't have a choice, really", he replies. "If you refuse to be part of what's happening here, you can either go into exile – I definitely don't want to do that – or you can continue to struggle. Palestinians don't have a choice; struggle is forced on them. So as long as they're resisting, and despite everything they are still willing to do it with Israelis, we can't afford to say, 'Sorry, I'm depressed, I can't make it today.' We can just be part of the struggle, tell people about it, and keep going so there will be people on both sides who know and trust each other. If we can keep these bridges alive, then maybe one day at least we will have something to build on."

12
The Generation that Matters

"I am not willing to be part of an organization committing war crimes, taking the lives of thousands of innocent civilians, an organization that, in the name of humanism and democracy, forces me and my peers to sacrifice a period of our lives, and our lives themselves, for false calm, for no calm shall come to pass until Israel decides to give up the policy of war and turn towards peace." After reading her shministim statement to a small crowd of supporters, Netta Mishly walked into Military Prison No. 400.

When I met Netta, she and her American boyfriend had lived in Jaffa only three days, and her parents in Tel Aviv were terrified for her safety. Although an increasing number of Jewish settlers are buying and building here, many Jaffa residents are still Arab-Israelis, Palestinians.

I sit with Netta Mishly and Raz Bar-David Varon in the living room of Raz's commune, up three flights in an old building on Yerushalayim Street. Eight people share the big apartment; three of them are preparing dinner at the moment, a large pot of bubbling vegan soup. The furniture is sparse and well used. It includes a fan, essential in the current heatwave, and a guitar propped in one corner. A livid poster cries out "Forty Years of Occupation!"

The two women ask if they can smoke. "It's your house," I reply, without much enthusiasm. "I suppose I should tell you to stop, but of course it wouldn't have any effect." They both laugh, and light up.

A CRACK IN THE WALL

The two of them were born in 1990: Netta in Tel Aviv, and Raz in a small town near Haifa. Both recall growing up on stories from the first Lebanon war, when their fathers took part in the 1982 Israeli invasion. "My father wanted me to be a paratrooper like him", says Raz. "On Purim, a holiday when you dress up in costume, mine in grade five was a soldier's uniform. I knew nothing about

Palestinians, only that Arabs were all around us, and we had to fight to stay alive because all of them wanted to kill us."

Netta nods in recognition. "I still have a photo of me at five or six in my dad's uniform, holding an M16 rifle, whch is taller than me", she says. "He told me a story: when he was walking around in Beirut, he met this man who wanted to go to Israel, he was born there but he wasn't allowed to go back. I couldn't understand this – why didn't he just go back? Ten years later I understood, he was a Palestinian refugee. We heard nothing about this in school."

On a tour to East Jerusalem at the age of 15, Raz Bar-David Varon got her first look at the separation barrier, an eight-metre concrete wall as far as she could see in both directions. "On this wall the Israeli government painted a big picture, a beautiful village with blue sky, trees, green grass. But then you see through a crack in the wall, and there is a real Palestinian village, with no trees, no grass. I thought, what is the government trying to hide from me? Suddenly I had a feeling that they had lied to me about many things."

In Jerusalem I met their fellow-refuser, Sahar Vardi, on her day off from work as assistant to City Councillor Meir Margalit (see Chapter 3). She came to talk with me at the home of my host, who became friends with Sahar's father in Ta'ayush, an Arab-Jewish activist group formed during the second intifada.

By the sixth grade Sahar was attending Peace Now demonstrations with her father, and in 2003 she accompanied him for the first time to the occupied West Bank. In Al-Nu'man, a small village south of Jerusalem, they planted olive trees, repaired water pipes, and helped however they could. "Most people there speak Hebrew or English, so it was easy to communicate", Sahar says. "Seeing the fence being built, being there right after the first houses were demolished, watching the checkpoint get built – witnessing that whole process, the imprisonment of a whole village – that was a very strong experience for me." By then she was 14.

Sahar grew up in the same military culture as Netta Mishly and Raz Bar-David Varon. "When I was in grade six," she recalls, "my brother had a poster of a woman soldier fighting beside a male soldier; it was when the army had just started a mixed combat unit. I remember thinking 'That's what I want to do, I'll show the guys that I can fight too.'"

To see for herself what was on the other side of the wall, Raz accompanied a friend to a village protest in the occupied West Bank, one of many as the wall advanced. The activists helped villagers create a cardboard wall, which they would then tear down in a gesture of defiance. But the soldiers got to it first. "When they started to destroy this art project, people sat down on the ground, trying to block them. The soldiers dragged people, they beat them, they threw tear gas on us. I was amazed. I'm an Israeli Jew; they tell you the army will protect you from the Arabs, this is their job. But they didn't protect us, they attacked us for trying to speak out non-violently against something we don't believe in. After that I started going to more and more demos, I learned more, and developed my own opinions." Raz was 15.

"I had the same experience", says Netta. "Your whole life they tell you that the army are the good guys, then you see how they behave. I felt very bad that these people represent me, they use my name and my security to justify what they're doing. I felt sort of like an ambassador, to show Palestinians that there are at least a few people that want to create a better future for all of us. Basically my government is shit, and their government is not so good either, so it's only people who can make things better."

A parallel shift occurred for Sahar Vardi. "Most of my early activism was from a left perspective, but still quite Zionist. For example, my best argument for getting out of the territories was that it would benefit the Israeli economy." In 2005 she joined a solidarity olive harvest with Rabbis for Human Rights. On the bus she talked with a member of Anarchists Against the Wall, about the hottest topic of that year, Prime Minister Ariel Sharon's plan to disengage from Gaza. "As a member of Peace Now, of course I supported the idea. But this guy started giving me the other side: the disengagement does nothing for the Palestinians, it will only make Gaza a prison, and with the settlers gone it will be that much easier for Israel to attack. I began to think this is more complicated than Peace Now was saying."

Earlier, Sahar had joined the youth group of Meretz, an Israeli social democratic party. There she met Netta Mishly, whose mother, a Meretz supporter, had encouraged her to join. It was a comfortable milieu for talking politics, feeling less isolated, and questioning the occupation, the military state, even Zionism. Though most youth members were more radical than the party elders, internal conflict was manageable – until 2006, when Israel invaded Lebanon again.

"The war started on a Wednesday morning", Sahar says. "On Thursday, Netta and I organized the first demonstration, at the Ministry of Defence in Tel Aviv. Others spread the word, and about 200 people came – we were shocked, we expected maybe 20. I got a lot of hate calls, and calls from the press, but the thing I wanted most was for Meretz youth to come. But on the day the war started, the Meretz party declared that they supported this attack, and therefore Meretz youth couldn't come to the demonstration. Right after the war, I officially resigned, and from that point I was no longer part of the Zionist left."

INTO THE FUNNEL

To resist here is one thing; to refuse, quite another. A woman whose child was about to enter the army described the process to me as a funnel, starting at birth then narrowing gradually until the age of 18, when it pours thousands of young people into the military apparatus, year after year. Given this kind of pressure, how did these three decide to refuse?

Netta replies, "Everything I saw in the West Bank made it clear to me that I couldn't join an army that does these things. Of course, I changed my mind 100 times, I should go to prison, I shouldn't. In the end I felt that if I did go to prison, it would give me more legitimacy, because people respect people who sacrifice for their beliefs. If I didn't go to prison there would be less hatred, but also less respect. Even my friends who went to the army told me they totally disagreed with me, but they respected the way I did it – I didn't just get out by saying I was crazy or something, I was willing to pay a price for my beliefs."

In 2002, Sahar attended support demonstrations for five imprisoned refusers, but still had no idea that she might do the same. On the contrary, she explains, "Everything you learn in Israel leads you to believe that going to the army is inevitable, it's perfectly natural, it's just what everybody does when they're 18." But each protest she attended – and getting arrested at several – further eroded her sense that army service was either natural or justified.

In 2005, Sahar signed the senior letter. Israeli high school seniors wrote the first letter in 1970, informing then Prime Minister Golda Meir that even though they would serve in the army, they would refuse to serve in the Occupied Territories. Similar letters followed, written by students in their final year of school, and co-signed by others in earlier grades. By 2001, says Sahar, about half the signers said they wouldn't serve in the territories; the other half said not in the army. "I think our letter in 2008 was the first that said we won't serve in the army, period. The more people saw that the mainstream Zionist left – Labour, Meretz, Peace Now – kept supporting the wars, the more they looked outside of that for change. And the problem with only saying that you won't serve in the territories is that when you're marking Palestinian houses to be bombed from an office in Tel Aviv, you are still enforcing the occupation and war."

Raz Bar-David Varon's rough education in the West Bank also moved her to refuse. "Your purpose is to make more awareness about this horrible situation," she explains, "but I was in conflict, how can I raise this subject? If you do, you get so much hatred from Israeli society, how can they hear anything you say? So I started to think that going to prison was the best way. It's good that we had the group. I don't know if I would have done it alone."

By chance, most of the 2008 shministim (refusers) were women. Was feminism a factor in their refusal? "Of course", Sahar replies. "The military is totally male-dominated. You can be a woman in it, but either you try and be just like the men, or you do the proper female functions like make the coffee. I actually had people tell me, 'Fine, don't go to the army, what difference does it make, you would only make coffee anyway.'"

"This is a new kind of feminism for Israel," says Raz, "not the liberal kind that says a woman should be able to be a pilot in the army, and we can kill Arabs just as well as the men. That's crazy. The oppression of Palestinians is connected to the oppression of women, it's a question of power. I don't believe my right to progress in this society should be at the expense of Palestinians."

"I learned that feminism is a liberation movement," Netta adds, "and when a society is oppressed, the women are oppressed twice; once by the oppressor, then again by the social structure of the society. As a feminist I can't oppress other women, my obligation is to be in solidarity with them."

In a state where army service is so deeply normal, what reactions did they get to their public refusal? "Constant conflict, all the time", Raz replies. "At family dinners, sometimes you ignore what's being said, but sometimes you have to say something and then it becomes an argument, you have to fight with your family and your friends. My family wasn't too bad, but I have a friend in the group who can't go to family events because when there is an ugly scene they blame her. She doesn't even have to say anything, the tension starts just because she's there."

Netta nods. "Many people end up having relationships only with other radicals, and some stop talking to their families, they just find it too hard to fight with people all the time. I didn't want to be like this, I wanted to keep all my friends, my family, but it's really hard. My father was very disappointed that I didn't go to army, and some of my friends resent me because they went to the army and they feel I'm not doing my share."

A veteran activist, Sahar's father supported her decision. In her final year of school, 2008, they tended her mother through a long illness, and then death. Though Sahar withdrew from many activities, she held firm in her decision. "The hardest thing for me was the relationship with my brother, a career soldier in the army", she says. "I got used to the fact that he's a soldier, but when things like the Gaza war happen, even though he's not a combat soldier I know he had an active part in bombing Gaza, which is everything that I'm protesting against. I've had conversations with him about it, but they all come to the same dead end. You just can't continue them, not if you want to have a relationship as brother and sister."

The three women identified New Profile (see Chapter 11) as a vital source of support. New Profile assigns to each refuser an experienced volunteer guide through the whole process from induction to release, so they know what to expect at each stage, including prison. Raz comments, "It's like going on a bad road; they can help you find the way."

FORSAKING THE ROAD OF VIOLENCE

One of the guides they all mentioned fondly was Haggai Matar. In 2001 he and others refused to serve in the army. (For more of his story, see Chapter 11.) Prior to their trial, Haggai and two friends were held in military prison. "That was interesting", says Haggai in a mild, thoughtful tone. "The worst of it was listening to long lectures, commanders yelling at you, making you do pointless things, and no time for yourself. The guards there had a saying, 'A soldier in prison is a soldier thinking, and soldier thinking is not good.' So they don't give you any time to think."

When the guards concluded that the young refusers were causing their fellow prisoners to think, they were transferred to civilian prison. With more spare time, they taught other prisoners Hebrew and literacy.

Due to an international campaign by New Profile and other organizations, Haggai received thousands of support letters from Israel, the Occupied Territories and other countries. One that moved him particularly came from a young Palestinian in the Occupied Territories. He wrote that he had grown up wanting to be a suicide-bomber. "But when I heard of your decision," he wrote, "I realized that there are actions which trigger greater echoes that any bomb ever could – and I have forsaken the road of violence."

As Haggai and his fellow-refusers left the prison, they were again ordered to report for duty in the army. Again they refused, and returned to prison, ultimately for two years. "Then finally they gave up", Haggai says. "The whole thing brought them a lot of bad publicity. They had pressure not only from left groups, which they always ignore, but also from prominent lawyers and judges in Israel and abroad. We were recognized as prisoners of conscience by Amnesty International and the UN. Even some prominent Zionist politicians said the army was going too far; already we were two years in prison, and no one in the army gets that for anything." In rare instances where Israeli soldiers are sent to prison for beating or even killing Palestinians, nearly always the terms are less than a year.

Anxious to minimize soldier casualties of the kind that forced it to withdraw from Lebanon in 2006, Israel launched its 2008–09 assault on Gaza with a terrifying barrage of remote-controlled high-tech weaponry, followed later by a ground invasion. I ask Haggai, by now a veteran of the refusers' movement, if such large numbers of soldiers would continue to be needed.

"For the time being, yes", he replies. "Israel has a lot invested in the notion of a people's army – the army is us and we are the army, it exists for our survival and protection, therefore it can't be questioned."

PRISON LESSONS

In Israel, the military funnel narrows at the age of 16, when the induction process starts with aptitude tests and visits to army units. It narrows sharply again at 18 with an order to appear on a fixed date at a prescribed base. "From this date until you're exempted," Netta explains, "it doesn't matter what you do or don't do, automatically you're a soldier. At 18 your health care stops, the army is your health care. Everything about you belongs to the army."

As soldiers, refusers are charged with a standard military offence, refusing an order, and tried in a military court. But first they may apply to a committee that will judge whether or not they qualify as conscientious objectors. "It's like a criminal investigation", says Netta. "You're really under attack there, I had five military people yelling at me and one civilian picked by the army, a professor of some sort to knock down any ethical arguments. In a situation like that, how can you explain yourself or even think?"

At Sahar's hearing, applicants that preceded her emerged from the ordeal in tears. "It's quite horrible. They insult you, they threaten you, they tell you that if you don't go, you'll rot in prison for ever. They also try to trick you by offering nice alternatives – maybe you'll go to the police, not the army, or maybe we'll make you a teacher in the army. They just want to see how you'll answer."

Refusers and New Profile members told me it's virtually impossible to fit the army's definition of conscientious objection. Netta says, "They ask you things like 'If you see someone raping your mother, would you do anything about it?' If you say 'Yes, I'd kick his ass', obviously you're not a pacifist. Even if you are a pacifist, if you refer even once to the occupation or Palestine, that makes you a political resister, so you fail anyway. They're a catch-22, these committees."

Knowing the committee would reject her appeal, Raz took the opportunity to tell them what she thought of the army and the occupation. When a young soldier on Sahar's committee asked her why he should go to the army and she not, Sahar replied that she didn't want him to go either. Netta called the head of her committee a murderer.

From autumn 2008 through spring 2009, as their draft dates came up, each of the shministim went to prison. Their comments on the experience are brief and pungent. Netta: "It's the most boring thing I've ever done." Raz: "The time passes so slowly, you could go crazy." Sahar: "It wasn't a nice experience, but not that bad. All day you clean, clean, stand, walk right, walk left, sit, stand, clean and eat." She didn't mention that she arrived at the prison wearing a T-shirt from Courage to Refuse (Israeli officers and soldiers who refuse to serve in the Occupied Territories). When she refused to wear the regulation army uniform, she was put in solitary confinement for the duration of her sentence.

Support from outside was crucial. As did the others, Netta received letters from Israel and abroad. "You think, why would those people care about you and what's going on here? It's good to feel that you're part of something broader." Raz adds, "Also these people remind you why are you doing this. In prison they make you so busy, you can forget why you are here. They want you to think it doesn't mean anything. Then you get so many letters, and it reminds you that what you are doing matters to someone; maybe it makes people think, maybe it makes a small change. It's kind of nice."

I ask them if anything positive had happened in prison. For all of them, instead of undermining their resistance, it actually confirmed their reasons for refusal. Sahar replies, "In there you see how the army treats its own soldiers – of course, it's less destructive than to the Palestinians, but still you encounter horror stories like one woman who was arrested for heroin use, and in her first three days in prison, no doctor saw her. She should have been in rehab, but to them she was just another prisoner. Or girls who wanted to change their jobs in the army, some of them to get away from sexual harassment, but they're not allowed to change, so they desert knowing that they'll go to prison, because usually after prison, they change your job! It's ridiculous. These girls are giving two years of their lives to the state, and it treats them like shit."

Raz and Netta both mention how, ironically, the closed world of prison had expanded their horizons. Raz explains, "In prison you could talk to people that maybe you wouldn't know in your life outside. You have to get along with everyone in there, otherwise it's going to be hell. I met one girl who said how much she hated Arabs, she wanted to kill them, but when you get behind the slogans and really talk, I discovered she has a good friend who is an Arab. All the girls there understood that they're screwed up by the system, the army is bullshit, and it won't protect them or help them."

Netta revised some of her assumptions about feminism. "I met women in prison who are probably the strongest I've ever met, but from the leftist point of view you'd say they're not feminist because they shave their legs, or because they don't have a more radical way of thinking; let's say they still believe a woman should cook for her family. But they've been through so much I can't imagine, and still the way they act is so strong, I thought, 'What is feminism if not this?'"

After each refuser had served a number of consecutive sentences, the army released them as mentally unfit for service. The exemption had to be approved by an army psychiatrist. Netta describes her bizarre encounter: "I told this psychiatrist that I saw a friend being shot by the army at a protest, and half of his brain spilled out. The psychiatrist said, 'Well, it's like you're stuck in an elevator, and you get traumatized by it, but the best solution is to go into an elevator again and deal with your trauma. So the best way for you to deal with this trauma of yours is go into the army.' I think I would rather have spent two more months in jail than have to face that crazy psychiatrist again." She laughs, a little bitterly.

To her, the "mentally unfit" label is a tactic to pathologize conscientious objectors. "It's not that there could be anything wrong with their system, you're just not fit or good enough for it."

Mentally speaking, these young refusers are not only fit, they are athletes. As shministim they have to be exceptionally strong and steady, to stand their ground under attack. It could be said that these virtues also define a good soldier, but with one key difference: the refusers aren't following orders.

THE GENERATION THAT MATTERS

When I met them in Israel, Sahar and Netta had just returned with other 2008 shministim from intensive speaking tours in South Africa and the United States. The tours were sponsored by Jewish, war resister and solidarity groups in the host countries.

On both tours the shministim encountered hostility and disruption from militant Zionists. In South Africa, says Sahar, "We had people yelling at us in discussions, not letting us talk, and in one case the organizers had to call in security when it looked like people were going to attack us." One of the South African sponsors reported, "The Shministim were called cowards and traitors. Their Jewish identity was questioned. Someone shouted 'They should be lynched', another shouted 'Knock some sense into them.'"

At one of the US events, too, security had to escort the speakers, Netta Mishly and Maya Wind, safely out of the hall. "People were yelling at us and throwing things", Netta says. "Israel is doing very good propaganda work in the US, so Jews there feel like Israel is theirs, it belongs to them. I was quite offended by their arrogance, telling me, an Israeli, that I was disloyal to Israel and I don't know what I'm talking about."

Raz jumps in. "You hear the same thing here, all the time. If you come as a soldier to a non-violent demo, you throw tear gas and you shoot at people, then you know for real what happened there, but if you come as a protester or even a journalist, then you don't know what happened. The only reality is the military point of view. It drives me crazy."

Still, for the travelling shministim, the benefits greatly outweighed the stress. Sahar was particularly encouraged by her encounters with young South African Jews. "One of the biggest Zionist youth movements there even has in its constitution that it's against the occupation", she says. "But they don't know what to do, they're so afraid that opposing the occupation automatically means opposing Israel. It was very important for us to say over and over, it is not antisemitic and it is not anti-Israel. The most positive thing is that in all the youth discussions we had, even if people disagreed with us, even if they came wearing IDF shirts, still they listened; we had conversations, we tried to understand each other. The only people who shouted at us, even in the youth meetings, were older adults. So I'm optimistic. This is the generation that matters now – no offence (she laughs disarmingly) – and at least they're open to having this discussion."

Sahar also took hope from her meetings with South African Muslims. "The last talk I gave in Johannesburg – at that point I was alone, the other two were in Capetown – turned out to be one of the most effective. About 200 people came from the Muslim community, and the meeting ended with a call for boycott, but they made a point of emphasizing that this was not antisemitic. As a Jew, obviously I don't want antisemitism, it's no more appropriate than any other racism. But also it's so easy for Israel to dismiss anything that can be seen as even remotely antisemitic. I think the most important thing right now is to separate Jewish from Zionist and from occupier, so go ahead, criticize, demonstrate against the last two, but not the first. Since the Israeli government keeps blurring them together very effectively, activists in Israel and in other countries have to keep making the distinctions very clear."

For Netta, the tour followed an earlier trip to the US a year before, with no planned events, just informal encounters across the country. The change, she says, was amazing. "I think that before Gaza lots of Jewish people were scared to open their mouths, but after Gaza, people are speaking out a lot more, they're more active. Also in Arab-American communities, after 9/11 people put their heads down, but now they're more open. This made me feel much better, because without the US we couldn't maintain the occupation. It's a very good sign that people there are starting to wake up."

SPREAD THE WORD

When I met Raz and Netta, both were working in Jaffa. Raz is volunteering for a year with Sadaka Reut, a community organization formed in 1983 to bridge the deep divide between Palestinian and Jewish youth inside Israel. The apartment where we met is a Sadaka Reut commune. "We meet separately, Jews and Palestinians, and then we meet together", Raz explained. "We talk about the conflict, the occupation, and prejudice in Israeli society. We try to make the conflict very personal, not something far away and only for leftists – it's about who we are. We also work in the community and in schools; this year with teenagers in Bat Yam." South of Tel

Aviv and Jaffa, Bat Yam is home to large communities of Jewish immigrants from Arab countries and the former Soviet Union, with glaring disparities between the affluent beachfront and the inner city.

Netta had just started to work with African refugees in Jaffa. "Many of them are having a hard time financially, and it's not easy to find jobs, housing and health care. My work will be to see what people's needs are, and how we can help. The organization is called the African Refugee Development Centre, it was created by refugees ten years ago. My bosses are all refugees, a nice break from the usual power structure where white people are always the bosses. Here it's someone from the community who knows the community, so they can help me find my way."

In Jerusalem, Sahar Vardi has two jobs, studies history part-time at university, and continues to engage in solidarity and protest actions. Besides her work with city Councillor Meir Margalit, this year she also took over from Haggai Matar as coordinator of New Profile (see Chapter 11) youth groups across Israel.

Recently Sahar forwarded an international call to action. It originated from Open Shuhada Street, one of the South African groups that co-sponsored the shministim tour. Formed after the Gaza war by Jewish, Muslim and other activists in Cape Town, its primary campaign focuses on Shuhada Street, formerly the main street in Hebron, which several hundred settlers and the Israeli army have rendered effectively, and illegally, out of bounds for more than 160,000 Palestinian residents.

Sahar added her own stirring call. "It is our hope that activists in cities around the world will agree to participate by symbolically shutting down a major street in their cities and/or organizing a demonstration in a strategic location (i.e. the Israeli embassy/consulate, city centre, college campus, etc.) on 25 February, in solidarity with the Palestinian residents of Shuhada Street. Please spread the word and join this global struggle for justice today!"

THE NEXT SHMINISTIM

The senior letter for 2009–10 opens, "We, the undersigned young women and men, Jews and Arabs from all parts of the country, hereby declare that we will toil against the occupation and oppression policies of the Israeli government in the Occupied Territories, and in the territory of the land of Israel, and therefore refuse to take part in actions related to such policies, which are carried out in our name by the Israeli Defence Forces."

Eighty-eight young Israelis signed the letter, which was sent to the prime minister. This year's refusers have already begun to serve prison terms, and veterans only a year or two older will guide them through.

The letter concludes, "Our objection to becoming soldiers of the occupation stems from our loyalty to our values and to the society surrounding us, and it is part of our ongoing struggle for peace and equality, a struggle whose Jewish-Arab nature proves that peace and coexistence are possible. This is our way, and we are willing to pay the price."

13
Naming Palestine

Near sunrise I'm awakened by the sounds of village life in Palestine: a goat bleating, the chug of a farm tractor passing the open window, and the eerie shriek of an Israeli war-jet.

In smoothly hilled farm country, Al-Jalama is five kilometres north of Jenin in the occupied West Bank.

My host Nasser Abufarha has been up for an hour, responding to his first batch of emails. A solidarity group in Ireland wants to know how prices compare for olive oil that's certified fair trade only, or fair trade plus organic. The opening chapter of Nasser's dissertation is ready to be published online. The first dozen of 40 stainless steel storage tanks from Italy should arrive tomorrow at the new processing plant in Burqin. Visibly relieved by this last news, Nasser laughs. "People will be surprised. These are not the kind of tanks that usually invade our village!"

WATER

Nasser Abufarha was born here in 1964, in this vaulted room that used to be the whole house but is now his living room. On the wall behind him, formal photos of his grandfather and his parents keep watch. The grandfather wears a keffiyeh, a practical head-covering for men long before Yasser Arafat turned it into a symbol of the struggle for Palestine.

In 1948, when Jewish soldiers occupied Al-Jalama, Nasser's father led a small band of local men to retake the village. Their success was fleeting, but not forgotten here. I note a direct line of resistance from father to son. "Oh, absolutely", says Nasser. "Some of our products actually carry a label that says 'Resisting the occupation by insisting on life.'"

Growing up under Israeli military occupation, he learned early to resist. "If you even spoke the name of Palestine, or showed the colours of the Palestinian flag [red, green, black and white], you could be arrested. So we would draw it or write it everywhere: in our notebooks, on walls, on tree trunks, on the ground. This became a kind of game for us with the Israeli army – we would raise the flag; they would chase us. It was one way to resist what they were trying to do to us, to make us forget who we are."

At the same time, Nasser experienced the crushing impact of military rule on farming, the primary livelihood for many in an area still known as the breadbasket of Palestine. His family used to grow citrus fruits and guava, but after the Israelis took control of the aquifers – Palestinians are forbidden to drill any new wells – the fruit groves died. For a while the family grew melons, which are less thirsty, until these, too, withered.

"Of seven wells in the village, only one is still viable," says Nasser, "and from that we only get half the water we did in the past. Now most farming here has switched to greenhouses, to conserve water, but even that is difficult as it gets drier. This is a totally different village from when I grew up. We used to farm in the open air, surrounded by citrus trees and lots of birds. Now we farm in plastic houses."

But still they also farm in olive groves that cover the dry hills, as they've done for centuries. Here among the ancient silver trees is the contemporary form of Nasser's resistance. Now the name of Palestine is written on products going out from Burqin to 14 countries on three continents.

Shortly before the new Canaan Fair Trade processing plant opened, Nasser gave me a tour. In any context it would be impresssive, but under the strictures of military occupation it's astounding. Set in an olive grove, the plant is huge: 4,300 square metres (46,000 square feet) on three levels, the lowest dug deep into bedrock.

Olives will arrive here from farmers across the West Bank, to be pressed, filtered and stored underground at a precise temperature in oxygen-free tanks, preventing the build-up of peroxide that would cost the oil its highest-quality extra virgin status. From storage it goes to bottling, labelling, packing and shipping. In other parts of the plant, olives, sun-dried tomatoes, spices and grains will be processed into a growing range of Canaan Fair Trade products.

In a time and place where jobs are scarce, Nasser says the plant has employed about 50 workers to build it, a similar number will be hired to run it, and about twice as many have been working with the suppliers, for most of which Canaan has been the main project through the summer. The tanks come from Italy, the grinding stones from Turkey, the ecologically-friendly furniture from reclaimed lumber in Indonesia. The plant even has its own nitrogen generator. "This is because we live under conditions which might make it difficult to get nitrogen tanks refilled", says Nasser, with an ironic smile.

We emerge from the cool interior into encircling olive trees, the heart of this enterprise. I inquire about a particular tree, thick and gnarled, with a broad canopy – it must be very old. "No," he replies, "that one is young, only three to four hundred years old."

Yesterday they had to uproot a tree of similar size so they could dig for underground water storage. Instead of cutting it up for firewood, as would happen where I live, they transplanted it to another spot in the grove. To my surprise, olive roots are shallow, which explains why the trees can be uprooted so easily by Israeli bulldozers. Since the tree would take a while to recover from being moved, and its olives wouldn't mature properly for eating or oil, Nasser harvested them on the spot. Before he picked me up in Jenin, he bought plastic buckets so his sister could pickle them. No olive is wasted here.

PRECIOUS COMMODITIES

In the second chapter of his PhD dissertation, "Land of Symbols: Cactus, Poppies, Orange and Olive Trees in Palestine", Nasser writes: "The olive trees, olives, and olive oil are precious commodities in the West Bank. They are an integral part of the Palestinian diet. A Palestinian home is traditionally well stocked with enough olive oil and wheat for the year until the next harvest season, and these staples constitute the daily breakfast for most Palestinians."

Beyond that, its unique qualities have made the olive tree a revered symbol of nationhood for Palestinians. Nasser writes, "These qualities are its dominance in the landscape of Palestine; its history of ancient presence in Palestine; the old age of the tree itself, which exemplifies the old Palestinian existence in Palestine and connects Palestinians to the lives of past generations in their family tree as the olive trees are passed on through the generations; and the communal life the olive trees create around their maintenance, harvest, and celebration."

Nasser's paper is the fruit of his other work, anthropology. His education started on the ground in occupied Palestine, and continued in the United States, at the University of Wisconsin in Madison, culminating in a PhD in cultural anthropology and international development. How does this combination work? "The two are at opposite ends of the theoretical framework", says Nasser. "Anthropology is hesitant to engage in how to do things, but more engaged in better understanding people. International development is more about planning, and how to do things. My idea of anthropology is not to be a commentator, but an engaged participant in what I'm studying, which is my own society. To engage you have to understand the culture that you're working in. The context of Palestine is one that I live and understand. Now I'm better able to have impact here through practices that are theoretically informed by anthropology, but also incorporate a planning approach to social change."

In Madison coffee shops Nasser encountered a practice that immediately struck him as relevant to Palestine – fair trade. "Usually it's understood as a means to address disparities between giant corporations and local growers. But then I started to think, 'How could this work for Palestinians?' – not just to address disparities, but even to make trade *possible*. Due to the occupation, export from Palestine – if you can do it at all – has many hurdles and conditions that result in extra cost. So we would need somehow to free ourselves from the tyranny of market pricing. I knew we could produce excellent products, but how could we sell them? Sometimes we aren't even allowed access to local markets, much less to the outside."

He returned home to Palestine in 2003, the third year of the second intifada. "Palestinians were under siege and very isolated, we could hardly move. Because of that, olive oil prices were extremely low, less than 7–9 shekels, or about US$2 a kilo, so farmers were losing interest in harvesting their olives – why do all that work when nobody is buying and you can't even cover your cost of production?"

He and some friends organized meetings with Palestinian farmers and people who ran oil presses. At the same time, they investigated what Nasser calls "the nuts and bolts" of international fair trade. From this inquiry emerged, within a year, two new entities: the Palestine Fair Trade Association (PFTA), and Canaan Fair Trade, of which Nasser is principal owner.

The PFTA is a union of local farmer cooperatives, pressers and traders. Each cooperative elects a representative; the resulting body elects the board, and it appoints the staff. One of the new organization's first and most radical initiatives was to set a base price for olive oil at 15 shekels a kilo, double the prevailing market price. Immediately farmers were interested, but leery – why would anyone do such a crazy thing? Where was the hidden trick?

Since the international fair trade certifying bodies hadn't yet developed any guidelines for olive oil, the PFTA had to develop its own, blending Palestinian farming traditions with fair trade experience in other commodities around the world. The resulting guidelines were ratified by the members in 2005, and by international certifying bodies shortly after.

While the PFTA takes care of the producers' interests, Canaan Fair Trade handles marketing and distribution. In order to export their olive oil, PFTA members had to meet European, Canadian and US import standards, as well as gaining the technical capacity to produce and distribute in much larger quantities. Nasser explains, "We began by bringing the oil into compliance with international standards, testing and monitoring for acidity levels and other factors. After a series of workshops with farmers and pressers, in 2005 the proportion of farmers' oil that fully met the standards increased from about 20 per cent to almost half, and when we moved into organic certification in 2006, the proportion increased to about 80 per cent."

What did they have to do to meet the organic standards? "Most olive farming is done by traditional methods, which are organic by nature", says Nasser. "Where the Israeli army won't allow them to go regularly to their groves, some farmers do use herbicides to control weeds, so they don't become a fire hazard in the summer. But with fair trade and organics we hope to encourage farmers to return to traditional methods as a way to protect the environment. Also, it's less expensive when you don't have to buy chemicals, and you're not held hostage by the Israelis who decide whether or not to let these products in. This is the question that has to guide us in everything – does it empower the community?"

FAIR TRADE

Though the standards weren't hard to meet, the cost of certifying large numbers of farmers and pressers proved too much for the fledgling organization. But by chance at the same time, Dr Bronner's Magic Soaps, the largest natural soap producer in the US, had just decided to make all their products entirely from fair trade and organic ingredients. In their international search for olive oil they contacted Canaan Fair Trade; it had access to oil and the necessary documentation of organic practices, but no budget for certification. The Dr Bronner people agreed to cover the cost.

After an intensive period of training and inspections, by harvest time in 2006 the Swiss certifying body, the Institute for Market Ecology, had certified 375 farmers as organic producers. Since 2007, Dr Bronner's Magic Soaps has been purchasing 90 per cent of its olive oil from Canaan and the Palestine Fair Trade Association. The rest comes from Palestinian and Jewish producers inside Israel.

In response to attacks for "dealing with terrorists", Dr Bronner's current president, David Bronner, argued, "Canaan Fair Trade was founded by Palestinians who support peaceful coexistence with Israel and see profitable olive farming as one means of improving Palestinians' economic situation. Canaan Fair Trade is an example of what fair trade is about: disadvantaged farmers facing the obstacles and difficulties of reaching markets in the midst of a conflict situation, are being organized on fair trade terms that help them and their families negotiate these obstacles and connect with markets in the west."

When I met Nasser Abufarha, he had just returned from launching Dr Bronner's Magic Soaps in Israel with David Bronner. Full circle, olive oil from Palestine comes home. Advances from the company on future purchases also helped Canaan to build the new plant.

My own connection to Palestinian olive oil began in a chance encounter with Robert Massoud at a farmers' market in Canada. Like Nasser, Robert is a visionary driven by dislocation. Born in 1957 to Palestinian parents who had fled from their village to Jerusalem, he emigrated with them to Canada in 1964. Growing up in Montreal, Robert followed his parents' example in suppressing his identity. "The PLO was forming then, and it's when the early hijackings occurred. All the progaganda said they had no grounds for doing these terrible things, they were just savages. How could you respond to that? At home we would call ourselves Palestinian, but out in the world we would say we were from the Middle East, from Lebanon – anything but Palestinian."

Over the next two decades, through university and a successful career in marketing, Robert Massoud gained knowledge, confidence and what he calls "a cumulative outrage" at what was happening in the Middle East and how it was reported/distorted in North America. In 2003, the same year Nasser Abufarha returned to Palestine, Robert searched for an effective way to engage with the long struggle. Eventually he found a vehicle that suited his passion and his skills: fair trade olive oil.

With a few activist colleagues, Robert organized bottling, labelling, publicity and distribution of 1,500 bottles. Zatoun was born. Zatoun is Arabic for "olive". Five years later, more than 30,000 bottles of olive oil and a range of other fair trade products from Palestine were sold by a far-flung network of volunteers in cities and towns, workplaces, schools, union halls, churches, synagogues and mosques throughout Canada and the United States. Some retail outlets now also sell Zatoun, but the project is still driven mostly by volunteers. They include a Jewish doctor who works in a low-income inner-city neighbourhood, a rural woman who grew up under the German occupation in Holland, an Israeli-Canadian who has become a fierce critic of Zionist policies, and me.

In the face of a brutal occupation, faithfully supported by most western governments including Canada's, Zatoun offers a rare form of practical life-affirming direct action that citizens can take from a distance. It provides farmers in the West Bank with an essential market for their olive oil. It funds the planting of olive trees to replace millions of trees destroyed by the Israeli army and settlers, as well as art and language programmes for children forced to grow up in refugee camps. But Zatoun has another less tangible role that Robert Massoud considers equally crucial in North America, where it's a challenge to find honest information about Palestine and Israel.

"The Palestinian experience is like being in a hurricane", he says. "You're trying to be heard, to tell your story and make your case, but in the uproar of hype and spin and fear-mongering, you can't be heard. This is what Zatoun is meant to address. We don't have access to the levers of media, nor to the politicians, but we do have access to the grassroots, to people. Now through Zatoun they can get beyond the spin and connect with something real."

In occupied Palestine, Nasser Abufarha explains the other half of the same argument, "The Israeli strategy is to deny the existence of Palestine, to make us disappear behind the wall, erasing us from the map and from the public mind. Having the name "Palestine" on the bottle or package, right there on the shelf, this is an assertion of our existence, and buying these products is an act of resistance against the erasure that policy-makers continue to promote. For us, this is what separates what we're doing from charity. We are doing an exchange based on equity. Palestinians take a lot of pride in their olive oil. As one farmer said, 'Germany has its BMW, we have our olive oil.'"

The fair trade connection has had a whole other layer of impact here. "When Israel was formed," says Nasser, "it was legitimized by the western powers and the UN; they simply looked the other way while Palestinians were ethnically cleansed from most of our land. The fact that this happened, and still happens, causes much resentment among Palestinians. So the olive oil sales tell us we're not alone, and the western world is not just one big homogeneous colonizing entity; in fact, there are a lot of people willing to stand by us. These distinctions are very important, just as it is for westerners to see Palestinians, Islam and Arabs as complex and varied."

PERMITS TO FARM

Still, for farmers here the most compelling argument for fair trade is survival, it makes farming possible again. In the tiny village of 'Anin I talked with two farmers, cousins, both of them weathered and strongly built. Mahmoud Issa took over his father's land a few years ago, and introduced organic farming to the village; his cousin Awad Milhim followed soon after. Mahmoud also represents the local cooperative's 50 member-families on the PFTA board.

Having an interest in organic growing, I wonder how they manage harmful insects without pesticides. "We use traps", says Mahmoud, with Nasser translating. "These traps are the same yellow colour as the flowers so they attract flies, which then get stuck. It works very well." Awad nods agreement.

What about water, do they have enough? "Not enough to irrigate", Mahmoud replies. "We can only afford to water new seedlings until they are strong, then they can survive on their own." Is there less water than in the past? "Yes. There is less moisture in the olives, we can see that they are thirsty. It means the fruit will not be as sweet. Also, when the spring season is as dry as it was this year, we have fewer flowers, which means fewer olives."

Before the PFTA, Mahmoud and Awad sold their oil to local merchants or to Israeli brokers, and were thankful if they could break even on their costs. Has this changed? The cousins look at each other and laugh. "There is no comparison", says Mahmoud, emphatically. "Now we can support our families, and our kids will be able to go to college."

Nasser explains, "The current market price for olive oil is about 14 shekels. Canaan pays an 18 per cent premium for fair trade, plus an additional 10 per cent premium for organic. This year, PFTA farmers are getting an average of 20 shekels for their oil, about 25 per cent above the market price. This is what we promised to pay even if the market price fell. The farmers see these things as real, not just hot air."

This feat is all the more remarkable for having been accomplished under military occupation, which is never far away. While we stood on the roof of the new plant yesterday, an Israeli military helicopter hovered above. Like many others here, Nasser hardly notices the war-jets any more, even when they break the sound barrier, but on the roof he stopped talking and watched the helicopter. Why the difference? "Unfortunately a helicopter often means they're going to assassinate someone in the area."

In 'Anin I ask how the occupation affects farmers. By way of response they take me out to see where their land is, downhill from the village, more than half of it now cut off by the wall – a broad white slash through the landscape, wavering in the heat.

To reach their olive groves on the other side, the farmers need to request permits from the military authorities. If a farmer is lucky enough to get one, it may allow him only one hour on the other side. Whether farmers can plough, prune, maintain and harvest the trees when these functions need to be done depends entirely on the whim of the soldiers.

Olive groves throughout Palestine are also subject to attack by both settlers and the army. Since the occupation began in 1967, it's estimated that at least a million trees have been destroyed, and the wall threatens to destroy or cut off twice as many. Even in a land so richly endowed with olives, the loss is catastrophic.

On the road to 'Anin, Nasser pointed out several large sheds on a hill across the valley – an Israeli agricultural settlement. Mahmoud's cousin Awad hasn't spoken much today, but now he talks about his almonds. "I didn't have much experience growing them, but with help from the PFTA I began to produce quite good almonds. When the settlers noticed this, they started to release pigs into our orchards. Pigs like to eat almonds, and to reach them they pull down the branches, breaking them. We chased them out, but the settlers keep letting them back in. It's terrible to see an almond orchard that's been torn apart. I'm starting to think I'll have to stop growing almonds. That's what the settlers want, but what can you do? If you try to defend yourself, the army will be here in a moment."

Nasser has to get back to Burqin now, to prepare for the arrival of those storage tanks. My parting question to the farmers: "What keeps you going?" Mahmoud replies, "To support my family I have to work my land. This is what I do."

A MOMENT OF OPPORTUNITY

By now, more than 1,700 farmers across the West Bank have signed on with the Palestine Fair Trade Association. From start-up in 2003, both the PFTA and Canaan have grown at an astonishing rate. The new plant is estimated to cost US$2.5 million, much of it from fair trade loans and advances. Does it make Nasser nervous? He laughs. "Of course, all the time."

Why the new plant right now; why take such a big leap? "Because this is a moment of opportunity", he replies. "We want to extend the benefits of fair trade to the widest pool of farmers we can serve, but not to the point where farmers have surplus olives that we can't sell. By marketing, especially in North America and Europe, we have been able to increase demand, so far by about 200 per cent a year. To meet that demand we had to upgrade our infrastructure as well as the quality and consistency of the product. This is why we need the new plant, to develop our storage capacity under premium conditions so that in years of low yield we can still meet the market demand, and in years of high yield we can store for the following year."

Demand for olive oil from Canaan grew dramatically with the recent addition of two major outlets: the international Whole Foods chain, and a chain of cooperative supermarkets in Britain. Not only is Palestine on the map, but so is Canaan Fair Trade. One day Nasser got a phone call from an official at the Tel Aviv office of the United States Agency for International Development (USAID). They had received complaints from private Palestinian olive oil trading companies, which are funded by USAID, claiming that they couldn't succeed because Canaan had driven the price too high. When farmers heard that PFTA members were getting 20 shekels for their oil, why would they sell to these other companies for so much less?

"My answer was to agree, why would they sell for less?" says Nasser. "When we started, we set the minimum price at 15 shekels, which was only three or four shekels above the cost of production. Within a few years the standard market price went to 14, but by then we were paying twenty or more, which includes premiums for certified fair trade and organic. The farmers deserve this premium, but even the basic market price of 14 is fair. Due to the military occupation, Palestinian olive oil has a lot of added production costs, so farmers here need to earn a little more than farmers in Turkey, or the big subsidized farmers in Italy or Spain. The approach of these

Palestinian companies is to keep the price very low so they can do business. Our philosophy is to add value by adding quality, plus the social values of fair trade and organic certification."

THE EARTH IS MY HOME

During the holy month of Ramadan, the daily dawn-to-dusk fast ends with a meal of traditional dishes. On my last day in Al-Jalama, we are invited to share the Iftar dinner with Nasser's nephew and his wife – soup; two lamb dishes: one made with mountain thorns (made soft in the cooking) and the other with okra; a Palestinian salad, and sweets made specially for Ramadan.

After dinner, as the evening cools, I join Nasser on a walk around the village. The whole village, or at least the male half, seems to be out on the street: children playing; men chatting, exchanging greetings and kisses on both cheeks. The atmosphere is remarkably safe and comfortable, though Nasser reminds me that the Israeli army has used Al-Jalama more than once for practice in village warfare.

He stops to chat with a local folk singer who promises to improvise a song for the olive harvest festival in November. Nasser introduces me to another man who says graciously, in English, "We are happy to see someone from the world."

We visit the village machinist-blacksmith, to see if he has finished building the metal handcart that will be needed to move the storage tanks into the plant tomorrow. He assures Nasser that it is 80 per cent ready. Afterwards, Nasser tells me with a wry smile, "I expect that means it's about 50 per cent ready."

We walk to the edge of the village, to the wall – a razor-wire fence here, with cameras – and the checkpoint, under harsh orange lights. Nasser points at headlights moving across a field – a military vehicle patrolling the fence. If Nasser didn't have an American passport, I comment, this is where his world would end. True, he says.

Later in the evening, an uncle and his wife come by for a visit. Nasser and his relatives all live within a few hundred metres of each other. Seeing how important family is to him, I comment that it must be hard to be separated from his other family, his wife and children in the United States. "It's very difficult, yes, for me and for them", he replies. "But I travel a lot, so I can keep staying in their lives, and keep them in mine. They'll be here, I hope, for our harvest festival in November. My kids have grown to be American

– they have a comfortable life in Wisconsin, that I wouldn't like to disturb. So I live in two worlds, and try to make the best of both."

Is he ever tempted to choose the comfortable life for himself? "Certainly", he says. "But Palestine is not something I can distance myself from. I can contribute here, be a positive force, and I don't think I could justify choosing a quiet life over that, teaching at a quiet university somewhere. To be honest, although the work I'm doing here is more tiring and more challenging, it is also a lot more meaningful. The results here are tangible, you see the smiling faces of farmers who had almost given up. Also I enjoy connecting with people who are doing good things around the world, not just be stuck away in one little corner. I feel the earth is my home, in the full sense of the word."

Does he worry that Canaan and the PFTA depend too much on him? "That was certainly the case for a while, but now the PFTA has trained staff, and we're about to add more positions. Canaan also has a good managing team. I still handle a lot of the marketing, but soon we'll be hiring dedicated marketing persons for the US and Europe. As the founder, I'll continue to be involved; but you know, I'm also an anthropologist, and there are many other things that I want to do."

* * *

For now, Nasser's day ends as it began, responding to another batch of emails. Suddenly he remembers that he has to call the electricity authority. The plant is running on a generator, but soon it will need full power, which could take some time to arrange. Then he returns to the plant. To receive the tanks tomorrow, the floor has to be smooth. They tried smoothing it by hand, scraping off chunks of concrete that had dripped wet from the ceiling during construction. When that didn't work they brought in a machine, a grinder/polisher. But the grinders were too smooth, so they had to change to a rougher grade. Then there wasn't enough power from the generator, so they had to find another ...

14
A Cure for Amnesia

We scan the rounded contours of fading hills, shadows of hidden valleys, tough little shrubs, and cultivated trees gone wild – fig, olive, pomegranate, and carob with long-fingered brown seed pods. Suddenly we have to yield the trail to a squad of speeding mountain bikers, helmeted, sunglassed and spandex-sleek, dispensing *Shalom*s (hellos), over their shoulders as they pass.

We are in Canada Park, a short drive northwest of Jerusalem. In the broad valley below, the separation barrier twists across the landscape. On the near side are the low, flat sheds of a large Israeli farm, built in the early 1980s on land belonging to the ancient Palestinian farming village of Beit Sira, which we can just make out on the far side of the barrier. The sprawling settlement bloc of Modi'in-Maccabim-Re'ut threatens further encroachments.

Official signs in Canada Park celebrate the area's rich and fabled past – biblical (the Israelite hero Joshua is said to have fought a key battle here), Hellenic, Roman, Byzantine and Ottoman. As to the four Palestinian villages buried here, there is only deep silence.

How did this happen? In a 1969 interview with the Israeli newspaper *Haaretz*, then Defence Minister Moshe Dayan offered an explanation: "Jewish villages were built in the place of Arab villages. You do not even know the names of these Arab villages, and I don't blame you because geography books no longer exist; not only do the books not exist, the Arab villages are not there either … There is not one single place built in this country that did not have a former Arab population."

REMEMBERING

The epic scale of this historical erasure provides fertile ground for the Israeli organization Zochrot. While leading an educational tour to Canada Park, Zochrot founder Eitan Bronstein conceived a remedy for the blanket amnesia that governs his fellow-citizens' view of Palestine: posting signs to identify what had been erased. A Hebrew word, Zochrot means "remembering".

"As a former kibbutz member, I was naïve enough to think that kibbutz people would be open to the idea", says Eitan. "So a journalist friend wrote an article which included a list of 30–40 kibbutzim, with the names of the villages that had been destroyed on that land. All we proposed was that people recognize what happened in the past, nothing more. My friend asked kibbutz members for their reaction to the idea. All were against it, 100 per cent. When I saw all these reactions, I understood how important it was that we should post the signs."

His conclusion strikes me as a good example of that much-hailed Jewish quality, chutzpah (audacity or gall). "Maybe", says Eitan, with a shrug and what I take to be a mischievous smile that lights his face. With close-cropped hair, open-necked, short-sleeved black shirt and black trousers, he could be a soldier on weekend leave.

Born Claudio in 1960, at the age of five he emigrated with his parents from Argentina to Kibbutz Bahan in the Hefer Valley. They changed their names to reflect their new-found home; Claudio became Eitan. It translates as "steadfast".

I asked him to describe his journey from Kibbutz Bahan to Canada Park. Accustomed as he is now to analysing historical shifts, he identifies several of his own. All of them occurred in times of conflict. "Like any good Israeli citizen, at 18 I went to the army", he says. "I was an excellent soldier: never questioned, never refused anything. When the first Lebanon war started in 1982, my army service had ended but they called me to go with the reserves. For the first time I refused, and they put me in jail for 28 days. I would say now that this was the most important crisis in my relation to the state." He was 23.

In 1987, when pent-up Palestinian rage against the military occupation erupted in the first intifada, Eitan was called up again for reserve duty. Again he refused, and again went to jail.

Eitan's next shift was sparked in 2000 by another intifada. By then he had been facilitating for almost a decade at the Neve Shalom Jewish-Arab school for peace. "During those years I learned a lot about the conflict, especially my part in it as an Israeli Jew. But then the question came, 'What can we do about it?' The only answer we could provide was to talk more; we had no ideas about what to do."

During the October 2000 protests, Israeli soldiers killed 13 unarmed Arab Israeli citizens. "That day I went to a demonstration," says Eitan, "and for the first time I was on side of the Arabs, facing Israeli police. In the school we talked about equality between Jews and Arabs, but now finally I understood that there could be no equality as long as the Jewish state was built on racism and colonialism. The best that Arabs or Palestinians can expect is to be second-class citizens in their own land. Finally I began to understand that the real issue here is Zionism. I couldn't say any more that I was a Zionist who supports equality. That doesn't work."

Within a year Eitan Bronstein started taking Israelis to sites where Palestinian villages had been erased from the map and from public memory. "When we first talked to the displaced persons committee (the National Committee for the Rights of the Internally Displaced in Israel) about the idea of these visits, they were surprised and suspicious. They questioned us, 'Why, what will you gain from doing this?' – it was not an easy test. But then they approached us to make a first visit, then another."

Zochrot was launched.

Eitan and his colleagues knew that to make any enduring impact, they would have to build an NGO with the capacity for systematic research and generating useful resources. They spread the word on their goals and intentions. "We were quite surprised when foundations approached us to offer support and money", says Eitan. "I was shocked, but then it confirmed that this was something worthwhile to do. But although we have more supporters outside the country, the most important push for us is the encouragement we get from Israeli Jews. Of course, they don't support everything we do, but it's enough that quite a few support the issue of knowing the past."

MEMORY LOSS

Canada Park is a pleasant refuge from the urban clamour of Jerusalem. Many Israelis come here to bike, walk and picnic on its 1,700 undulating acres. My Israeli friend takes me on a short walk from the main parking lot, through rows of pine trees to a small fenced ruin. The fast-growing pines were planted in many places by the Jewish National Fund (JNF), she says, to solidify Israeli claims to the land.

An official sign beside the ruin carries the title "Department of Archeology, Civil Administration for Judea & Samaria". It means we are standing on occupied land; "civil administration" is a euphemism here for the apparatus of military occupation, and "Judea & Samaria" the Judaic name for the occupied area more generally known as the West Bank.

My friend identifies the ruin as a Roman bath – we note water channels, round bowls carved into stone, a dry rectangular pool with a disintegrating mosaic floor. She draws my attention to three small domes, decaying but still clearly discernible on the roof. This was an Islamic shrine, where Muslim pilgrims came to pray. Beside it, outside the fence, weathered stones mark a graveyard. With a practised eye, it is also possible to read in a tumble of stones the skeletons of former houses.

These scattered fragments are the visible remains of 'Imwas, a Palestinian village known in Christian scripture as Emmaus. When Israeli forces swept into the area in 1967, their commander (later prime minister) Yitzak Rabin ordered the villagers to evacuate immediately. Poignant images taken by an Israeli photographer show streams of people carrying away children and bundles – all they could carry – under the watchful eyes of Israeli soldiers. Within hours 'Imwas, Yalu and Beit Nuba were bulldozed to the ground. A fourth village, Dayr Ayyub, had already been demolished in 1948.

Canada Park was built on the rubble of these four villages. In the early 1970s the Canadian branch of the JNF raised $15 million in donations to establish it. The park continues to be managed by the JNF, and maintained by donations primarily from Canada. Across the road from the ruins, a series of stone walls carry plaques naming hundreds of donors. The Canadian government still regards donations to maintain the park as charitable and therefore tax deductible.

When Eitan Bronstein got the idea to post signs here and in other sites of historical erasure, his original impulse was partly symbolic. But it also turned out to be a deep challenge to the dominant version of history.

In 1948 two major historical shifts occurred here, simultaneously: for the Jews, the gaining of a homeland; for the Palestinians, the loss of theirs, the Nakba, the catastrophe. Everything that followed appears to confirm that these two experiences of history are at odds. As it happens so often in the human story, the official version is written by the victor.

Shortly after Zochrot was born, it sought permission from the Jewish National Fund and the Civil Administration to post signs in Canada Park recognizing the villages of 'Imwas and Yalu. After more than two years of negotiation and a court challenge by Zochrot, finally in May 2006 the JNF posted two discreet signs. One disappeared shortly after, and the Palestinian reference on the other was obliterated with black paint.

In response, Zochrot requested that the JNF post signs to mark disappeared Palestinian villages not only at Canada Park, but at all the sites it administers throughout Israel. Researchers had already identified more than 80 destroyed villages. Zochrot offered help in identifying the remains and researching life stories. The JNF turned down their help, but accepted the list of villages. In 2008, JNF authorities agreed that in any park where signs detailed the local history, references to destroyed Palestinian villages would be added, with text subject to approval by the JNF.

At Canada Park, we notice, the posts for the signs recognizing 'Imwas and Yalu remain empty.

THE PAST IS PRESENT

Study tours to disappeared villages have become a staple in the Zochrot programme, and the most public face of Zochrot. Coordinated by Palestinian staff member Umar Ighbariyyeh, each tour draws from 100 to 200 people, mostly Israeli Jews. They trek through fields and up hills, and clamber over terrace walls to explore village ruins, which sometimes appear to be little more than random piles of rock. Nearly always the visitors are accompanied by refugees from the destroyed village, people who know how to interpret the random rocks, reconstructing their lost villages from memory.

After the August 2009 study tour to the destroyed village of Al-Damun, Umar Ighbariyyeh reported: "The refugees on the tour came from different families, and had been born in different neighbourhoods. The competition among them was obvious – displaying their knowledge; deciding which story to stress; choosing who would tell it. They argued about the exact location of the mosque, the exact name of the mukhtar [village leader], the boundary of the eastern neighbourhood. They brought the charred remains to life. The remains belonged to them, and their arguments were serious and emotional. Their pain is evident as they speak. Sixty-one years after their Nakba, they continue to refer to their property in the present tense."

For Israeli Jews, Zochrot tours can evoke other kinds of loss, including the shedding of illusions. Hava Keller joined a tour to the destroyed village of Alsumeriyya. A founding member of nearby Kibbutz Sa'ar, as a young woman she watched the villagers being expelled in 1948. "I naïvely believed that the refugees would soon return to their homes", she told the tour. Then one day, returning from work on a local moshav (farm), she noticed that all the village houses had been demolished. "After that day," she said, "I wanted nothing more to do with Zionism. I understood that Israel has no intention of living in peace with the Palestinians, but intends to expel them from the country."

Zochrot's stated mission is "to commemorate, witness, acknowledge, and repair".

As Eitan and his colleagues deepened their own witnessing of the Nakba, they came to understand that it is not a finished historical event, but an ongoing disaster. Every protester shot, every house demolished, every olive grove uprooted, every metre of separation barrier extends the Nakba, and the damage to be repaired.

For eight years Zochrot has spread this concept through tours, speakers and exhibits at the Zochrot centre, the magazine *Sedek*, and occasional bursts of attention from the mainstream media, some of it relatively positive. But still, to acknowledge the Nakba at all remains a marginal, even alien activity for most Israelis. Zochrot activists kept running into the same obstacle: how could they reach more people, especially those whose minds have not yet closed? One obvious answer: schools.

THERE USED TO BE PALESTINIAN VILLAGES

On my first visit to Tel Aviv, Zochrot education coordinator Amaya Galili hosted me in her compact downtown apartment, an easy walk from the Zochrot centre. In her early thirties, Amaya is a kind host and patient guide; energetic, articulate, and fiercely dedicated to changing the way her fellow-Israeli Jews regard their country, their neighbours and the landscape.

She has been deeply engaged in the challenge of creating a Nakba curriculum for Jewish high schools. Despite a major deadline looming for the project, she took time to share her own story. We talked over lunch at her kitchen table.

Born in 1977, Amaya grew up on Kibbutz Amir in the Galilee, near Israel's northern border with Lebanon. She recalls a junior high school visit to an Arab Israeli village about 30 minutes' drive along the valley. "This was the closest Palestinian village", she says. "I didn't think about it at the time, but later it did seem strange, since there used to be Palestinian villages where we lived."

In high school Amaya took seriously the teaching that she should play an active role in the affairs of her society. "In 1994 when the settler Baruch Goldstein murdered the Palestinians in Hebron, we organized a protest at a junction near the kibbutz. We did the same thing again after the suicide bombing in Afula [a town in the Galilee]. We felt that our response had to be equal." When she was 17, the neo-liberal privatizing mania that swept through Israel threatened to close her school. She and her schoolmates protested that, too.

I asked Amaya how her identity as an Israeli Jew had evolved. A key shift occurred for her in learning about the Holocaust. "I studied it very intensely, learned the history, read testimonies, and looked at the influence it has on Israeli society. I read Tom Segev's book, *The Seventh Million*, about how the Jews in Palestine dealt with the Holocaust, and how they reacted to survivors from Europe. This was the first time that someone supported what I was starting to think about how Israel uses the Holocaust. The last chapter is very strong: it talks about how youth are prepared for the army, and how the Israeli state shapes its collective memory on military, not humanitarian grounds. By grade twelve, when I went to Poland on a Holocaust tour, I differed for the first time from the group I grew up with. I still participated in the tour, but I refused to support some of the activities they made us do. This was an important moment for me, when I began to understand how the state shapes who we are."

A year later she did her compulsory army service, hated it, and returned to the kibbutz as soon as it was done. Here, Amaya experienced another profound shift. She decided to research the life of her grandfather, who emigrated to Palestine around 1938, helped establish the kibbutz, learned Arabic, and functioned as an informal diplomat between the kibbutz and its Arab neighbours in the surrounding villages. He died the year Amaya was born.

"I started to interview people who knew him", she says. "They told me a lot of nice stories about him, including how he helped the refugees after 1948. But when I asked them what happened in the war, suddenly they were embarrassed, they wouldn't say much. I couldn't understand this, I felt that something was being hidden. Later I found out that my grandfather was part of a unit in the Hagannah (pre-1948 Jewish army) that collected intelligence. While he was building relationships with the Arabs, being their friend, at the same time he was collecting information about their villages, so the Hagannah could have a file on every village, which helped them a lot in fighting the war. Here was the answer to my question, how the kibbutz could have had so many Arab neighbours before the war, but now there are none. It was really shocking to discover these two sides to my grandfather. For me this was an important breakthrough."

After studying sociology in university, Amaya worked for several years as a community organizer in low-income Jerusalem neighbourhoods, developing her own analytical and critical faculties along the way. Then she won a year-long scholarship to a Middle East social work studies programme at McGill University in Montreal, Canada. Though she didn't find the programme particularly useful, she emerged from it with a Master's degree in community social work.

Back home in Israel, Amaya worked for a while with people being processed into the made-in-the-USA Wisconsin Plan, under which public welfare is gutted, and the already disadvantaged are forced into jobs that either don't exist or that pay wages often below liveable minimums. "After a year I started to understand more clearly what we were doing. I met a Palestinian woman doing similar work, and we wanted to work together in community advocacy. But the organization that employed me didn't want me to work with Palestinians – they wouldn't say this directly, but it's what I felt quite clearly."

Then a friend at Zochrot – co-founder and associate director Norma Musih, who also grew up on Kibbutz Amir – told Amaya that the organization was looking for an education coordinator. She applied, and got the job. "When I went to Zochrot," she says with a smile, "my family and some of my friends were quite shocked. 'That's a very radical place', they said. 'It's okay to support social issues, but this business of facing the Nakba, it's too much.'"

To an outsider like me, facing the Nakba seems essential. But then I wonder, how many Canadians would be prepared to face the equivalent catastrophe for original peoples in North America? How did Amaya herself come to terms with the Nakba? "Where I grew up," she replies, "it's a beautiful valley, mostly agricultural. Often I walked through fields and forests, but I didn't see the ruins of the Palestinian villages, even the ruins were invisible to me. So now I want to help people to see the landscape through different eyes. We also need to develop ways to hear the Palestinians – not just to hear that we all believe in peace, but what did they really go through in the Nakba; what do they still go through today?"

SO DARK A MIRROR

Three years ago, a group of Israeli teachers took up the thorny question of how to introduce discussion of the Nakba into Jewish schools. It would be Amaya's primary task as Zochrot education coordinator to organize their work into a formal curriculum packet.

They consulted back and forth, then tested a prototype with about 20 high school students and teachers. Amaya incorporated their comments into a close-to-final product, the deadline for which is rapidly approaching when we meet.

Why is it so important for Israeli Jews to grapple with the Nakba? "First, it's an injustice against Palestinians, our neighbours", she replies. "But it's also about us, about who we are. My grandfather helped to throw out his Palestinian friends, and then he tried to compensate by helping the refugees. My grandparents knew a lot about this; my parents less; and by my generation, nobody talked about it. This is the silence of ignorance, but then it also becomes the silence of ideology. To talk about the Nakba raises a lot of fear and anger. But we have to talk about it, we have to deal with it."

I ask again, why? "I want to stay here in Israel, in Palestine; this is my home. But I don't want to be part of a colony, always at war, more and more closed in by walls and fences. To live here in peace, with justice, we have to integrate more into the Middle East. That means we have to stop oppressing another nation and other communities within Israel. The first step is to acknowledge the Nakba, and what we did to the Palestinians in 1948. I don't think we have any other option."

Amaya's case sounds reasonable and compelling, but rather utopian at a time when the current Israeli government is increasingly hostile to public acknowledgement of the Nakba. First the Yisrael Beiteinu party of Foreign Minister Avigdor Lieberman moved to criminalize any public commemoration of the Nakba on the same day as Israel's Independence Day. Then, after some ministers objected that this initiative would damage Israel's image abroad, a new bill was introduced to ban state funding to any group that organizes or funds activities related to the Nakba. If passed, the law would have the same silencing effect as the original proposal.

These heavy-handed manoeuvres provoked a public response from Eitan Bronstein. "We should not underestimate the challenge facing Israeli society: to recognize Israel's part in the expulsion of most of the Palestinian inhabitants of the land in 1948, the destruction of most of their localities (upwards of 500), the annihilation of urban Palestinian culture, and tens of massacres, rapes, incidents of looting, and dispossession. Looking into so dark a mirror takes courage and maturity."

I asked Eitan why he believes it so important to look into this mirror, to recover buried memory. "Without memory, we can't function", he replied. "When you repress or manipulate collective memory, you are touching at the root of our human existence. Of course, memory is never pure and without influences; it is always shaped not only by political forces but also by forces in our own lives. Still, it is a fundamental aspect of human life, and silencing or hiding it is one of most powerful, brutal ways to oppress people."

I commented, "What's distorted in the past will necessarily distort the present."

"Of course", said Eitan. "When we talk about the Nakba, we are not talking about something which is gone, but something which is still here, now, in everyday life. As long as we refuse to see this, how can we ever have true reconciliation between the two peoples?"

In mid 2009, the completed Zochrot learning packet was introduced to more than 200 Israeli high school teachers. *How Do We Say Nakba in Hebrew?* is designed for students aged 15 and older in a variety of courses. Using maps, literary texts, artwork, historical material, film and other media, the packet includes accounts of Palestinian communities before and after 1948, a history of events surrounding the Nakba, personal testimonies of refugees, a virtual tour of a destroyed village, and a discussion of the refugees' right of return.

According to the Israeli newspaper *Haaretz*, the Education Ministry was not pleased: "'The education kit was not approved by the ministry. Teachers using materials not approved by the ministry are acting against ministry procedure and policy.' The ministry also said it would conduct 'an immediate investigation.'"

Simultaneously, the education minister ordered that the word "Nakba" be removed from a school textbook for Arab students in Israel. It had only been inserted two years before, when an earlier minister allowed its use for the first time, in Arab schools only.

FIGHTING FOR HOPE

Setbacks and attacks are not new to Zochrot. In the Israeli media they've been called murderers, antisemitic, a marginal organization of lunatics, an example of Jewish pathology, an expression of narcissism and moral obtuseness, and Hamasniks, collaborators with the enemy. In 2009, after Eitan Bronstein urged Israelis to join in Nakba commemorations, he received a series of anonymous death threats. In 2010, the Knesset moved toward outlawing commemoration of the Nakba on Israel's Independence Day.

In such a climate, one Zochrot initiative that particularly enrages its critics is the promotion of public discussion on the return of Palestinian refugees to their homeland.

During and immediately after the 1948 war, three-quarters of a million Palestinians fled or were expelled from their homes, villages and land. The 1967 war caused a further exodus of some 350,000.

Right-of-return proponents cite a founding document of the United Nations, the Universal Declaration of Human Rights. Article 13 states, "Everyone has the right to leave any country, including his own, and to return to his country."

In December 1948, UN General Assembly Resolution 194 confirmed the right of Palestinian refugees to return to their homes. The General Assembly has voted almost every ensuing year to reaffirm these rights, but they remain abstract; General Assembly resolutions do not carry the force of law.

In Israel, where many Jews regard even Arab citizens as a threat to the Jewish state, any mention of refugee return provokes fear and outrage. Since 1948, Israeli authorities have used a range of means from legislation to military force, to prevent the return of Palestinian refugees. By contrast, the 1950 Law of Return ensures the right of Jews from anywhere in the world to settle in Israel and gain Israeli citizenship. The intent is clear: Israel is and must always remain a Jewish state. As long as it also professes to be a democratic state, the Jewish state can only be ensured by maintaining a Jewish majority. In such a context, any proposal of refugee return is anathema.

When Zochrot stepped into this minefield, it did so boldly. In June 2008, it invited Israelis to a public conference on the return of Palestinian refugees. There they were asked to grapple not with abstract questions on the right of return, which the planners accepted as a given, but the practical matter of how an actual return might work. In his opening remarks, Eitan Bronstein explained, "Whenever we talk about the Nakba and the return of Palestinian refugees, we're asked, 'Okay, so what do you propose? What can we do now? Go back to the countries we came from? Swim away in the ocean?' All the fears of Israeli Jews float to the surface. That, exactly, is what this conference is about."

Zochrot planners thought they would do well if 150 people showed up. In fact, even though the conference had to be on a work day, some 300 participants arrived. They worked together through one long day, trying to imagine a more inclusive future than the one set out in the Zionist programme. How could it be determined who was eligible to return, and who did or did not want to return? How could Israelis and Palestinians prepare for the profound changes that return would entail? How might new maps help people to view the country differently? How would citizenship be defined in an authentically multicultural society?

Given current trends in Israeli politics, it could be argued that such an exploration goes far beyond the visionary into the realm of fantasy. Yet many participants, including Eitan Bronstein, emerged from the conference with renewed hope. "Two things gave me hope", says Eitan. "First, in all the endless discourse about refugees here, talking about practical aspects of an actual return is something totally new. Even among Palestinians it remained abstract, so one of our goals was to encourage our Palestinian friends to imagine how we might live together in ways that don't depend on occupation and resistance. The second hopeful aspect was the reaction of people. Some of them had come to Zochrot events in the past, so they already understood the need to acknowledge the Nakba. But this conference was about visions for the future. People were curious to know what it could mean, and so were we – these possibilities haven't existed before, we have to invent them. The willingness of people to imagine gives us hope."

In fact, Eitan argues, Zochrot is in the business of fighting for hope. "If you look at the news rationally, every day we are declining and probably there isn't much reason to hope, so what we have to do is fight to maintain hope. If I look at Zochrot, the mere fact that we are growing is grounds for hope. Zochrot isn't just a peace group, something for people who want to love each other. It challenges the very basics of the Jewish state as it is presently constructed, so if people are coming to come and see what we offer, it means there are Israelis who want to think radically about change. When you think only in terms of more or fewer checkpoints, one checkpoint less may be better but this won't bring peace or reconciliation. When we really try to think about reconciliation in practical ways, this can give some realistic hope."

Closer to home, Eitan took it as a sign of hope when his eldest son, one of four children, refused to serve in the army – not just in the Occupied Territories as Eitan had done, but in the military altogether.

WALLS COME DOWN

While we clean up after lunch, I ask Amaya Galili where she stands on the question of hope. "It depends on which day you ask me", she replies. "I want Israel to change itself before it's too late, but I'm afraid that we are approaching the moment when it could already be too late. Things are getting worse – the wall, the racism. Maybe the state will last 50 or 100 years, but not the way it is now. The problem is, Palestinians can be very nice, but as long as Israelis continue to get more fascist, more and more colonizers, why should they be nice? I hope that what I and others are doing will open people's eyes, change their way of thinking, so that if somehow peace can come, it will have a foundation, something to build on. But if there isn't a big movement of people who want real change, and leaders who believe that a just peace is the only way, there will be a disaster. So you see," she concludes, with what I read as a rather melancholy smile, "I have good days and bad days."

Should I conclude that this is a bad day? Amaya laughs. "Not so bad", she says. "I talked recently to a woman who grew up in East Germany. When the wall came down in 1989, she remembers that in one night everything changed – one day the teachers were communists, the next day they weren't. I found this quite inspiring. Of course, I don't think it happens like this very often, the walls coming down so fast. I would say that one of our goals at Zochrot is to encourage critical thinking. I don't believe this will lead to revolution, or that we'll convince millions of Jewish Israelis to see what happened in the Nakba and to say 'Yes, the refugees can return'. When I think about how political change occurs, I doubt that it will come fast. It means working slowly, with patience, person by person, knowing in the end that this is work which has to be done."

15
The Tempo of History

We park in a pool of thin shade by a small, parched tree. Though Ramadan holy month has emptied the streets of Kufr Qara, the Workers Advice Centre (WAC) is open.

Inside, Wafa Tayara talks intensely with five young women. Two of them wear hijab, as does Wafa; the others, jeans and long-sleeved shirts. One has sunglasses perched on her head.

At another desk, Dani Ben-Simhon speaks rapid Hebrew into the phone, running a restless hand over his bristled head. Interpreting for me today is Michal Shwartz, a founder of the Workers Advice Centre. Her lively gaze follows the two exchanges.

"Dani is trying to persuade a Jewish farm-owner to employ these five Arab women – it's harvest now so they need workers to pack produce. Wafa is trying to convince the women to work with us instead of with a subcontractor who skims 1,200 shekels from their wages every month."

On a hot September morning we drove here from Haifa in WAC's well-used Toyota Corolla. Dani drove, already at work on his mobile phone, while Michal and I talked in the back.

WAC's work is done entirely within Israel. As we drive into Kufr Qara, Michal tells me that, like every Palestinian village, most of its land has been confiscated by the Israeli state. The latest confiscation is for an American military base. At the same time, the government gives virtually no support for industry in Arab villages. We pass small garages, a few shops. If people here want to work, says Michal, they have no choice but to work in Jewish farms and factories.

In the office, Wafa continues to negotiate with the five women. "Wafa is telling them it's a good place to work," says Michal, "not too heavy, putting things in boxes, and it's not under the sun." Dani leans into the phone, as if to add weight to his case.

Discernible in this small local drama are the grim outlines of a much larger battle. "On the big Jewish farms," Michal explains, "local Palestinians are being replaced by foreign workers. Already more than half the farm-workers in this country are from Thailand. They are brought here for five years by manpower companies, 'shackled', as we say, meaning they are tied to one boss – it actually says so in their passports. They work like slaves. Since they live on the farm, they are available at all times to work 14, 16 hours a day, at 13 shekels an hour. The legal minimum wage is 20. For this the farm-owner gets a subsidy from the Israeli government. As a result, you can see what a struggle it is to get Arab workers hired even temporarily."

While we watch Wafa reason with the women, Michal explains, "Eighty per cent of Arab women still don't work outside the home, and most who do are professionals, teachers, nurses. Farm-work is regarded as the lowest of the low. But there is a lot of poverty here; many husbands are out of work, injured or in prison, so the women need to work."

From outside, the muezzin's songful voice, amplified, calls the faithful to prayer.

WAFA TAYARA

One of nine sisters and two brothers, Wafa was born in Kufr Qara in 1973. Her father worked in factories, picked fruit, raised chickens, ran a small grocery, did what he could. The young Wafa wanted to work too, but married as soon as she finished high school, and before long she had four children. Her husband worked in construction, until a disc ruptured in his back.

With no professional training, farm-work was the only field open to Wafa. "My husband's family thought that this work was not respectable", she says. "People would say that if I had to do such work they must be destitute. I don't think that way, neither do my own family or my husband, but unfortunately my mother-in-law represented the way that most people think."

From necessity she persevered, working on a variety of farms. On one she suggested that she and her co-workers ask for a raise, but most feared that if they made any demands, the boss would replace them. Wafa also ran into trouble with her neighbour, a Palestinian subcontractor who supplied workers to farms in the area. "He said I was making these women think too much, while he was doing them a favour just by allowing them to work, so I should shut up."

At the time, the WAC was launching an initiative to organize farm-work for women. Dani Ben-Simhon visited Wafa and Nur, her husband – as a construction worker he was already a WAC member – and invited Wafa to join. She would get the full minimum wage, the rights of a worker under Israeli law, a pay slip – rarely provided to farm-workers, but essential to obtain any social benefits – and the support of a union. To Wafa it sounded too good to be possible. "But things were so bad," she says, "I thought, why not give it a try?"

She organized a group of four women to work with her on a farm near Kufr Qara, cramming themselves into her small car each day. "That first day was a very big event", she says. "At the end of the day we calculated our earnings. We had worked this many hours, therefore the sum on our pay slip will be such-and-such. Is it possible that we will get so much money?"

When other village women heard that Wafa earned one-third more they did, they started coming to her for work. They pleaded with her not to tell the subcontractor. But of course, he knew; this was a village. "He went to the fathers and husbands, he said, 'What do you want, more money or someone to protect your daughters and wives?' He even threatened to burn my car. But these tactics didn't work", says Wafa. "More and more women came, so many that finally the subcontractor asked if he could work with us." As Wafa recounts this in Arabic, Michal laughs merrily.

After a year, Wafa accepted a paid job as full-time organizer with WAC. Its 30 workers across Israel are all paid equally, a little above the minimum wage.

Dani comes off the phone grinning: The farm-owner will hire the five women, at least for now. But how will they get to the farm without a car? Now it's Wafa who works the phone. "This is our Achilles' heel", Michal explains. "In Arab villages there is no public transportation, so if you have no car you stay home. Farm-owners solve this by having a subcontractor with a car, but he takes a big cut. We have to find a woman with a car big enough to take four others, then we ask the farmer to pay for the gasoline."

As if on cue, Wafa's husband pulls up in a car big enough to get the five women to work – today. For tomorrow, another solution will have to be found.

Dani is already back on the phone, chasing farm-owners.

DANI BEN-SIMHON

Born in 1960, Dani grew up an outsider, the child of Arabic Jews who emigrated from Morocco to Israel in the 1950s. People like them were wanted in the new state because they were Jewish, but segregated in "development towns", Kiryat Gat in their case, away from the main centres. They were treated as second-class citizens because they were not of European origin, in a country that turned its face from the beginning toward Europe, and away from the Arabs.

After his army duty, Dani left Kiryat Gat to study art in Tel Aviv. "My painting was not a question of esthetics", he says. "I was looking at ways to influence people toward thinking about racism and equality, especially the issue of east and west in Israeli society. But then I went to Haifa, and suddenly one kilometre from my house I felt I was in a refugee camp. For years I had been talking about racism between Jews, European and Oriental, but of racism against Arabs, of the occupation, nothing. For 15 years I had been sleeping."

Working in a hotel to support himself, he volunteered at the Workers Advice Centre, teaching Arab children in Jaffa how to make their own art. As his awareness deepened, he learned to speak and write Arabic. Through the 1990s he also became aware of neo-liberal globalization, a rapidly spreading disease. "It wasn't hard to see what was going on – the rich against the poor, and exploitation regardless of nationality or religion. Step by step, I became more and more involved."

I asked Dani why he shifted from art to organizing. He replies, "I understood, both as an artist and a person, that your power to influence things is very small, maybe you can do a few good things for a few people. But if you want to make social change, you need to go deeper to the roots, and join with other people."

He joined the Organization for Democratic Action (ODA), WAC's political entity, moved to Haifa, and immersed himself in the struggle.

OLD SOCKS

Another day, we drive from Haifa to the new WAC office in the village of Baqa. On the highway we dart among heavy trucks. In Israel there are 40,000 truck drivers, Michal says. Twenty-five years ago the big national transport companies were unionized, and the drivers paid well enough to qualify as middle class. But when the neo-liberal wave swept through Israel in the 1990s, it left in its wake hundreds of smaller companies and subcontractors, hardly any union jobs, and legions of drivers at the mercy of their bosses.

Like farm fields, highways provide fertile ground for organizing. After meeting for several months with truck drivers, WAC organizers got a vivid picture of their situation. Many work 300 hours a month, which comes to ten hours a day, seven days a week. At best they earn 6,500 shekels a month, an hourly rate around the minimum wage. Most have no pension, no insurance. If they complain, they are fired. Since the drivers are often people who can't get other work – Russians, Eastern Europeans, Arabs – many can't read or speak Hebrew, a further disadvantage. Drivers who seek help from the big state union, the Histadrut, find it indifferent to their plight. As one driver told Dani, "The owners can throw us away so easily, we are like old socks."

To negotiate a fair contract, bargaining committees need to be organized in each company. WAC organizers go to ports, quarries and truck stops, where they hand out leaflets in Hebrew, Russian and Arabic. Then they wait for calls.

Last night Dani met with drivers from a small company. One of them had called to say he was interested, and Dani suggested he try to persuade others to come along. Six showed up, aged 25–55. A WAC volunteer translated between Dani's Hebrew and the drivers' Russian. "These men have worked for this company for six to eight years", says Dani. "They know they're being cheated but they don't know what to do about it."

Dani argued the case for joining WAC, and then electing a committee to bargain with the owner for a contract. "By law you need only one-third of the workers to establish a bargaining committee", says Dani. "Last night they already had more than one-third of the drivers in this company. I think there is a good chance they will agree."

Is it hard to organize disparate groups who've learned to be enemies? "Yes", Dani replies. "When I explained that our goal is to build a union for everyone, one driver said 'Agh, we don't need the Arabs.' I said, 'Why not? You're being exploited by the same boss, the same methods. The boss can hire [to pit] them against them, or you against them. If we want change, we need to work together.' They said, 'Yes, yes, you're right.' When you talk with workers about their reality, they understand, they can recognize that we are trying to find a good solution to a shared problem."

Michal adds, "From the beginning people see that our literature is in Hebrew and Arabic, or trilingual, so it's clear that we are not a Zionist organization like the Histadrut, interested only in Jewish workers. When people decide to work with us, they know where they're going. The decision may not be so easy to make, but those who make it know what they're doing."

"In WAC," Dani adds, "we are trying always to reinforce this idea of shared working-class interest, regardless of nationality. This is different from other organizations that talk about coexistence here. Either they talk and talk but say nothing about politics, or they eat hummus together and that's it. We're talking about something much bigger, mutual working class interest to make a change in our society."

From my reading of history I'd say this is a long, steep uphill battle. Since Michal has been at it longer than anyone else I know, I asked her how she reads history. She pauses a moment before responding: "We are not people who lack patience, who think we can change history with our own hands. We look around, we see how things have gone in the past and how they are going now, and we work at the tempo that history forces on us. Sometimes you have to run very fast to remain in the same place. But experience shows that when you're active you build something, and if you don't stop in the middle and leave in despair, it will bring results. Even if you won't live to see them, at least you know you're doing something that's needed."

By way of results, Michal mentions a recent breakthrough. For two years WAC has been trying to organize diggers, manual labourers who work in archeological sites and stone quarries. As in agriculture and trucking, in the excavation business bosses collaborate with manpower companies to create a virtual slave market, picking and choosing from the most excluded, and thus most desperate for work – Palestinians, Ethiopians, the elderly, women.

WAC focused its organizing efforts on a quarry company in East Jerusalem. Half the workers come from the occupied West Bank, half from occupied Jerusalem. "In the beginning," says Michal, "the quarry company said 'Who are you? You don't represent anyone, we don't need to deal with you.' Now after two years of struggle, including going to the labour court, we succeeded in forcing the company to allow elections to form a workers' committee, with WAC as the union, to start negotiations with the company. Now for the first time the workers get pay slips, and already the company had to give them toilets and masks. This is a big step forward."

In May 2010, after the quarry management halted negotiations, all 40 production workers went on strike. They refused management's offer to resume negotiations without WAC. Three days into the strike, management agreed to marathon negotiations toward a collective agreement, the first in 27 years at the quarry.

MICHAL SHWARTZ

Michal's long view of history took a while to mature. She was born in Jerusalem in 1949. "It sounds like millions of years ago, doesn't it?" she says. Her close-cropped hair is grey, her face weathered, but her smile is warm and she radiates calm determination. I asked her how she had evolved as a political person. Already I think of Michal as a revolutionary, but I'm shy of that loaded and much-abused word.

She dates her first awakening to army service in the 1967 war. At 18 she worked as secretary to an officer who served as Israeli liaison to the United Nations agency responsible for Palestinian refugees. "We were stationed at the Allenby Bridge," she says, "and there I witnessed what was happening to the endless stream of refugees that crossed from Israel into Jordan. Until then I was very naïve; I thought that Israel wanted peace but the Arabs didn't. Then gradually I saw that things were not as I had been led to believe, and little by little I began to understand the colonialist nature of Israel."

After the army Michal went to university and joined with other Israelis in opposing the occupation of the West Bank and Gaza. Then questions began to arise for her about the situation of Palestinians still living inside Israel, who had suffered military rule from 1949 to 1966, under which much of their land was confiscated. In March 1976, after the Israeli government announced plans to expropriate thousands more dunams of land (one dunam is equal to a quarter of an acre) for "security and settlement purposes", finally decades of resentment spilled over. Marches and a general strike were called in Arab towns and villages throughout Israel.

"Israeli forces went into the villages and murdered 13 young people, all of them unarmed", says Michal. "These events were another landmark in the political growth of many people, including me."

As Michal's engagement deepened, the risks rose. "The political group I was part of realized in the mid '80s that in this struggle there were two camps: on one side was the US, Israel, and unfortunately the majority of the Israeli population; on the other side, the Palestine Liberation Organization and the Soviet Union. We decided to be part of that camp. So when the first intifada broke out in 1988 – really a popular uprising, not an armed struggle – we worked closely with the left and the PLO in the West Bank. For that our newspaper was banned and four of us were imprisoned on the charge of belonging to a terrorist organization. They made a big public case of it, everybody said we were traitors and we should get 40 years. In the end the state made a plea bargain, and we were sentenced to one and a half to two and a half years. As you can imagine, this was a very strong experience."

Shortly after Michal emerged from prison in 1989/90, a wave of euphoria washed over Israel in the form of the Oslo Accords: peace was at hand, and with it a solution to the Palestinian "problem". Once again, Michal and her comrades found themselves on the other side of the wave.

"From the beginning we could see that Oslo would only serve Israeli interests, and for the Palestinians it would be a disaster. Along with the Paris Accords, it gave Israel total control of the Palestinian economy, and it also finished the PLO as any kind of liberation organization. Because of it many Palestinians had to seek work in Israel, and when Israel more and more blocked them, they became totally dependent on foreign donations. This was the main idea of Oslo, to get Palestinians out of the Israeli cities and let Arafat deal with them."

When Michal says "we", she's talking about two organizations she helped to form: the Workers Advice Centre and the Organization for Democratic Action. The long-term goal of both is to build working-class strength in Israel. While WAC does the kind of practical, day-to-day-survival work I witnessed at Kufr Qara, the ODA publishes magazines of political news and analysis in Arabic and English, and runs candidates in national and local elections. "We have never got into the Knesset or a municipal council," says Michal, "but we feel it's crucial to keep putting our programme before the public as a real alternative to what is offered by anybody else. Our candidate for the current municipal election in Tel Aviv is quite unique – not only working class but also a woman and an Arab: a young Arab woman, 35 – and pregnant! We don't think she'll win this time, but it's enough for now to present a candidate, make our ideas known, and see what support we get."

This time the ODA candidate didn't win a place on the municipal council, but did garner about 2,000 votes. "This is not very much," says Michal, "but for us it's a lot. Next time it can only get better."

BAQA

We leave the truck-crowded highway for the winding village streets of Baqa, or rather the two Baqas. Until the 1948 war, Baqa was one village. The armistice line cut it in two, Baqa Al-Gharbiya on the

Israeli side and Baqa Al-Sharqiya on the Palestinian side, but traffic and commerce between them continued – until the separation wall was built a few years ago.

Here there is no defiant graffiti, only blank concrete slabs two storeys tall topped by razor wire. On the ground, Israeli soldiers patrol in Hummers. "Where we are standing," says Michal, "it used to be very lively, with a big market where Israelis and people from the West Bank came to buy produce from the local farms. Now, as you can see, everything is closed."

WAC's rented office here is bright, sparsely furnished but spacious, with several offices opening off the small central hall where we meet. One wall is covered in exuberant colour photos of the WAC contingent at this year's International Women's Day march in Tel Aviv. Wafa arrives late, with apologies – she had to take one of her children to the doctor.

She has a new job, coordinating women's empowerment activities. Michal described this WAC initiative on the way. "It's a feminist project," she says, "not Canada-style, but adapted to needs here. Women meet once a week with a facilitator. There is a lot of emphasis on going out to work, how to organize things at home, and how to get husbands to participate in the work of the house, which is quite a revolution here. Some women succeed in making these changes, some just end up doing double chores and get very tired. On the other hand, many of them say that going out to work relieves stress. Because their world is larger, they meet other workers, they have their own bank accounts, it's a very big change for them. So these meetings are a chance to think and talk about who they are, and what they want. We believe that women in a traditional society can be its most traditional source, but they can also become a powerful force for change."

That's the theory. How does it play out in reality? For Wafa, her own family was the first test. "I am certainly no superwoman," she says, "so we had to put a lot of effort into changing the family. At the age of eleven, my older son took charge of the other children. In the morning he made them sandwiches, he changed nappies, and he took the youngest one for somebody else to look after. My husband changed his life too; he did things in the house – but on condition that no one would see. For example, he wouldn't put out washed clothes because the neighbours would see, but he did do other things inside the house. If I didn't have to work outside, I don't see how we could have got free from the old ways."

While Wafa is talking, another woman enters the office – Mofida Abumah, in black hijab to the shoes, with white embroidered patterns on wide sleeves. She and Wafa briefly compare their struggles with dieting. Mofida laughs easily, and uses her hands often for emphasis.

Born here in 1963, she works about 20 dunams of land in the village, half of it inherited and half rented, on which she and her children grow vegetables for market in Tel Aviv. The current economic crisis has cut deeply into her sales. "Now we have a lot of onions ready," she says, "but with no market we don't even pick them, we leave them on the land. During the Jewish holidays, so many Jews travel that we could hardly sell anything. But what choice do I have? This is what we do."

Mofida heard about a WAC women's meeting, and decided to give it a try. "First I came because I wanted to see people, to have a social life. I was tired of just working at home and on the land, I needed something else."

What happens at the meetings? "The facilitator asks all the women questions, and each of us talks about her life, her problems. The facilitator says all the time that women have rights, we are not less than men, we can speak, we can do, we can earn. In this way women become stronger and stronger."

Did she recruit other women for the meetings? "Yes", she replies. "Some came, but others were afraid of their husbands." Michal adds, "It's a strong tradition here that when the husband comes from work, the woman should be there to serve him. She can't just say I cooked, here's your food, now I have to go somewhere."

Did Mofida find the meetings helpful? She laughs, and points at one of the International Women's Day photos on the wall. There she is, front and centre. "If I didn't go to the empowerment meetings, I would never have gone to Tel Aviv", she says. "I wouldn't have had the courage to leave home, to go anywhere. Now if I'm going to a meeting I just tell my husband, I don't even ask his permission." She laughs with delight.

THE MOSHAV

Wafa arranged for us to meet a small group of WAC members at the end of their shift on a large moshav, a farm near here.

To reach Gan Yoshiya we pass several Arab villages. People have farmed the broad fertile valley here for centuries. But since 1948, says Michal, the Israeli state has confiscated 90 per cent of

Palestinian lands. With hardly any land left of their own, many Palestinians have to work for Israelis.

The small town of Gan Yoshiya has its own security barrier that trundles open once Wafa identifies herself to the guard as a WAC representative. Inside, tree-shaded streets are lined with bungalows and lush gardens. It looks like a suburb.

On the moshav, flat fields stretch away to hazy low hills. Six women are waiting to speak with us. They look to be in their twenties and thirties, dressed for work in jeans and shirts. For the past five days, a heatwave has driven daytime temperatures into the high thirties, even higher under the sun in the fields.

The women can't stay long; up before dawn, they've been working in the fields since 5.30 a.m., and will soon have to go home to prepare the evening meal. To avoid trouble with the boss, they ask that their names not be used.

For one of them it's the first week of work. She heard about the WAC at a women's empowerment meeting. Because she's pregnant, she wavered about going out to work. "But the economic situation is so bad," she says, "I decided that I should do it, as long as I can."

Another woman says she has four children. "To come here in time I have to get up at four. I try to cook the day before so I won't have to do it when I get home."

Transportation is always an issue. "The woman who used to bring us stopped coming", says another woman. "My husband makes a special effort to bring us this week, but after that we'll have to find someone else." Waiting nearby, her husband raises a hand.

Are there Thai workers on this farm? Several women nod. "Yes, many. We just work when the owner needs extra. No matter how well we work, when there is less to do we'll be the first to be kicked out. The Thai workers always stay, they sleep here."

Do the women resent them? "We have no problems with them", says one woman. Wafa adds, "We are all workers. But the Thais get a lot less money, so it's hard for the local workers to compete."

I asked if WAC has made any difference here. Energetic nods. One woman says, "I earn more money, I get out of the house, I meet people. There is no comparison to before." Another adds, "Before WAC, when I worked the subcontractor would take whatever he wanted, and I never knew how much I would earn. Now all my rights are protected."

Still, their situation remains precarious. The woman who's pregnant says, "If the owner kicks us out, where will we go?"

A HIGH STANDARD FOR A GOOD DAY

On the way back to Kufr Qara where Wafa lives, I ask her what she wants from the future. First she addresses the collective picture: "What I really hope is that we succeed in organizing the workers, and build a big union." Then she turns to herself. "Always I have dreamed about academic study, but never reached it. Now I have started. I have a lot of fears – will I have enough time, will I be able to learn, to remember so many new things? But if I encourage other women, I have to encourage myself too."

She takes two courses at the Open University, English and history. "With English the big challenge is learning how to speak it. This is important for me; it's part of solidarity with the world. Michal is helping me. I envy her because she can speak three languages, so she can talk with many people. I hope that I, too, will be able to know three languages."

And history? "At first I thought it would be boring," she says, "but actually it helps me to see a longer view of what we are doing. Sometimes everything is down, other times things go up. At first I thought academic learning was like a flower that you put on your breast to show off, or to make a lot of money. Now I understand that it is not only for a certain strata of people, but open to everybody, and it widens your horizon. I wish that workers could work a little bit less, and have more time to learn – they hardly even have time to read the daily newspaper." Full circle back to the collective.

At the WAC office in Kufr Qara, half a dozen Arab-Israeli teenagers kneel on the floor of the big front room. Members of the WAC youth movement, they are making posters for an evening event to close the second week of Ramadan. Two boys have gelled hair, and two others have mobile phones which they check every few minutes. Their leader is an energetic young woman. To be facilitated by an experienced Palestinian storyteller, the event will feature the telling and acting of stories drawn from their young lives.

Michal explains, "Some very touchy issues come up – relationships with parents, the value of women, equality – but this woman really knows how to get them to talk, both males and females. We have already seen how much better they can communicate among themselves and with their parents, especially the mothers. So you see, the work here is very rounded, it's not just trade union stuff."

In the office, Wafa and Dani meet with a group of women, young to middle-aged, who have come from their shift in a nearby aluminum factory, jobs organized by WAC. In this case WAC replaces the subcontractor, but doesn't skim off a third of their wages. Instead, WAC members voluntarily pay union dues of 35 shekels a month, equivalent to US$8–9.

Wafa and Dani are urging the women to join the WAC pension plan. In 2007, after six months of arduous negotiation with an Israeli pension firm, WAC won a pension plan with much lower administrative charges than the usual plans, and insurance that maintains 75 per cent of a worker's salary if she or he can't work due to injury or illness. The women listen intently and ask many questions. Michal adds a comment now and then. I notice that when she speaks Arabic, suddenly her hands move more expressively.

Wafa hands out pension application forms. Three women sign on the spot; the other two put the forms into their bags.

As we leave the office, I ask Dani if it was a good day. "Not bad", he says. "It wasn't so good. We only got work for one group of women."

Like his comrades, he sets a high standard for a good day.

16
Hello?

Michael: "Hello, is this Dr Yaghi?"

Dr Yaghi: "Yes, this is he."

Michael: "Hello, Dr Yaghi. I tried calling you on the landline. I could hear you saying 'Hello?, Hello?', but I think you couldn't hear me."

Dr Yaghi: "No, I couldn't. There is a problem here in Gaza with telephones and mobiles. Maybe you can try again."

Michael: "All right, but if it doesn't work, can I call you again on your mobile? I'll pay any charges, so the Palestinian Medical Relief Society doesn't have to."

Dr Yaghi: "Okay."

He hangs up. I dial his landline again. Three rings ...

Dr Yaghi: "Hello?"

Michael: "Hello. Can you hear me?"

Dr Yaghi: "Yes."

Michael: "Good. Shall we continue on this line, but if we lose it, I'll call you on the mobile?"

Dr Yaghi: "Hello?"

Michael: "I'm here, Dr Yaghi, can you hear me?"

Dr Yaghi: "Hello? ... Hello?"

The line changes, I hear more static.

Michael: "Dr Yaghi, can you hear me?"

Dr Yaghi: "Yes, I hear you."

He can only give me 30 minutes. Under the circumstances, it seems generous.

Aed Yaghi was born in Gaza City in 1967, of refugee parents.

The Gaza Strip is 41 kilometres (25 miles) long, and 6–12 kilometres (4–7.5 miles) wide, a total area of 360 square kilometres (139 square miles). About 1.5 million Palestinians live there. By contrast, the rural county where I live has twice that area, with some 23,000 people. Gaza is surrounded by the Israeli state on three sides, an 11-kilometre (7-mile) border with Egypt, and the Mediterranean Sea.

Eighty-five per cent of Gazans are refugees from other parts of Palestine, who fled or were driven from their homes and villages during the 1947–49 war. Three generations later, more than half still reside in Gaza's eight refugee camps.

Why did Aed Yaghi become a doctor? "To help people", he says. In 2002 he moved from another practice to join the Palestinian Medical Relief Society (PMRS). Now he directs all its programmes in Gaza. Why did he join PMRS? "We deal with people who are suffering from poverty, especially people living in marginal and rural areas. This is my idea of working with people in most need." He supervises a wide variety of programmes, carried out by more than 100 staff and many more volunteers.

Founded in 1979 by a group of Palestinian health professionals, the non-profit PMRS struggles to fill ever-deepening voids in a health care system devastated by decades of Israeli military occupation. Throughout the Occupied Palestinian Territories, the PMRS focuses on children's health, women's health, a mobile clinic, physical rehabilitation, pharmacy, counselling and health education. In rural areas, primary health care centres offer general medicine, child health, management of chronic disease, emergency care and provision of medications.

I ask Dr Yaghi to describe his working conditions. "We have been living under chronic economic emergency since 2000", he replies. "I feel we are living inside a big prison, like the 11,000 Palestinians who are living in Israeli jails. Now, as I am speaking to you, there is no electricity where I live. In the Gaza Strip there is only one main power station. The fuel comes from Israel. Israel doesn't supply fuel continuously or regularly. So the power station cannot produce enough electricity. At this moment there is no electricity in one-third of Gaza City. It is winter now and cold, so it is hard for people."

The day we talked, Israel blocked delivery of fuel at the Kerem Shalom crossing into Gaza. That night, two-thirds of Gaza had no electricity, and it was feared that the plant would have to shut down entirely.

How do the power cuts affect health work? "It affects all of life here," says Dr Yaghi, "but I will focus on the medical aspect. Electricity is needed for many things we do in our clinics, and for equipment in many departments of the hospitals, especially surgery, newborn children and intensive care. There is a generator, but it's not enough, and it also depends on fuel controlled by the Israelis."

ON THE BRINK

Palestinians differ in their assessment of when Gaza became a ghetto. Some say 1948, when Palestinians from Yafa and Bedouins from the Negev poured into refugee camps which they believed would be temporary. Some say 1967, when full-scale Israeli military occupation began. Or 1987, when the first intifada/uprising against the military occupation erupted, or 2000, when the second intifada broke out. Or 2005, when the Sharon disengagement plan turned the Gaza Strip into a prison, cut off from the outside world by land, sea and air.

The Israeli siege tightened sharply in 2006, when Palestinian voters in the West Bank and Gaza elected a majority Hamas government. It tightened even more drastically in 2007, when Hamas fighters defeated a US-backed coup attempt by Fatah forces that had lost the election, and further again when Gazan fighters, some unaffiliated with Hamas, fired homemade rockets into southern Israel, killing four civilians. During the same period, the UN reported that Israeli attacks on Gaza killed 59 Palestinians, nearly all civilians.

By that time, more than 90 per cent of Gazans depended on international humanitarian aid for basic survival. Then in 2006–07, Canada, the US and Europe cut off economic aid to Gaza. Medicines and fuel ran out, power generators shut down, then water and sewage treatment, and UN food aid dwindled at times to a trickle. Gazan farmers were attacked from air and ground, and fishing boats from the sea.

By late 2008, the blockade by Israel and its allies had denied the 1.5 million Gazans so many basic life supports that the UN Relief and Works Agency declared Gaza "on the brink of a public health disaster". Officials admitted privately that the situation was already well over the brink.

On 9 December 2008, UN Special Rapporteur for Human Rights Richard Falk issued a report on Gaza. The American professor emeritus of international law stated: "Such a policy of collective punishment, initiated by Israel to punish Gazans for political developments within the Gaza strip, constitutes a continuing flagrant and massive violation of international humanitarian law as laid down in Article 33 of the Fourth Geneva Convention. It would seem mandatory for the International Criminal Court to investigate the situation, and determine whether the Israeli civilian leaders and military commanders responsible for the Gaza siege should be indicted and prosecuted for violations of international criminal law."

LOOKING AT ANTS

On 27 December 2008, the Israeli military and the Labour government of Prime Minister Ehud Olmert launched a massive bombardment of the Gaza Strip from air, sea and land, followed by a full-scale ground invasion.

Leaders in Europe and North America – including the new President of the United States – remained silent or supported Israel's assault. Arab regimes allied with the US remained silent. With few exceptions, mainstream western media condoned the attack.

Israeli soldiers who took part testified later to the Israeli soldiers' organization Breaking the Silence:

If you face an area that is hidden by a building – you take down the building. Questions such as "Who lives in that building?" are not asked.

When your company commander and battalion commander tell you, "Go on, fire!", the soldiers will not hold back. They are waiting for this day, the fun of shooting and feeling all that power in your hands.

There was no need for such intense fire, no need to use mortars, phosphorus ammunition. Others as well as myself have a certain feeling that the army was looking for the opportunity to hold a spectacular manoeuvre in order to show its muscle.

The amount of destruction there was incredible. You drive around those neighbourhoods, and can't identify a thing. Not one stone left standing over another. You see plenty of fields, hothouses, orchards, everything devastated. Totally ruined. It's terrible. It's surreal.

You feel like an infantile little kid with a magnifying glass looking at ants, burning them.

By 18 January 2009, when Israel suspended its attack, between 1,385 (B'Tselem Israeli human rights organization figure) and 1,417 (Palestinian Center for Human Rights figure) Palestinians had been killed, of which 762 (B'Tselem) to 1,181 (PCHR) were non-combatants; 313 to 318 were children. More than 5,300 Palestinians were wounded, and more than 20,000 left homeless.

In that same period, three Israeli civilians and one soldier were killed in southern Israel, and nine soldiers within the Gaza Strip; four by their own forces.

In September 2009, Judge Richard Goldstone and his Commission presented their Report of the United Nations Fact Finding Mission on the Gaza Conflict. A former South African Constitutional Court judge, Richard Goldstone served as the chief prosecutor of the United Nations International Criminal Tribunals for the former Yugoslavia and Rwanda. The 575-page report followed a six-month inquiry, in which Israel refused to cooperate.

The report states: "We came to the conclusion, on the basis of the facts we found, that there is strong evidence to establish that numerous serious violations of international law, both humanitarian law and human rights law, were committed by Israel during the military operations in Gaza. The mission concluded that actions amounting to war crimes and possibly, in some respects, crimes against humanity were committed by the Israel Defense Force."

Even though the report also accused Palestinian armed groups of committing war crimes by firing rockets into civilian areas, Israel and its allies dismissed the report as biased. It was endorsed by the UN Human Rights Commission and the UN General Assembly.

WHAT CAN WE DO?

Dr Aed Yaghi reports that 30 medical personnel were killed in the attack, 33 ambulances destroyed, and 14 hospitals or primary health care centres partially or totally destroyed. "Since the war," he says, "some ambulances have been donated by international organizations, but we haven't been able to repair the hospitals and health care centres because the Israelis don't allow any building materials to enter Gaza."

> Michael: "How do the destruction and the ongoing siege affect water supplies?"
> Dr Yaghi: "Hello?"
> Michael: "I'm still here. Can you hear me?"
> Dr Yaghi: "Hello? ... Hello?"
> Michael: "I'm going to try and connect on your mobile number."
> Dr Yaghi: "I can hear you now. You were asking about –"
> Michael: "Water."

Dr Yaghi: "In each 48 hours, water is supplied in Gaza City about 12–18 hours, sometimes less, but not more. The water is not good for drinking. We must treat it before drinking, with filters, and people buy water in tanks."

Michael: "That must be very hard for people with little or no money."

Dr Yaghi: "Yes, of course. But what can we do? Without water you cannot live."

The Gaza Strip's already degraded water and sewage infrastructure was heavily targeted in the Israeli bombardment. Reconstruction materials and parts are forbidden entry into Gaza. By September 2009, the International Committee of the Red Cross warned that Gazans' access to drinking water was in danger of collapse, and the World Health Organization (WHO) said widespread outbreaks of hepatitis A and parasitic infections were imminent. The water in 90–95 per cent of all wells is undrinkable by WHO standards.

I ask Dr Yaghi about medications, are they getting through the blockade? "It takes a lot of time, at least four weeks, for medications to enter Gaza. Sometimes we are still waiting after four months. Save the Children donated equipment in August 2009 for our physical therapy centre. It's called Short Wave [controlling pain and increasing blood flow to damaged tissue by deep heat]. There are many people here with injuries. Only last Tuesday [February 2010] we received this equipment. A lot of things, they don't let in at all. In the last report of WHO, 72 kinds of medication were not in the stock of the Ministry of Health. Hundreds of items, medical supplies, zero stock at the Ministry of Health."

Michael: "If you don't have these necessary things, what do you do?"

Dr Yaghi: "Nothing, because we have no medical alternatives. So we do advocacy work, we try to put pressure on the Israelis to let these medications come in. Sometimes we ask international NGOs to bring some kinds of medication with them, but they can only bring enough for personal use, so it would only be for one or two patients, not for all who need it."

A year after the attack, the Israeli Physicians for Human Rights organization (see Chapter 9) reported that over 100 amputees in Gaza still lack prosthetics. Among them is "S", aged 48, of Gaza City. On 15 January 2009 an Israeli rocket hit the top floor of her house, while she was in her children's bedroom. When sections of the ceiling and walls collapsed, S was trapped under the rubble until her husband could extricate her. Her left leg was badly damaged, and her right leg had to be amputated above the knee. A year later, she still lacks the necessary prosthetic.

Nutrition in Gaza has deteriorated steadily since the Israeli noose tightened in the early 2000s. According to the UN Relief and Works Agency, 6,600 dunams (about 1,650 acres) of agricultural land were destroyed in the 2008–09 attack, and seven poultry farms housing more than 1 million chickens. How does the continuing siege affect nutrition? Dr Yaghi replies, "Malnutrition in children under five has reached about 80 per cent. More than half the children under five now suffer from anaemia, and in some areas 75 per cent."

The intense focus on child health is not surprising, when almost half the Gazan population is 14 and younger. But under such a brutal blockade, how much can actually be done to remedy malnutrition? "Since September 2009, PMRS has a nutritional programme for children under five years in many areas", says Dr Yaghi. "We distribute iron, and follow up with home visits and education in health and nutrition. We do what we can."

The people of Gaza have been through so much, in such severe isolation and for so long. How do they find the strength to survive, to continue struggling? A silence follows my question, long enough that I think I've lost contact. But then Dr Yaghi says, "I think the main strength is that Palestinians here in Gaza believe that we must continue to live, that we must resist Israeli aggression. That is the main strength here, the belief that we are living in our land, and we must struggle again and again, and finally we will win." He says this quietly, no slogans, without bravado.

LIFELINES

The will to live is manifest in the tunnels. For at least a decade, hundreds of hand-dug tunnels under the Israeli wall between Gaza and Egypt have provided a lifeline for the Gaza ghetto. Originating in basements of houses or in olive groves, tunnels can run as deep as 15 metres (49 feet), and almost a kilometre (two-thirds of a mile) in length. Under repeated attacks by Israeli aircraft and ground forces, they are constantly re-dug, rebuilt.

In December 2009, echoing Israeli claims that tunnels are used to smuggle weapons into Gaza, the Egyptian government announced construction of a massive steel wall above and below ground to shut off access to them. Heavily funded by the US, the Mubarak regime continues to be a faithful ally to Israel. The BBC reported that the wall's steel panels were engineered and manufactured in the US. In Egypt the project is known widely as "The Wall of Shame".

I ask Dr Yaghi if he ever feels helpless. Without hesitation he replies, "No, I don't. We don't have time, there is too much to be done. I believe we must continue our life, and we must help our people."

Gazans repair and rebuild what they can. Gaza's only cement plant was destroyed by Israeli rockets, but the attack left behind some 420,000 metric tons of rubble. Using hand-cranked grinders, Gazans are remaking some of it into building bricks.

A series of international solidarity and aid flotillas have attempted to break through the Israeli blockade. While a few boats did succeed in reaching Gaza, others have been forcibly blocked by the Israeli military. In July 2010, Israeli commandos boarded one of the ships illegally in international waters and killed nine flotilla participants.

Although the usual justifications ensued from Israel's allies, widespread popular outrage outside Israel caused the authorities to announce that they would "ease" the land blockade, permitting more goods to enter the besieged enclave. Aid and human rights organizations argue that the changes are more cosmetic than substantial; that they will benefit Israeli commerce far more than Gazans; that as collective punishment on a civilian population the blockade remains illegal under international law, and that only a full lifting of it could even begin to undo the catastrophic harm of the long siege.

In the meantime, for Palestinians in Gaza, life goes on. After a long drought, in January 2010, heavy rains caused flash floods in low-lying parts of the Gaza Strip, where many people have lived in damaged buildings and tents since their homes were destroyed during the 2008–09 Israeli assault. With other agencies, the PMRS moved in to help.

The PMRS website features an impressive list of programmes and priorities. But when so many basics are lacking, and so much is determined by outside forces – even the weather – how do Dr Yaghi and his co-workers set priorities on the ground? "The first priority is to end the siege on Gaza," he says, "to open the borders, to let not only infrastructure materials but all products enter Gaza. We need the international community to put more pressure on the Israeli government to end the siege and the occupation, and at the same time to continue their donations for Palestinian programmes."

As he responds to my question, at first I think he has misunderstood its practical, day-to-day focus. But in fact, he went directly to the heart of the matter.

Still, as a writer I want to pursue the question a little, to get a clearer sense of how Dr Yaghi and his co-workers adapt to shifting and often unpredictable conditions.

Dr Yaghi: "Hello? … Hello?"
Michael: "I'm here, Dr Yaghi. Can you hear me?"
Dr Yaghi: "Hello?"

He says "Hello?" five more times. I respond, without effect. Then he hangs up.

Several times I dial both numbers, land and mobile, but am unable to restore the connection.

17
Cracks in the Wall

In September 2009, the Norwegian Ministry of Finance announced that it had dropped the Israeli company Elbit Systems Ltd from its national pension fund portfolio. Minister of Finance Kristin Halvorsen told reporters, "We do not wish to fund companies that so directly contribute to violations of international humanitarian law."

Elbit products are on display throughout occupied Palestine – surveillance cameras, pilotless aircraft and other systems for population control; or, as the Elbit corporate website puts it, "defense and homeland security applications".

While downplaying the impact of Norway's decision, the Israeli government criticized it sharply, and summoned the Norwegian ambassador for a reprimand.

To the growing international movement for boycott, divestment and sanctions, the Elbit divestment was a major victory, the first time a foreign government had publicly divested from an Israeli corporation for violating international law.

It was a crack in the wall.

FOR THE SAKE OF JUSTICE

In the sixth decade of Israeli occupation, in 2004 the International Court of Justice declared: "the construction by Israel of a wall in the Occupied Palestinian Territory and its associated regime are contrary to international law".

That same year, a coalition of Palestinian academics and intellectuals launched PACBI, the Palestinian Campaign for the Academic and Cultural Boycott of Israel.

A year later, 170 Palestinian civil society organizations issued a broader call to the world: "We, representatives of Palestinian civil society, call upon international civil society organizations and people of conscience all over the world to impose broad boycotts and implement divestment initiatives against Israel similar to those applied to South Africa in the apartheid era. We appeal to you to pressure your respective states to impose embargoes and sanctions against Israel. We also invite conscientious Israelis to support this Call, for the sake of justice and genuine peace."

The call makes three demands, all based in international law: end the occupation, which includes dismantling the walls and settlements; recognize the right of return of Palestinian refugees, and institute real equality for Palestinian citizens of Israel.

Earlier attempts at boycott had occasional, isolated success, but these direct calls from Palestine to the world have galvanized organizing efforts in many countries. For Palestinians, they had an additional impact.

Palestinian-Canadian poet and activist Rafeef Ziadah explains, "The Oslo process was meant to fragment the Palestinian people from each other, disconnecting the West Bank and Gaza Strip into separate bantustans. They had already been cut off from Palestinian citizens of Israel, and from Palestinians in diaspora. These demands acted against this fragmentation by speaking of Palestine as one entity, not just the West Bank and the Gaza Strip but historic Palestine, including, for example, the area in Haifa where my family was kicked out from."

As a third-generation refugee, Rafeef has first-hand experience of fragmentation. Her Palestinian grandparents were expelled from Haifa in 1948, to refugee camps in Lebanon. In Israeli-supported Phalange militia attacks against Palestinian refugee camps in the late 1970s, both Rafeef's grandparents and four uncles were killed in Jisr el-Basha Camp. This left an 18-year-old daughter, Rafeef's mother, to care for the survivors. They included the three-year-old Rafeef, born in 1979 in Nazareth, her father a Palestinian citizen of Israel. Forced into exile once again in 1982, the family sought refuge in twelve countries; eventually Rafeef landed in North America.

"It's very complicated", she says. "Palestinian refugee women lose their status if they marry a non-refugee man, and my father lost his Israeli citizenship when he went to Lebanon. So neither of them had any status, which meant that my siblings and I were all undocumented. This affects every part of who you are and what you do. All your life you live with the fear of having no papers, of being deported. But my story isn't unique, it's the Palestinian story of exile and statelessness. This is our daily life. It's how we survive."

I ask Rafeef when and how she became an activist. She pauses for a moment, then replies, "We're born into it – born into refugee camps, born knowing the name of the village you come from, knowing you can't go back there, knowing you have no country to be registered to. You learn the history, the oral narrative of

Palestinians, how we were thrown out during the Nakba, and your parents ingrain in you the right to return to the land they were kicked out from. This is not something we come to as adults. The taste of injustice is with you from birth."

But not all Palestinians become activists, so there must be some decision, some choice. "Absolutely", says Rafeef. "I'm not saying that Palestinians have no choice, only that a politicized identity comes very early. Personally, I became active in North America, around the anti-globalization movement in the early 2000s. The second intifada was starting then, and I think it was a big awakening for Palestinians in diaspora. During the Oslo process we were numbed. It took us a while to realize that this was just a waiting period, a cover while Israel continued to build settlements in the Occupied Territories. With the intifada, we woke up to what was planned for us – bantustans for a South African-style apartheid domination. After that, organizing happened very quickly on university campuses."

A PhD student in political science at York University in Toronto, Canada, Rafeef is a founding member of the Coalition Against Israeli Apartheid (CAIA), and later joined the steering committee of the PACBI.

THE OUTPOST OF CIVILIZATION

In addressing their calls for BDS (boycott, divestment and sanctions) not to governments but directly to "people of conscience all over the world", the Palestinian initiators had learned from the international movement against South African apartheid. For many years it, too, was a loose network of widely-scattered grassroots initiatives, an apparently quixotic effort to marshal popular power against an immense, implacable enforcer. The struggle was then and seems now impossibly unequal, with the entire apparatus of western power in full support of both regimes. Both were/are seen as effective bulwarks against the dangerous prospect of freedom for huge subject populations in the regions under their control.

From the late nineteenth century to the present, the Zionist movement and the state it created have made themselves indispensable to western power. Never again would Jews be on the wrong side, the losing side of history. In 1898, Zionist founder Theodor Herzl wrote in *Der Judenstaat* (The Jews' State): "To Europe we would represent a part of the barrier against Asia; we would serve as the outpost of civilization against barbarism."

This symbiotic arrangement is spectacularly evident today: the Obama administration drops all demands on Israel to stop the settlements, while handing over the next instalment of US military aid; US and British authorities collaborate in blocking the Goldstone report on war crimes in the Gaza assault (no doubt having been reminded by Israeli officials that they, too, could face similar charges on Iraq and Afghanistan); the US and Europe impose sanctions to force Iran to quit developing nuclear power, while they continue to grant carte blanche to the Middle East's only actual nuclear weapons holder, Israel. In May 2010, despite Israel's failure to meet several of its basic requirements, the influential OECD welcomed Israel as a new member.

The global BDS movement asks "people of conscience" to defy this wall of elite power, to break through it, eventually to push it over. But why, of all things, does PACBI call for a boycott of cultural and academic institutions like the Israel Ballet, a target in early 2010? Isn't that a bit rarified?

Rafeef Ziadah explains, "Israeli academic and cultural institutions are deeply implicated in how Israel treats Palestinians. At universities there is a lot of research in military technology and tactics, architecture for the settlements is advanced, and the demographics of Palestinians are studied to find better methods of population control – these are just a few examples. As for cultural institutions, their role is to beautify the image of Israel, to whitewash Israeli apartheid, and to divert attention from what Israel is doing to Palestinians. PACBI tries to hold these instutions accountable for what they do. We argue that Israel can't present itself to the world as a progressive cultural entity while at same time it is massacring Palestinians in Gaza."

As I write, the Israel Ballet is on tour in Florida and the northeast US. A coalition of US groups called for a boycott of its performances, noting that the company receives about US$1 million annually from the Israeli government, and is promoted as a cultural ambassador by the Israeli Consulate in New York.

Who decides what to boycott? "In the BDS movement, organizations around the world are autonomous", says Rafeef. "As long as they respect the terms of the call from Palestine, they are free to decide and initiate as they see fit. We believe local activists know best how to work in their particular situations. It could be a union resolution, or a consumer boycott against a particular product, or the Israel Ballet coming to your city. These decisions don't come from the Boycott National Committee in Palestine or from PACBI, but we do have working relationships with many organizations around the world, and often it makes sense to coordinate our activities."

In Canada, the Coalition Against Israeli Apartheid connects groups widely scattered across the country and working in a range of sectors. "For example, there's a Labour for Palestine section, which works toward passing resolutions for boycott, divestment and sanctions within unions. There is Students Against Israeli Apartheid which, among other things, organizes Israeli Apartheid Week on university campuses; there is Queers Against Israeli Apartheid, and there are specific boycott campaigns at different times in different places. It's not one big coordinated national campaign, but people initiating many types of action that are relevant to local context."

BOYCOTT!

Among those who heard the call from Palestine was Kobi Snitz. He was born Israeli in 1971, to a European-Canadian mother and American father who had emigrated to Israel. After finishing school there, Kobi went to university in Toronto, Canada, then to Maryland for his PhD in mathematics, returning to Israel for post-doctoral work.

"My politics developed while I was away", Kobi says. "Meeting Palestinians and Arabs at school in Toronto and Maryland heightened my sense of the need to build new kinds of relationships with Palestinians here. When I came back to Israel in 2003, that seemed the most important thing for me to do."

Wanting to do practical work on the ground, he joined Anarchists Against the Wall, participating in protests and direct actions against the wall and occupation throughout the West Bank, actions led by popular committees in Palestinian villages. This arrangement turns upside down the power structure of the occupation.

Kobi explains, "We Israelis have got into the habit of feeling it's natural for us to lead, to call the shots. But the struggle for Palestinian liberation should be led by Palestinians, and Israelis in the resistance movement need to be conscious of this at every level. For example, at demonstrations the soldiers prefer to speak to Israelis. Nothing in their training has prepared them for a situation where Palestinians might actually be in control. So it's important for us to say to soldiers, 'It's not my village, it's not my land, you should be speaking to the Palestinians.'"

As repression escalates in Israel, Palestinians remain the primary targets, but Israelis have also been arrested, beaten and even shot by soldiers at protests. Kobi has been arrested several times, and jailed while trying to block a home demolition in the Palestinian village of Kharbatha.

He puts the experience in perspective. "For Jewish Israelis," he says, "arrest is nothing compared to what it is for Palestinians. In our case it can be boring and annoying, but it's quite predictable. Usually we're charged with the same offences, which aren't severe, and we're rarely kept for more than 24 hours. There is little uncertainty for us, which is one of the scariest things for Palestinians when they're arrested – you don't know what's going to happen to you, how belligerent the police will be, what you'll be accused of, how much bail will be, and when or even if you're going to get out."

In response to the Palestinian call for BDS, members of Anarchists Against the Wall formed the nucleus of Boycott!, soon joined by other Israelis. Its subtitle is "Supporting the Palestinian BDS Call from Within". While the movement gathers momentum abroad, Boycott! has tended to evolve more slowly. "As the movement in South Africa did," Kobi explains, "here in Israel, the occupying power, we have to address some complicated questions, so we're still in a stage of development and study. These are things I'm not used to doing as an activist, but they're necessary to understand and explain what we need to do here."

What's so complicated? Why not just identify the harm and the culprits, then boycott them? "The harm is very clear," says Kobi, "but after that it gets more complicated. The Palestinian call is for an institutional, not a personal boycott. That's based on the premise that institutional boycott has more impact than individual boycott. But also, how do you distinquish which individuals deserve to be boycotted? Would you have a committee that decides who's a good boy and who isn't? You want to do as little harm as possible to individuals. It's true that pressure on an institution could cause pressure on individuals – if you boycott a factory, people may lose their jobs – but the principle remains: it's more legitimate to boycott institutions than individuals."

Boycott! endorsed and helped spread the call to boycott the Israel Ballet tour in the US. Does receiving state support necessarily mean that an institution represents the state? "In Israel it does", Kobi replies. "The Foreign Ministry is very frank about the purpose of sending Israeli art and science abroad. It promotes a positive image of Israel, and it diverts attention from Israeli policies that we consider criminal. So if you choose to be an emissary for the Foreign Ministry, you should be held accountable for that."

Where does Boycott! fit in the global movement? "A couple of years ago," says Kobi, "people in other countries would often ask for a statement of support from us in Israel, to protect them against accusations of antisemitism. Now that the international movement is stronger, I think this kind of support from us has become less crucial. Right now I'd say the most useful thing Israelis are doing for BDS is a project called 'Who Profits from the Occupation?'."

WHO PROFITS

When Israel scolded Norway for the Elbit divestment, Norwegian officials hastened to assure Israel that the Elbit decision would not affect its other investments. In fact, the Who Profits from the Occupation database lists 31 corporations still in the Norwegian pension portfolio that continue to profit from Israel's occupation of Palestine.

None of this information is secret, says Merav Amir, research coordinator for Who Profits. "We don't send in spies", she says, with a quiet laugh. "We only collect information that the companies publish themselves, or that different branches of government or similar organizations put out. Since the occupation has become so normalized in Israeli society, companies here are not afraid or ashamed to publish this information. They don't see anything wrong with what they are doing. Some are even proud of it."

Born in Haifa in 1972, Merav grew up in a family that was "somewhat left but not active politically". In the Israeli education system she learned little more of Palestinians than that they were to be feared. "I sensed that something was wrong with this picture," she says, "but I had no resources to form an independent opinion." At university she began to ask more questions, and when the second intifada broke out in the early 2000s, she was drawn to engage more deeply. In 2005, Merav joined MachsomWatch, a women's organization that monitors checkpoints (see Chapter 5).

Most of her duty-shifts were at the Huwara checkpoint, which controls traffic in and out of Nablus, the largest city in the occupied West Bank. "There you see, directly, with no filters, how Israeli soldiers deal with Palestinian civilians", says Merav. "You see the power relations of military rule, its impact on daily life, on the possibility of living. It's quite a blunt learning experience."

Merav heard that members of the Coalition of Women for Peace had begun to investigate economic forces involved in the occupation. "I found this initiative really exciting", she says. "Much attention is paid to the political and ideological aspects, but not enough to the economic interests that have fuelled the occupation for more than 40 years. It's a missing piece of the picture."

WE DON'T PRESCRIBE

Merav joined the Coalition of Women for Peace and the project in 2007, and with the launch of the online database in February 2009, she became research coordinator. The Who Profits website calls the project a "community research effort". What does this mean? "The research is coordinated by a team of three, including me," Merav replies, "but we actually rely on a much broader range of activists to accomplish the work. We underestimated the scale of this project when we started, it's huge. There are hundreds of companies in our offline database for which we are still compiling information, so that we can get them into the online database. It needs a very extensive team to accomplish this."

The project is well situated in the Coalition of Women for Peace, a grassroots organization of activists in ten women's peace and anti-occupation groups. The members are Jewish and Palestinian/ Arab-Israeli, in their early twenties to late eighties. "It's good to have both the experience of women who've done this kind of thing for a long time and the energy of the young. With that combination you can get a lot of things done." The Coalition was one of the first organizations to bring people into the streets against the second Lebanon invasion and the attack on Gaza.

Who Profits collects corporate data not only from company and government sources, but also from field research on the ground. When I travelled in the West Bank with Daphne Banai of MachsomWatch (see Chapter 5), and Dorothy Naor of New Profile (see Chapter 1), I noticed how meticulously they observed changes in settlements, outposts, industrial zones, and villages along the way.

"This is how it works", says Merav. "Over time you learn how to read the different facets of Israeli control. On one hand, it's quite simple: the military occupation of a civilian population, but when you look more closely you see a hugely complex and sophisticated system of economic-military control."

In the face of Israeli and western propaganda on growing prosperity in the West Bank, a February 2010 report by the World

Bank presents a rather different picture: "The apparatus of control itself has gradually become more sophisticated and effective in its ability to interfere in and affect every aspect of Palestinian life, including job opportunities, work, and earnings ... It has turned the West Bank into a fragmented set of social and economic islands or enclaves cut off from one another."

In a 2010 report, Merav Amir and her colleague Dalit Baum, project coordinator of Who Profits, detail how neo-liberal policies have succeeded in turning the occupation from a costly burden into a highly profitable enterprise for Israeli and international elites. "A potentially competitive Palestinian economy was actively de-developed, the movement of Palestinian workers and goods was regulated to the benefit of the Israeli market, and the Palestinian consumer market has become a captive market for Israeli goods. Israeli manufacturers, employers and merchants have used this economic-military control to secure profits."

Who Profits organizes corporate data into three categories: the settlement industry, economic exploitation, and population control. Each of these is subdivided into specific activities; under each are listed companies known to profit from these activities, along with the products or services they provide, annual revenues, subsidiaries, major shareholders, website and contact information.

Elbit Systems shows up in two aspects of population control, The Wall & Checkpoints, and Specialized Equipment & Services. Amid a long list of Israeli companies, here, too, are bulldozers from Caterpillar and Volvo, widely used to destroy Palestinian houses and olive groves, as well as various surveillance systems and electronic fences from Motorola, Ingersoll Rand, and Hewlett Packard.

As in the case of Norway and Elbit, the BDS movement makes good use of data published by Who Profits. But on the project's own website there is no call to action, no mention of boycott, divestment or sanctions, only a quiet plea: "We hope to promote a change in public opinion and corporate policies, leading to an end to the occupation."

Why the reticence? "Partly it's for legal reasons", Merav replies. "What we offer is not a boycott list or a blacklist, but an information centre. There are different things you can do with this information. We even have settlers writing to us, 'Oh, thank you, now I know who to support.' That isn't our goal, of course, but there you go – we simply provide the information, we don't prescribe what should be done with it." It occurs to me that non-prescription would qualify nicely as a feminist approach.

"Exactly", says Merav. "I also see what we're doing as making good use of our privilege. As Israelis who speak Hebrew, we have access to this information, to the different places where it's published or available. It would be much more difficult for Palestinians or people in other countries to get it. So this is how we use our privilege."

BDS

Israel and its backers have reacted to the BDS movement as their counterparts did to the earlier movement against South African apartheid. First they ignored it, then they ridiculed it. But as its impact deepens, they take notice.

In 2004, the Presbyterian Church in the United States initiated a "phased, selective divestment" from certain American corporations operating in Israel.

Under the banner "Stolen Beauty", "bikini brigades" in American cities and "bathrobe brigades" in European cities urge shoppers not to buy Ahava cosmetics. The company manufactures products in the illegal Mitzpe Shalem settlement in the occupied West Bank, but labels exports to the EU as originating from "The Dead Sea, Israel".

Following the 2008–09 Israeli assault on Gaza, members of the South African Transport and Allied Workers Union refused to unload a ship filled with Israeli goods in Durban, despite threats from the shipowner. In June 2010, after Israeli commandos killed nine Freedom Flotilla participants in international waters en route to Gaza, Swedish dockworkers refused to load or unload Israeli cargoes; similarly in Oakland, California, dockworkers refused to cross a protesters' picket line blocking access to an Israeli cargo ship.

BDS groups in France and Belgium pressed the Dexia Bank to stop financing illegal settlements in the occupied West Bank. In January 2010, the bank notified regional councils in Judea and Samaria (the Israeli term for the occupied West Bank) that it was cutting off their lines of credit.

In Scotland, Strathclyde University students staged a successful sit-in to force the school administration to stop buying water from Israeli-owned Eden Springs, which extracts water from a spring in the Israeli-occupied Golan Heights.

In Oregon, USA, the student body at Evergreen College voted to divest from "Israel's illegal occupation".

In 2010, a range of musicians withdrew from commitments to perform in Israel. They included Elvis Costello, Carlos Santana,

The Pixies, Devendra Banhart, Snoop Dogg, The Klaxons, and Gil Scott-Heron.

In July 2010, the US organization Jewish Voice for Peace launched a major campaign to persuade TIAA-CREF, one of the world's largest retirement funds, to divest from corporations that profit from the Israeli occupation.

A STRATEGIC THREAT

Inevitably, the growing BDS movement has become a target. The backlash can be seen as a perverse form of tribute.

In February 2010, a prominent Israeli security think-tank, the Reut Institute, urged the government to treat the BDS movement as "a strategic threat", part of a global campaign for the "delegitimization" of Israel, denying its right to exist – code for a Holocaust-in-waiting. According to the Institute, the "delegitimizers" are few and marginal – Palestinians, Arabs, Muslims, migrants, radical political activists. But even these few are "a strategic threat". London, Madrid, Toronto and the San Francisco Bay Area are targeted as "hubs" of "the delegitimization network". The Reut Institute recommended that Israel's embassies serve as "front positions" in a counter-attack, and that "Israel should sabotage network catalysts".

Apparently, the authors of the report failed to notice that in South Africa, with apartheid gone, the state still stands. But more telling is their relentless focus on the language of war. They note that the crisis in Israel's "legitimacy" could "cripple" its ability to unilaterally launch "harsh" military attacks.

Shortly after the Reut documents circulated widely on the internet, the words "sabotage" and "attack" were removed from later official versions.

To Rafeef Ziadah, the Reut report offers valuable insight into the mindset of Israeli power. "They know how to make war – of course, who wouldn't with the fourth largest military in the world? But they don't have a clue how to deal with average people around the world who are fed up with the lies we've been told, who are saying 'What you're doing is wrong, it's against international law, and therefore we have to boycott.' These are the same things that galvanized people to act against South African apartheid."

In the Israeli backlash, as usual, it's Palestinians who face the greatest risks. Mohammad Othman lives in the wall-encircled West Bank village of Jayyus. He is a youth coordinator with the

Grassroots Anti-Apartheid Wall Campaign (Stop the Wall), and a prominent advocate for boycott, divestment and sanctions. Returning from Norway via Jordan in September 2009, Mohammad Othman was arrested at Allenby Bridge, the only exit-entry point for West Bank Palestinians. A strong international campaign won his release in January 2010, but only after he was interrogated and held in military prison for 113 days, without charge or trial. Since then, Stop the Wall's offices have been invaded by Israeli soldiers, and computers and video equipment stolen.

For Israelis, too, backlash is looming. Merav Amir explains, "As the BDS movement has a few successes, businesses here start to feel the pressure. These companies and the government expect this from what they call pro-Palestinian organizations, which means solidarity groups abroad, but when they find an Israeli organization connected to it, that makes them really angry. Like any racist viewpoint, it's supposed to be us against them. It has nothing to do with justice or peace, only us against them."

In January 2010, the Israeli right-wing organization Im Tirtzu ("If You Will It") accused 16 human rights organizations of collaborating with the enemy, after evidence they gathered was incorporated into the Goldstone report on Gaza (see Chapter 16). Among Im Tirtzu's targets are the Coalition of Women for Peace, Who Profits, and two Coalition member groups: New Profile and MachsomWatch.

"This report of theirs got headlines in the Israeli media," says Merav, "and what's worse, instead of criticizing it as fascistic, most of the media actually commended it."

In August 2009, Israeli academic and activist Neve Gordon wrote in a *Los Angeles Times* editorial that, after painful reflection, he no longer felt he had any choice but to support boycott, divestment and sanctions against his country. As well as receiving death threats, he was immediately attacked by the president of his university, by government ministers, and by US donors who threatened to withhold funding until he was fired.

Kobi Snitz is also an Israeli academic, also publicly committed to BDS. Does he fear this kind of backlash? "As it turned out," he replies, "it [the backlash] wasn't enough to get Neve fired, not even to remove him as chair of the department. Perhaps most important, there were more faculty members in support of him – or at least his right to express his opinion – than there were against him. I actually find that encouraging."

As the impact of BDS deepens, the Israeli backlash escalates. In June 2010, amid a deluge of anti-democratic legislation, the Knesset passed first reading of a law to criminalize support for BDS. To retaliate against a growing Palestinian boycott of goods produced in the settlements, the law would withhold funds which international law obliges Israel to transfer to the Palestinian Authority, and divert them instead to affected Israeli companies. The law would also fine Israelis who initiate, encourage or even provide information for any boycott or divestment action, and force them to compensate companies for lost business. It would also forbid entry into Israel for any foreigner who publicly advocates BDS.

ISRAEL'S NEW BEST FRIEND

In Canada, the backlash to BDS takes two forms. Rafeef Ziadah explains, "We are regularly attacked by Zionist organizations, but by now we're used to that. In the absence of any real arguments, they just keep fear-mongering, repeating the same tired accusation of antisemitism. Of course, it has no merit. We are not speaking about Judaism, but people do have a right – and a responsibility, I'd say – to speak out against an apartheid state. Recently we've also seen the growth of the Jewish Defence League, which is more aggressive and thuggish – ironically it's considered to be a terrorist group in the US, but not in Canada. I expect we'll see more of this kind of thing as the BDS movement continues to grow."

The other source of managed backlash in Canada is government. In early 2006, immediately following the election of Hamas, Canada rushed to be the first country in the world to boycott the new government, even before the US did. In 2009, Canada was the only country among 47 to vote against a UN Human Rights Council resolution condemning the Israeli assault on Gaza. Israeli Foreign Minister Avigdor Lieberman commented, "It's hard to find a country friendlier to Israel than Canada these days."

In 2009–10, Canadian government agencies cut funding to the Al-Mezan Centre for Human Rights in Gaza; the UN Relief and Works Agency, which provides clothing, food, health and education services to some 4.7 million registered Palestinian refugees; the Canadian-Arab Federation, which works with immigrants; Kairos, a Canadian faith-based ecumenical organization that works for social change; the Israeli human rights organization B'Tselem; and Mada Al-Carmel, a ten-year-old social research centre based in Haifa, effectively shutting down a major study on the marginalization of women in Arab-Israeli society. In making these arbitrary cuts, government ministers acknowledged that lobbying by Zionist organizations was a significant factor.

YOU CAN'T SHUT DOWN A MOVEMENT

To speak with me, Rafeef wedged some time into a schedule that included two jobs, and last-minute preparations for Israeli Apartheid Week. This annual series of events in late winter has been denounced by the leaders of Canada's two largest political parties; banned outright at two Ottawa universities; and at York University in Toronto, even the sponsoring group, Students Against Israeli Apartheid, was banned and fined. On other campuses, posters have been banned and room rentals refused.

"This is really sad", says Rafeef. "You'd think that academic institutions would want to encourage people to think, to speak out, to fight for justice, but instead they try to shut us down."

"Is it possible to shut you down?"

"They can harass us with tactics like taking away room bookings," she replies, "but if necessary we'll hold our events outside in the cold. They don't seem to understand that you can't shut down a movement like this. Ironically, in fact, the more you try to shut it down, the more it grows. If I was doing strategic thinking for their side, I would say don't try to shut it down, that just galvanizes people on a very basic freedom of expression level, the right of people to voice their opinions. Israel as an apartheid state, yes or no – that's an intellectual debate based on facts that we should be allowed to have. People can understand that, and they don't like to be bullied."

IS THIS WORTH A PRESS RELEASE?

In a poem on her music-backed CD "Hadeel", Rafeef Ziadah speaks of a nine-year-old Palestinian girl, killed by an Israeli shell in Gaza. "Who, who will tell Hadeel that we went out for coffee, and carried on the day she died? Nothing stopped, not a pause, not a tear, next meeting, next cigarette, next train, check email and sigh – over another Palestinian gone. Is this worth a press release? Maybe not. Solidarity from afar ...."

This bitter, helpless feeling, solidarity from afar, I can appreciate. But in Rafeef's case, it must be compounded many times by her own story. "That's true", she says. "To sit in Canada as a Palestinian and watch the bombing of Gaza, it's devastating. You're watching something that's been happening to us for more than 60 years, over and over. When Beirut was invaded in 1982, I lived through the siege; those are some of my first memories as a child. To see the same thing happen to people in Gaza, only with more efficiency, more sophisticated weaponry, it's – killing. What do you do? You just keep plugging away at the work. Unfortunately, solidarity work can become very routine – put out another press release, another poster. But I have to say, the BDS movement actually gives you something real to do, something beyond writing press releases. When students ask their university to divest from Israeli apartheid, that's a real, concrete action you take against complicity, refusing to let business go on as usual. I think this is one of the main strengths of the BDS movement that keeps people going, despite all the crimes, despite all the devastation."

MY GRANDFATHER'S HOUSE

Judging by the South African experience, sanctions – the "S" in BDS – come later, when popular pressure builds enough to force one government after another into breaking ranks with the apartheid regime. The primary goal of sanctions is to increase the cost of ignoring international law. For example, Israel's acceptance into the United Nations in 1948 was conditional on its implementation of UN Resolution 194, which affirms the right of all Palestinians to return to their homes and lands from which they were exiled, and the right to compensation for those who choose not to return. UN Resolution 194 has yet to be implemented by Israel.

While I understand refugee return as a legitimate right entrenched in international law, in this case it strikes me as rather abstract. What does it mean personally to Rafeef, who was actually displaced? "I don't think of it abstractly at all, but very concretely", she says, without rancour. "I know exactly where my father's village is in Palestine. If I go to Haifa I can locate my grandfather's house. We have real ties to Palestine, and we have a right to return, also a right to restitution for more than 60 years of exile and statelessness. When Zionists say 'Why don't we dialogue?', I say 'Sure, let's dialogue about how Palestinians should go back home – by bus, train, airplane?' Without the right of return there can be no justice, and without justice, how can there be peace?"

SOON AFTER

While work proceeds slowly but steadily on international sanctions, grassroots campaigns for boycott and divestment grow rapidly in number, range and sophistication.

Following the divestment action of the Norwegian State Pension Fund, one of Norway's largest life insurance companies, Kommunal Landspensjonkasse, divested from Elbit Systems Ltd.

Soon after, Denmark's largest bank, Danske Bank, did the same. Bank official Thomas H. Kjaergaard explained, "We do not want to put customers' money in companies that violate international standards."

Soon after, one of the largest Danish pension funds, PKA Ltd, sold its US$1 million worth of shares in Elbit.

Soon after, one of the two largest pension funds in Holland, ABP, sold its US$2.7 million worth of shares in Elbit Systems.

Soon after, the Swedish pension fund Första AP-Fonden divested from Elbit.

Soon after, Deutsche Bank, Germany's largest, divested from Elbit ....

*   *   *

Cracks in the wall.

18
The Safety of Sleep

"The whole village now has the feeling that we hate night", says Lamyaa Yassin. Her voice is steady, her hands clasped firmly in her lap. "Night is supposed to be restful and quiet, but now it's just the opposite: no rest, no comfort. It's hard for us; especially for the children. Even though we're here with them, they don't feel safe. We wish every day would only be day, with no night."

On an October afternoon in the village of Bil'in, occupied West Bank, we're sitting in the airy parlour of Lamyaa and her husband Mohammed Khatib, a leader of the Popular Committee Against the Wall and Settlements. He couldn't meet with us as planned because he had to go hospital in Ramallah with severe diarrhoea, after soldiers beat him with rifle butts during a recent night invasion.

Lamyaa speaks through a two-step translation, Arabic into Hebrew via Leena, an Arab-Israeli student nurse who came with us today, and then into English via Emily Schaeffer, the American-Israeli lawyer who drove us here from Tel Aviv in an ancient borrowed Subaru. Timna, an Israeli videographer, tapes the conversation.

Lamyaa Yassin wears a black robe, and a headscarf of soft lavenders. Her face is side-lit by afternoon sun through open balcony doors. Across a shallow valley, the massive bulk of the Modi'in Illit settlement spills over a hill. In between is one of the roads the Israeli army uses on its night assaults.

A few months earlier in mid-summer I'm sitting in Toronto, Canada, with Mohammed Khatib and Emily Schaeffer. We're in the airy, comfortable kitchen of Miriam Garfinkle, a physician and activist who helped organize their Canadian tour. Miriam's back door opens onto a small tree-shaded garden, bright with bloom. From out there float calm, leisurely murmurs of Saturday morning in a quiet residential neighbourhood.

In jeans and a T-shirt that says "Remember Our Friend Bassem", Mohammed has dark hair, greying at the temples. Emily, dark blonde, wears shorts, a T-shirt and a light-blue scarf. The two of them are in Canada to launch a ground-breaking civil suit in the Quebec Superior Court. To be presented jointly with Canadian lawyer

Mark Arnold, the case accuses two companies legally registered in the Province of Quebec – Green Mount International and Green Park International – of illegally constructing settlement buildings on land that belongs to Bil'in, contravening both international and Canadian law.

Prior to the hearing, Emily Schaeffer and Mohammed Khatib are touring Canadian cities to inform people about the case, and about five years of creative non-violence in occupied Bil'in.

THIS IS OUR EXPERIENCE

Mohammed was born in Bil'in, October 1974, seven years into the Israeli military occupation. "For most people, occupation is only a word, you can't really understand it unless you live under it. For example, the Mediterranean is only 25 kilometres from my house. Some days we can see it, but we are not allowed to go there. My son thinks the sea is a small body of water, like a bathtub or a small pool after the rain. Because of the occupation we cannot take him there."

To attend high school in the next, larger village, then university in Ramallah, Mohammed had to pass through military checkpoints. A particular incident distils decades of abuse: "At one *machsom* (Hebrew for "barrier") we were not allowed to pass by car, only by foot", says Mohammed. "One day the soldiers took a small tape from a cassette, a very thin tape, and they tied it one metre (about three feet) high, so if you want to pass, you have to go under it, you have to bow. We accept to be humiliated like this because we have to live, go to school, go to work, to the hospital. But one of our friends, he refused to be humiliated. He walked through the tape, breaking it. That is all he did. The soldiers responded by shooting him in his leg. Then they kept him there for a long time in front of everyone. We called the ambulance; it came, but they refused to give him to the ambulance. He died there in front of everyone. They said he endangered the life of the soldiers. So they do a crime, then they lie. Sometimes they open an investigation, but nothing happens. This is our experience."

In 1991, Israel confiscated 200 acres of Bil'in farm land to build the Kiryat Sefer settlement. Villagers protested, without effect. Then in the early 2000s, as the separation barrier/apartheid wall sliced through Palestinian land, most villages in its path resisted as well as they could. When the bulldozers approached Bil'in late in 2004, the villagers learned that more than half their land, most of it cultivated, would be taken. "When the wall comes," says Mohammed, "the occupation comes to your door. You have no chance to escape, so you have to resist."

Village leaders called a public meeting, which elected a core group to launch the Popular Committee against the Wall and Settlements. Mohammed Khatib would be its first coordinator. "For three months we tried to stop the bulldozers, but from protests in other villages the army has learned how to keep people away from the bulldozers. So we failed, the wall continued, and olive trees were destroyed. But one day when they came to destroy more trees, they found us in their way. This was new thinking for us, a change of strategy. We went very early in the morning before the army came, chained ourselves to the olive trees, and waited for them to come. For them it was a surprise. From that day, this is how we have continued."

Every Friday into the present, villagers and their Israeli and international supporters have continued to invent non-violent tactics to resist the wall and maintain crucial media focus on their struggle. Still, by the end of 2005 the Bil'in section of the wall was almost complete, a measure of the enormous power gap between the Israeli military state and the popular resistance. About 1,700 people live in Bil'in.

Committee leaders concluded that they had failed to clarify to the world outside how the wall connects with the spread of settlements. "Israelis say all the time that the wall is for security reasons", Mohammed explains. "At Bil'in you can see very clearly that it is only for confiscating land and expanding the settlement. But how could we bring people to understand this?"

THE OTHER SIDE OF THE WALL

Ironically, Israeli border police provided a clue. When Palestinians from the occupied West Bank travel to the outside, they must exit and return via the Allenby Bridge that connects the West Bank with Jordan. On one such return, Mohammed was interrogated by border police. "I spoke freely about what we do," he says, "because nothing we do is illegal. When I talked about the settlement being built on our land, one of them said to me, 'You are failing to send your message out. Now that the wall is built, all your themes are useless.' He was right, it's true. When I heard that, I thought, 'Instead of just waiting for the settlers to do what they want, how can we can take the struggle to the other side of the wall?'"

One morning, soldiers discovered that villagers had placed a house trailer on land which still belongs to Bil'in by international law, but which Israel now claims. The army destroyed the trailer, but by next morning the villagers had replaced it. This time when soldiers came to remove it, the villagers asked them why. Mohammed explains, "By this time we had discovered through Israeli activists that this settlement was illegal not only by international law but also by Israeli law, because they had made some changes without approval from the authorities. So we asked the soldiers, 'Why do you not stop the settlement, which is illegal by your own law, but instead you come and take our house?'"

The army retorted that the villagers' building was illegal because it lacked a foundation, was less than ten square metres, and didn't have a roof, window or door. "So one night we built a house," says Mohammed, "with a foundation, a roof, a window and a door. It was not easy to do all that in one night, but we did it. The house is still there, people live in it."

In parallel, after several attempts, finally in late 2005 Bil'in and its lawyers succeeded in getting the Israeli High Court to hear a complaint on illegalities in the expansion of the Mattityahu-East settlement onto Bil'in land. Eventually the Court ordered that construction stop on housing units in Mattityahu-East.

The settlers hardly paused for breath. When Mohammed and two other village leaders tried to stop a settler crane from lowering a trailer onto Bil'in land, settlers beat them up. The assailants were arrested, but released by police a few minutes later without charges. Again and again, settlers invaded Bil'in land, the villagers tried to block construction, and the police arrested not the illegal invaders but the legal Palestinian protesters. This is the logic of occupation.

On the legal side, Bil'in won a rare victory in September 2007, when the High Court ruled that the route of the wall must be altered. In theory, this ruling would allow the village to recover almost half of its lands that had been confiscated in 2004. A year later, the court confirmed its ruling and found the Israeli government in contempt for not having complied the first time. A year later, work began on the new route. If completed, it will return about 650 dunams (160 acres) of stolen Bil'in land to the village. About 1,300 dunams will remain on the Israeli side of the wall.

As Friday protests at Bil'in continued to attract supporters and international attention, Israeli military reaction escalated – water cannon, then water with noxious chemicals; rubber bullets (one of which fractured the skull of a Bil'in protester), then live ammunition; tear gas in round containers, then in bullet-like projectiles.

In June 2008, army snipers shot Bil'in videographer Imad Bornat three times, nearly destroying his leg. He had documented the Bil'in resistance from the beginning.

In April 2009, a soldier shot Bassem Ibrahim Abu Rahmah in the chest from close range with a high-speed tear-gas projectile. He died en route to hospital. Bassem was much loved in Bil'in, and nearly always in the front line at weekly protests. At the moment he was shot, he was shouting at the soldiers in Hebrew: 'Stop, stop shooting, you've injured an Israeli protester!' This is the Bassem that Mohammed Khatib's T-shirt urges us to remember.

EMILY SCHAEFFER

Tyranny works best in the dark and in isolation, forcing its victims to feel alone and helpless. This is one of the reasons why Mohammed Khatib and Emily Schaeffer are in Canada. Emily explains, "We want to make clear for people how the occupation and the court case are linked, but also we want to connect them to Bil'in. If they feel helpless and frustrated with what's happening over there, there are things they can do about it here. For example, boycott, divestment and sanctions – it's very important for people to hear an Israeli Jew saying that I support BDS, even though at some point it might affect me negatively." (For more on BDS, see Chapter 17.)

Born in 1978 in the New England state of Massachusetts, Emily grew up in a progressive Jewish milieu – family, Hebrew school, reform synagogue. I ask what she means by "progressive". "It was about charity, social justice, how to give to others", she replies. "I understood Jewish people to be good people, who try to promote justice in the world."

At about six she became absorbed with antisemitism, the Holocaust and Israel. "I learned what happened in my own family – one side came from the Ukraine during pogroms in the early twentieth century, and another part from Austria. During the Nazi period some of them fled and some were sent to the camps. I learned that Israel was our refuge from all that."

At 15, she went on a synagogue youth tour to the Promised Land, and fell in love with Israel. Four years later, Emily returned to take her third year of university studies in Jerusalem. "It was 1998, before the intifada, so I met Palestinian students in my classes and in the student residence. Because I was hearing different stories from them and the media, I wanted to see for myself what was happening, so I started going with them to the West Bank and Gaza. It didn't take long for everything to click in my mind, and then everything I believed fell apart."

I asked her what exactly fell apart. "Everything I had been taught about Israel," she replies, "and much of what I had assumed about Jews being good, just people. I grew up thinking we were an oppressed minority, that all Jews are victims, and that includes Israelis. Now suddenly I realized how privileged I am. This was a big angry moment for me, I even called my rabbi in Massachusetts and yelled at him for lying to us. I told him that the Jewish values he taught me did not apply in Israel. Yes, we were victims in many other periods, but now we were making someone else the victim."

Emily joined the mainstream Israeli peace movement – the Meretz party and Peace Now. For several years she moved back and forth between Israel and the US. "I would flee to the US, too angry to stay here, then I'd come back to work with a specific organization or project – ICAHD (the Israeli Committee Against House Demolitions), Ta'ayush, Anarchists Against the Wall."

Why did she choose law? "I wanted to work full-time as an activist", she says. "I chose law because you can use it to get tangible things done on the ground; for example, in human rights cases, but it can also work as a political tool to get out the larger message – that's just how my brain works."

When Emily graduated from law school in 2005, she found an ideal home in the law firm of human rights lawyer Michael Sfard. By the time Bil'in Popular Committee members came to Sfard's firm for legal help, Emily was already immersed in the struggle for survival that the village embodied.

COURTING JUSTICE

At Miriam Garfinkle's house in Toronto, Emily and I chat in the kitchen. Out in the garden, Mohammed Khatib paces while he talks on the phone with his children in Bil'in. Tomorrow their Canadian tour resumes, and by the end of the week Mohammed and Emily will be in a Montreal court. I can hardly imagine the mountain of legal research a case like this must require.

"In the Israeli court that's true", says Emily. "Israel has adopted bits and pieces from military and property law of several former rulers: Ottoman, British and Jordanian; whatever suited its purposes. But here, we reject all that, and simply argue that Israel is subject to international law. Under international law, civilians of an occupying country aren't allowed to live in occupied territory. By building the settlements, these two companies registered in Canada have enabled Israeli civilians to live on occupied land that belongs to Bil'in. This is a clear violation of international law, which Canada has legally adopted into its own laws."

An Israeli friend calls the Israeli High Court a "court of occupation". In four decades of military occupation, it has permitted and justified deportations, home demolitions, administrative detentions (imprisonment without trial), land confiscations and the building of settlements in occupied territory.

Can Emily, an activist, still expect justice for Palestinians from this court? She nods; it's a familiar question. "That's a big, big dilemma for conscientious human rights lawyers in Israel", she says. "To what degree should we participate in the system? At what point does it make us collaborators? As a lawyer, you're supposed to look after your client's interests, but as a human rights lawyer, you have to look at the bigger picture. Sometimes those interests contradict one another. By participating, we allow the court to claim that it listens to Palestinian complaints, and sometimes it even rules in their favour, so the system can sleep well at night, and the Israeli public can keep waving this flag that we're the only democracy in the Middle East, the most moral army in the world, and so forth. It makes you crazy. Sometimes people talk about boycotting the High Court. But if our clients still come to us for help, and we know there's a fairly good chance we can accomplish *something* – get someone out of prison who shouldn't be there, or recover an olive grove to put food on someone's table – how can we turn our backs on that?"

On 22 June 2009, Emily Schaeffer argued Bil'in's case before a judge at the Quebec Superior Court in Montreal. The judge reserved his decision for later.

HOME INVASION

At about 2.30 that same night, two squads of Israeli soldiers invaded Bil'in, raided several houses, and detained two young villagers.

A few months and many night invasions later, we are talking with Lamyaa Yassin. Mohammed called a few minutes ago from hospital in Ramallah; they still had to do more tests.

Daughter Ward (five) snoozes on the sofa, her head nestled in Lamyaa's lap. Son Khaled (three) careens into the room on a tricycle, with a young red-haired woman in pursuit – she's an international solidarity volunteer, here to witness and help however she can.

While Lamyaa strokes Ward's tumble of black hair, she describes the first invasion of their home. "When they surrounded our house, Mohammed wanted to talk to them, to find out what they wanted so they wouldn't come into the house. We were trying to protect the children. But before he could get to the door they broke it open with their weapons. The baby started to cry. Khaled was shocked, he just stood there. They put the whole family into one room, then they searched the house. Three soldiers stood at the doorway with their weapons, and their faces painted black. Khaled didn't cry, he didn't say anything – he just stared at them.

"We stayed in that room more than an hour while they searched. Then Captain Fouad, as he's known, came and said, 'As of now Mohammed is under arrest.' Mohammed kissed the children, then they put a blindfold over him. At that moment all the children started to cry, except for Khaled. When the soldiers took Mohammed downstairs, we followed them. I heard screams and calls for help from the neighbour's house. The soldiers had arrested three people there; they beat everyone. When they took the arrestees out, the soldiers wouldn't let us follow, so we watched through the window; we saw them push Mohammed into the jeep. When the soldiers left our house, we went outside. We heard ambulance sirens. Then I saw my brother Abdallah covered in blood. When we saw him like that, I put Khaled down, and he threw a stone at one of the army jeeps. That was his only reaction the whole night."

Accused of "incitement to damage the security of the area" and held for three weeks in the Ofer military prison, Mohammed was the latest but not the last of many Popular Committee members to be arrested. His wife Lamyaa was not allowed to visit him, but, as his lawyer, Emily could. They spoke by phone through security glass.

Standing on the balcony at Lamyaa's house, Emily told me, "A couple of day after I saw Mohammed, I made sure to visit her and the children. She was glad that at least someone she knew had got in there to see him. The children were all over me, I being at that point the closest they could get to their baba."

While Mohammed was in prison, the army invaded and searched their house again.

BREAKING THE WALL

When we stop for lunch in Miriam Garfinkle's sun-speckled garden, I watch Mohammed and Emily talking quietly in a blend of Hebrew and English; Mohammed reporting on his phone call to

Bil'in, Emily going over plans for the rest of the day. Noting their easy, stress-tested rapport, it occurs to me that when Israelis and Palestinians work together like this, refusing to see the other as enemy, they break through the wall.

In August 2009 the wall was breached for a moment when the Elders arrived in a convoy of twelve black-windowed American SUVs. Started by former South African President Nelson Mandela and funded primarily by two British and American tycoons, the Elders function as high-level international witnesses and diplomats. The delegation to Bil'in included Archbishop Desmond Tutu of South Africa, former US President Jimmy Carter, former Brazilian President Fernando Cardoso, Indian community organizer Ela Bhatt, former President of Ireland Mary Robinson, and former Director-General of the World Health Organization Gro Brundtland.

Emily Schaeffer was invited to brief them, then accompanied them to the village. Popular Committee members escorted the Elders to the wall, to the grave of Bassem Abu Rahmah, and to the village council where they heard testimony from villagers and Israeli supporters. When reporters asked for comment, Archbishop Tutu said, "Mahatma Gandhi, as a simple man, led his people to freedom through non-violent methods. Rosa Parks followed in his footsteps, and now the people of Bil'in will do the same." Former President Jimmy Carter added, "We are standing here on Palestinian land, and on the other side of the wall is also Palestinian land. This occupation must end."

A few days before the Elders came to Bil'in, Mohammed Khatib was released from military prison. In a hearing on his case, military prosecutors accused him of throwing stones during a demonstration. As evidence they submitted a photograph, along with the "confession" of a Bil'in youth in military custody, who had identified Mohammed Khatib in the photo. It was a simple matter for Mohammed's Israeli lawyer, Gabi Laski, to prove that when the photo was taken, the accused man was on tour in Canada.

Despite the revelation of falsified evidence, the military court would only release Mohammed on several restrictive conditions, including an order to report every Friday afternoon to a military base. Of course, this meant he would be unavailable for the weekly protests.

In September 2009, the Quebec Superior Court dismissed the Bil'in civil suit against the two Montreal companies, on the grounds that the claims should be heard by the High Court of Justice in Jerusalem. By then, the companies had already completed 500 residences in Mattityahu-East, and another 1,500 were in various stages of planning and construction.

A month later, the villagers' Canadian lawyer Mark Arnold filed an appeal against the decision. Among several grounds for appeal, he argued that the Geneva Conventions, one of which prohibits an occupying power from transferring its own citizens into occupied territory, had been incorporated into Canadian law, but not into Israeli law. Since the two construction companies are based in Canada and allegedly violating Canadian law, it is appropriate for the case to be heard in a Canadian court.

In Bil'in the night invasions continued. "As time goes on," says Lamyaa Yassin, "the soldiers get more violent. I think they see that everyone here is still strong, still struggling, and this bothers them very much. They must think that by now, after so many home invasions, jail and beatings, people would be too afraid, but this is a struggle for our land and our lives, so we continue."

After midnight on 16 September, Israeli soldiers invaded the village again. "We were on the roof with international solidarity activists", says Lamyaa. "We saw many jeeps coming. Then Mohammed got a call: soldiers had invaded Abdallah's house. He wasn't there. Mohammed thought he could help, so with a few international activists he went over to the house. Hearing the children screaming from inside, he went in to try and comfort them. The soldiers started beating him with their rifle butts: they hit his face, his chest, his back and his stomach. They said to him, 'If you don't shut your mouth, you will have the same fate as Bassem.'"

Very likely this is why Mohammed had to go hospital in Ramallah today. A photo taken of him that night shows a face swollen and purpled with bruises. But Lamyaa recounts his ordeal calmly. People here can't afford to dwell too long on the horror, or the rage.

ABDALLAH ABU RAHMAH

Like everything else in this imprisoned village, it is only a short drive to Abdallah's house, in a courtyard garden behind an impressive metal gate. A tall man with a gentle handshake, Abdallah Abu Rahmah came here today specifically to meet with us, but he can't stay long. He is on the army's wanted list, due to charges from 2005 for his involvement in non-violent protests. After we leave, he'll return with his young daughters Layan (five) and Luma (seven) to a safe house in Ramallah.

He showed us the results of the latest army attack, starting at the gate. "On 16 September my wife heard a sound outside", he says. "She saw soldiers trying to open the gate [he bangs on it to illustrate], but it was locked. Then six or seven soldiers climbed over and opened it from the inside. Many soldiers came in. They came to the main door of my apartment and started to break it, but my wife came quickly to open it."

He shows us the bent front door, broken handle, and a battered inner door to a room where placards and banners for Friday protests are stored. Abdallah tells us, "When the soldiers didn't find me or any material they wanted, they destroyed many things in this room."

He leads us outside to another entrance off the courtyard. "This is where my mother lived. When she died on 15 August, we closed this room in mourning; no one is allowed inside. [While his mother lay dying in a Jerusalem hospital, Israeli authorities denied Abdallah the permit necessary to visit her.] The soldiers broke the door, and checked everything in that room. Then they went to my brother's apartment and did the same. Soldiers stayed in my apartment more than one hour, they gave my wife an invitation for me to meet the Shabak leader. They told her if I didn't come, they would find me and do the same as they did to Bassem."

"Shabak" is an acronym for the Israeli General Security Service. Its agents operate throughout Israel and the occupied Palestinian territories, issuing many such "invitations".

"They came back four days later on the holiday [Ramadan]", says Abdallah. "They gave my wife another invitation for me to come to the Shabak. They took my number from her and called me many times, but I know the number is for Shabak, so I didn't answer; I put my phone on silent. If I answered, they would use pressure to make me meet them, and put me in jail for many months like Adeeb."

Another leader of the Bil'in Popular Committee, Adeeb Abu Rahmah was arrested by soldiers at a Friday protest in July 2009. A taxi driver, he is the sole provider for a family of eleven. In July 2010, after Adeeb had already been held for a year in the Ofer military prison, an Israeli military judge sentenced him to a further two years.

In the garden, Abdallah Abu Rahmah pours us glasses of orange juice. His wife Majida sits beside him, their nine-month-old son Laith in her lap. Abdallah was born here 39 years ago, in an old building on this small piece of land. He teaches Arabic full time at Birzeit high school, and Jerusalem history part-time at Al-Quds open university. He also raises chickens in a coop behind Mohammed's house.

How did he get involved in the struggle here? "We were students at school in the first intifada, then at university we also used non-violence in demonstrations. When they started to build the wall here, we knew that all of our agricultural land, 2,000 dunams, would disappear behind it, so the village established the Popular Committee. We read about Gandhi and Nelson Mandela – we want to use the same methods here, but in our own way, for this place."

I ask him what it's like to be a fugitive. "I feel tired, very tired from doing this", he replies. "Today I finished school, ate my lunch, and came quickly here to meet with you. After we finish, we will go back to Ramallah. It's difficult to live this way. Many times I find checkpoints on the roads. Two nights before now, I came to a checkpoint, but, lucky for me, ten or eleven cars were waiting there, so I could turn and go another way. It was more dangerous, a small road between the olive trees. The soldiers followed, but they did not find me."

The afternoon is waning; soon Abdallah will have to leave. One of his daughters is already sleeping in the car; another is with an uncle in the village. "They don't want to sleep in this house because they are afraid the soldiers will come in the night. The last time they came, the children woke up to see a large number of soldiers with masks, black faces and guns. It's difficult to go to sleep every night in another house. On Thursday night I decided to stay here, but in the middle of the night my daughters said 'No, we can't sleep here', so we drove to Ramallah. We need peace and safety for my family, so I won't stay here again until they stop following me and trying to arrest me."

The village was shaken by the "confession" that prosecutors tried to use against Mohammed. Abdallah knows very well that, regardless of his own record of non-violence, and the fact that every protest is well documented on both sides of the fence, the same could easily happen to him. "One of the children they arrested," Abdallah tells us, "he said that we told them to throw stones. When they come out of jail, we must ask them 'Why did they say this, why? Why do they lie like this?'" It's the first time he has raised his voice, a momentary overflow of anger, grief and fatigue.

Emily gently offers a response, "They're children, they're being interrogated." Timna adds, "For children, it's difficult to endure this kind of pressure." Leena, the student nurse, adds, "They scare them in so many ways; they beat them, they make them say what they want them to say – if you tell us what we want to hear, then we'll release you."

Abdallah sighs, looks at the ground. "Yes", he says. He knows. But still, *why?* He raises his head again. "Something has changed here", he says, in a tone less weighted. "For two weeks there have been no raids, no calls to come to the Shabak. Something has changed. I hope that in one or two months they will forget this case and I will come back to sleep here in my house."

At this point a neighbour arrives, Ashraf Abu Rahmah: he will stay overnight as a protector in the house. Bassem was his brother. At 28, Ashraf is also a veteran of the struggle here, already jailed and injured several times in non-violent actions – most notoriously last year: while he sat on the ground handcuffed and blindfolded, an Israeli soldier shot him in the foot.

Visiting hours have run out for Abdallah. He has to leave Bil'in now with his daughters, and find a safe route to Ramallah.

Two months later, nine Israeli military vehicles surrounded Abdallah's home, broke down the door, blindfolded and arrested him. At his first hearing, as expected, the military prosecutors charged him with throwing stones, with incitement, and – here was a surprise – with the possession of arms.

It turned out that the "arms" were empty Israeli tear-gas canisters and used concussion grenades, many hundreds of which have been fired by the Israeli army at protesters in Bil'in. People gathered up the spent items, displayed them to journalists, and recycled them creatively in their actions, arranging them into a large peace symbol, and hanging them on a Christmas tree. Stored in Abdallah's house, the waste products of Israel's occupation were the only arms he possessed.

In July 2010, the military judge found Abdallah Abu Rahmah guilty of the charges that stemmed from his role in organizing non-violent protests in 2005. Already imprisoned for more than half a year, he was sentenced to a further two months. Abdallah awaits a further trial in military court on charges from his arrest in 2009, which also result from his role as a leader of the Bil'in Popular Committee.

His lawyer, Gabi Laski, commented, "The military court threads a dangerous path of criminalizing legitimate protest in the West Bank."

DREAMS OF FLIGHT

In the Friday protests, sometimes the discipline of non-violence holds; sometimes enraged young men throw stones over the fence at soldiers. Either way, the soldiers fire. Given how much violence and brutality Bil'iners endure, I ask Mohammed Khatib how he and his fellow-villagers maintain the high level of non-violence that they do.

He replies, "It's our right as Palestinians to resist the occupation, but we must choose the method that we think will have the most benefit. Why engage your opponent in a fight that you know you will lose? Instead, you compete in a way that you think you can win, and show what we have as Palestinians. We don't have an army, or tanks, or nuclear weapons, like Israel. What we have is our rights and our own power. How can we show this power, show who is victim and who is victimizer? By using non-violence."

Like other occupiers, from its inception Israel has met non-violent resistance with escalating violence. As Lamyaa says, it bothers armed soldiers very much when people without arms refuse to submit. Mohammed concurs. "What we are doing is more dangerous than to shoot a gun and then run away. If you tie yourself to a tree, you wait for the army to come; maybe to shoot you, to kill you. You also have to learn how to control yourself, because when you react to violence with violence, you are out of control, and in that field your opponent will win."

People safely outside the situation sometimes ask, "Why don't more Palestinians use non-violent protest?" The question ignores the long history of Palestinian attempts to seek justice through non-violent means, and the equally long history of official Israeli violence in suppressing these attempts. Still, as someone whose belief in non-violence has been through trial by fire, Mohammed knows a lot more about the subject than I do. So I asked him: "Why don't more Palestinians use non-violent protest?"

"There are a lot of reasons", he replies. "First, some people think that if they use non-violence, it cancels your right to resist in a military way. Some people think that it's not effective, that what's taken by force can only be returned by force. Also, there aren't many examples where people can see that non-violence succeeds. What we've achieved so far in Bil'in is good, but these things aren't visible enough to people outside. For all these reasons, to practise non-violence is not easy. It needs courage, a lot of time and effort, real leadership, and a strong belief in what you are doing."

Bil'iners are not alone in their strong belief. Across the West Bank, in Gaza, and within Israel, people are resisting the occupation and the military state. So far the authorities have succeeded in keeping these local struggles relatively separate, but Bil'iners aim to overcome this enforced isolation. "We are forming a coordinating committee for local non-violent resistance," says Mohammed, "so it isn't just this village and that village by itself, but more national. This committee is not just one party, it is for everyone." Mohammed was elected first coordinator of the new committee.

In another attempt to reach out, in 2006 Bil'in hosted the first International Conference for the Joint Non-violent Struggle against the Wall, drawing several hundred participants from Palestine, Israel and a dozen other countries. In April 2009, the fourth annual conference was dedicated to the memory of Bassem Abu Rahmah, killed by soldiers the week before. By the final day of the conference, protest Friday, the number of participants doubled. Under attack by Israeli soldiers, Popular Committee members managed to build a memorial to their lost friend Bassem.

In March 2010, the occupying army announced that the area surrounding the separation fence would henceforth be declared a closed military zone from 8 a.m. to 8 p.m. every Friday; Israeli citizens and foreign nationals would have to evacuate the village during those hours. The order applies to land between the separation fence and built-up areas in Bil'in. An even more restrictive decree was imposed simultaneously on the village of Ni'lin. These orders effectively criminalize legitimate protest, and justify escalating military violence.

In Palestine, many martyrs are buried. At 35, Mohammed is still young. He has four children. In Miriam Garfinkle's kitchen, I'm moved to ask, 'Does he fear for his own life?' "Yes", he replies. "After all these crimes of the Israeli occupiers, and so many people killed, I don't want it to become a regular thing for us Palestinians to die like this, as if we were born only to die. I don't want this to be the basis of struggle. But after Bassem I feel we are closer to death. I am not afraid, personally. When we go to these demonstrations I expect the worst; I know that maybe this time it can be me. I don't know why I'm not afraid of death – maybe because I believe in what I'm doing, and if you die for good things, it's an honour. So I would say that first we care about our lives, we care about our friends, but we are also not afraid to die." Emily adds quietly, "We need you alive."

In Bil'in, Israeli videographer Timna asked Lamyaa Yassin what impact the army invasions have had on the village. "The biggest impact is on the children", she replied, "This is what worries everyone the most. They have seen and experienced so many terrible things. For us, the worst thing is the impact on Khaled. Even when Mohammed is home, Khaled wakes up often in the middle of the night; he wets his bed. Also, now he hits his brothers and sisters. He never did that before."

Later I stood on the balcony with Emily Schaeffer, looking over the village as the sun sank and day cooled. She told me about the night she stayed here. "It was very frightening. From 10 p.m. to 5 a.m. I didn't get a wink of sleep. When I came home to Tel Aviv in the morning and got into my own bed, I had never before felt so much appreciation for the safety and quiet of sleep. And that was one night. Here, it's night after night. Everyone here is always tired, always on edge."

In Miriam's kitchen I asked Emily if she ever experienced despair. "Of course", she says. "In this movement it's very easy to despair. But the Palestinians can't afford to lose hope – without hope you don't have life. One thing we remind each other of is that even when we feel defeated we are still preserving humanity and the connection between the two peoples for the future. If this is all we accomplish, still it's something."

It's late, and the two friends from Palestine–Israel are due at the next public event on their Canadian tour. My last question for Mohammed: "What would you do if the occupation ended?" He smiles. "I would be a pilot."

Emily looks surprised. "I've never heard you say that before."

Mohammed stands, preparing to take off. "I dream all the time that I'm flying", he says. "We are not allowed to fly. To become a pilot I would have to go outside the country, and then I wouldn't be allowed to come back. But when I dream it, it gives me hope, so that I can do things. This is the first time I've told this, but some of the creative things we did, first I dreamed it. In the night you dream about the idea, and in the morning it exists. This is why I dream of flying."

Index

9/11 149

Abraham (biblical figure) 136
Abu Dis 57, 58
Abufarha, Nasser 152–7, 158–63
Abu Mazen/Mahmoud Abbas, former
    president, Palestinian National
    Authority 122
Abumah, Mofida 186
Abu Rahmah, Abdallah 224–7
Abu Rahmah, Adeeb 225
Abu Rahmah, Ashraf 227
Abu Rahmah, Bassem Ibrahim 215,
    219, 223, 225, 227, 229
Abu Rahmah, Laith 225
Abu Rahmah, Layan 224
Abu Rahmah, Luma 224
Abu Rahmah, Majida 225
Abu-Zeina, Tharwa 48
Administrative detention(s) 128, 221
Afghanistan 202
African Refugee Development Centre
    150
Afula 81, 170
African-Americans 83, 84, 122
Ahava, cosmetic 208
Akiva, youth movement 69
Al-Aqsa Mosque 36, 37, 54
Al-Bustan 32, 38, 93
Al-Damun 168
Al-Ittihad 80, 87
Al-Jalama 152, 162
Al-Jazeera 45
Al-Kamandjati Music Centre 27
Al-Mezan Centre for Human Rights 211
Al-Najah University 43, 45, 48
Al-Nu'man 140
Al-Quds (open) University 22, 49, 225
Al-Ram 54, 62
Al-Yasmeen Hotel 46
Aliyah 7, 29
Allenby Bridge 183, 210, 217
Allenby Street 105
Almonds, growing 160
Alsumeriyyah 168
Amer, Hani 10, 11–12

Amer, Munira 10, 11
American 208
  -Israeli 215
  military base 177
  University, Beirut 100
  University, Washington DC 82
Amir, Merav 205–8, 210
Amman, Jordan 49, 50
Amnesty International 145
Amputees 195
Anarchists Against the Wall 137, 141,
    203, 204, 220
Anata 33
Anaemia, childhood 196
Animal Farm 27
'Anin 159, 160
Anthropology(ist) 154–5, 163
Antisemitic(ism) 148, 149, 173, 205,
    210, 219
Apartheid 31, 37, 74, 77, 138, 209, 211
  regime 213
  state 212
  wall 216
Arab-Americans 149
Arab-American Anti-Discrimination
    Committee 82
Arab
  citizens of Israel 87, 119, 120–1
  -Israeli(s) 87, 117, 118, 120, 123,
    139, 165, 169, 188, 206, 212
  municipalities 81
  regimes 193
Arabic
  Jews 179
  (language) 58, 63, 80, 98, 104, 105,
    106, 170, 179, 180, 184, 189,
    215, 225
Arab-Palestinian 87
Arab(s) 55, 56, 81, 105, 114, 115, 118,
    122, 128, 129, 140, 141, 143,
    147, 159, 164, 165, 170, 173,
    174, 177, 178, 179, 180, 181,
    183, 184, 186, 203, 209
Arad 130–1

Arafat, Yasser, former chairman, Palestine Liberation Organization 117, 152, 184
Area A 102, 110
Area C 74, 102
Archeology, 91, 93, 94, 95, 99
    community 92, 94
Archeologists 92, 95
Argentina(ian) 29, 165
Arna's Children 20
Arnold, Mark 215–16, 224
Art Action 24
Asia 201
Assassinate(ion) 159
Associated Press 59
Association for Civil Rights in Israel, ACRI 82, 83, 131, 136
Atout, Samah 47
Austria 219

Backlash, Israeli, to BDS 209–11
Banai, Daphne 54, 55–6, 57, 58–9, 60–1, 64–6, 206
Banhart, Devendra 209
Bantustans 201
Baqa 180
    Al-Gharbiya 184
    Al-Sharqiya 185
Bar-David Varon, Raz 139–49
Bargaining committee(s), union 181, 182
Barghouthi, Petra 24–5, 26
Basic Laws 121
Bat Yam 149–50
Baum, Dalit 206
Bedouins 31, 106, 192
Beinish, Dorit, President, Supreme Court 78
Beirut 100, 140, 213
Beit Arabiyeh 33
Beit Nuba 167
Beit Sira 164
Belgium(ian) 17, 18, 208
Ben-Simhon, Dani 177, 178, 179–81, 182, 189
Bhatt, Ela 223
Bible, the 31, 92, 93, 96, 104
Bil'in 215, 216, 217, 218, 219, 221, 223, 224, 227, 228, 229
    Bil'iners 228
    Popular Committee Against the Wall and Settlements 215, 217, 220, 222, 223, 225, 226, 227, 229

Binyamina 129, 130, 133
Birzeit 225
Blau, Uri 68, 69
BMW 158
Bombs, sound 59
Border Police 35, 43, 60, 129, 217
Bornat, Imad 219
Bosnian Serb 98
Boycott, Divestment & Sanctions, BDS 66, 132, 137, 149, 199, 201, 203, 204, 205, 207, 209, 210, 211, 213, 214, 219
Boycott! 204, 205
Boycott National Committee, Palestine 202
Breaking the Silence 131, 193
Bridge to the World 42
Britain 132, 161
British Broadcasting Corporation, BBC 45, 197
British colonial
    authorities 80, 202
    occupation 99
    period 31
    regime 101
Bronstein, Eitan 164–6, 167, 169, 172–3, 174–5
Brundtland, Gro, former director-general, World Health Organization 223
B'Tselem 34, 79, 193, 211
Buddhism 64, 67
Bulldoze(d)(r) 27, 28, 32, 55, 130, 154, 167, 207, 216, 217
Bullets, rubber 218
Burqin 152, 153, 160
Byzantine(s) 91, 95

California 7, 126
Canaan Fair Trade 153, 155, 156, 157, 159, 161, 163
Canaanite(s) 91, 93
Canada(ians) 2, 18, 71, 156, 157, 158, 167, 171, 185, 192, 203, 211–12, 213, 220, 221, 223, 224, 230
Canada Park 164, 165, 166, 167, 168
Capetown 149, 150
Cardoso, Fernando, former president, Brazil 223
Care and Learning 19
Carmel Ridge/neighbourhood 113, 114, 123
Carter, Jimmy, former president, US 223
Caterpillar 51, 206

Central America 69–70
Checkpoints, 22, 50, 56, 57, 60–1, 102,
    103, 107, 109–10, 112, 140, 162,
    175, 205, 206, 216, 226
  Huwara 42, 205
  Kalandia 54, 57, 59–60, 61–2, 63–4,
    66–7
Christian(s)(ity) 80, 114, 115, 167
Church(es) 158
Chutzpah 165
CIA 18
City of David, el ir David 39, 89, 90,
    93, 96, 98, 99
Civil
  Administration 73, 74, 75, 107, 166,
    167
  rights 83
  society 124, 126, 134, 199
Closed military zone 66, 229
CNN 13, 25, 45
Coalition
  Against Israeli Apartheid, CAIA 201,
    203
  of Women for Peace 206, 210
Collaborators 106, 221
Collective agreement, union 181
Colony/colonist(ism)(izer) 7, 166, 172,
    176, 183
Committee for Educational Guidance
    for Arab Students, CEGAS 116
Communist(s) 176
  Party 19, 80, 113
  Youth 101, 113, 115
Congress, US 122
Conscience 126
Conscientious objector(s)(ion) 145, 146,
    147
Conscription 135, 136
Constitution 121–2
Costello, Elvis 208
Courage to Refuse 146
Court(s), Israeli 32, 83, 119, 120, 221
  High/Supreme Court 73, 74, 75, 76,
    78, 83, 97, 98, 119, 121, 122,
    135, 217, 221, 223
  labour 182
  Petitions to 73, 75, 76, 77, 78, 79,
    93, 97, 135
Crusaders 92
Curfew 23, 45, 46, 131
Curriculum, school 81

Daana 25–7
Danske Bank, Denmark 214

Darwish, Mahmoud 27
Database, Who Profits? 206
Dayan, Moshe, former minister of
    defence, Israel 164
Dayr Ayyub 167
Dead Sea 130, 208
Declaration of the Establishment of the
    State of Israel 122
Delegitimization 209
Demolitions, house/home 10, 29, 30,
    32, 38, 39, 41, 66, 93, 117, 221
Demolition orders 59, 74, 76
Deportations 221
Deutsche Bank, Germany 214
Dexia Bank 208
Diabetes 104
Diaspora, Palestinian 200, 201
Diggers, archeological and quarry 182
Dirasat, Arab Centre for Law and Policy
    84–8
Dolev,
  Ariel 130
  Diana 129–32, 133, 136–7
  Sharon 130
  Yaara 130
Dr Bronner's Magic Soaps 156–7
  David Bronner 157
Drama therapy 24–5
Drones 65
Dubai 49
Durban, South Africa 208

East Germany 176
East Jerusalem 32, 33, 35, 36, 37, 39,
    40, 42, 54, 57, 69, 71, 78, 89, 90,
    94, 98, 140, 182
Eden Springs, corporation 208
Egypt(ian) 49, 132, 190, 196, 197
  government 196
  "Wall of Shame" 197
Ein Yabrud 75
Efrony, Neta 54–5, 56–8, 59–60, 61–2,
    63–4, 66–7
Elad, Ir David Foundation 89, 90, 93,
    94, 95, 96, 97, 98, 99
Elbit Systems Ltd 199, 205, 206, 214
Elders, the 223
Elections, Israeli
  municipal 34
  national 34
Electricity 191
Elkana 10

Emek Shaveh, Valley of Shaveh 94, 95, 98
Emmaus/'Imwas 167
Ethiopians 182
Ethnic cleansing 31, 130, 159
Etkes, Dror 68–71, 72–9
European 208
    Parliament 124
    Union, EU 85, 208
        Heads of Mission 39
Europe(ans), 71, 108, 115, 156, 161, 163, 180, 192, 193, 201, 202
    Eastern 181
Evergreen College, Oregon 208
Exams, national 81
    psychometric 84
Exploit(ation) 180, 181

Fair trade 152, 155, 156, 157, 161
Falk, Richard, UN Special Rapporteur for Human Rights 192
Farah, Jafar 113–25
Farm
    owners 177, 178, 179
    work(ers) 177–8, 179
Farmers, farming 159–60, 179
Fascism(ist)(istic) 115, 120, 133, 176, 210
Fatah 116, 192
Feminism(ist) 132, 133, 143, 147, 185, 207
Fieler, Dror 20
Fieler, Pnina 20, 100–1, 102, 103, 104, 105, 108–9, 110, 111, 112
Florida, US 202
Flotilla(s),
    Freedom 208
    international aid and solidarity 197
Ford Foundation 85
Första AP-Fonden, Sweden 214
Fouad, Captain 222
France 208
Freedom of Information 68, 74
Freedom Theatre 17, 19, 23, 25–6, 27
    School 24–7
French Hill 69

Galilee 80, 169, 170, 175–6
Galili, Amaya 169–72, 175–6
Gandhi, Mahatma 223, 225
Gan Yoshiya 186–7

Garfinkle, Miriam 215, 220, 222, 229, 230
Gaza (Strip), 30, 34, 35, 65, 81, 103, 106, 107, 108, 110, 126, 130, 131, 132, 183, 190, 191, 192, 194, 195, 197, 200, 202, 212, 219, 228
    bombardment of 193, 195, 213
    City 190, 191, 195
    disengagement from 141, 192
    ghetto 196
    invasion of 193
    Ministry of Health 195
    siege/blockade of 107, 192, 194, 196, 197
    tunnels 196–7
    war on 144, 145, 149, 150, 196, 197
Gazans 191, 192, 195, 197
Geneva Convention(s), 224
    Fourth (Article 33) 192
Geographic information system, GIS 70, 75
Georgetown University, Washington DC 83
Germany, Germans 98, 100, 115, 158
Gil, Amiram 101, 107
Globalization 180
    anti- 201
Golan Heights 208
Goldstein, Baruch 7, 169
Goldstone, Richard, Judge 194
    Commission 194
    Report (of the United Nations Fact-Finding Mission on the Gaza Conflict) 110, 194, 202, 210
Gordon, Neve 210
Graffiti 58, 185
Grassroots 158
    Anti-Apartheid Wall Campaign (Stop the Wall) 209–10
Greater Israel 30
Greenberg, Professor Rafael 92
Green Line 6, 36, 56, 109
Green Mount International, corporation 216
Green Park International, corporation 216
Greenpeace 130
Grenades, concussion 227
Guantanamo camera 98
Guardian 37, 39

Haaretz 68, 69, 76, 85, 116, 118, 164, 173
Hadeel 212
Hagannah 170
Haifa 83, 113, 114, 116, 117, 124, 130, 139, 177, 180, 200, 205, 211, 213
Haifa University 31, 113, 115, 116
Halvorsen, Kristin, Minister of Finance, Norway 199
Hamas 107, 192, 211
   Hamasniks 173
Hantoli, Salem 46–7, 48, 53
Haram Al-Sharif 36
Hares 12, 13, 14
Har-ha Bayit 36
Hebrew 58, 99, 101, 104, 114, 116, 129, 140, 144, 164, 177, 181, 208, 215, 216, 219, 222
   school 219
   University 31, 81, 105, 131, 137
Hebron, 7, 169
   South 31
Hefer Valley 165
Hegemony 38
Hellenic empire 164
Hepatitis A 195
Herzl, Theodor 201
Hewlett Packard 207
Hezbollah 38
Highjack(ings) 3, 157
Hijab 50–1, 104, 105, 177, 186
Hiller, Ruth 126–8, 132–3, 134, 136, 137
Hiller, Yinnon 127
Histadrut, Israeli trade union federation 29, 181
Holland 46, 104, 158
   APB, pension fund 214
Holocaust 7, 30, 114, 115, 170, 209, 219
Holy City 92
Holy Land 53
Homeland security 199
How Do We Say Nakba in Hebrew? 173
Human rights 106, 107, 109, 122, 124, 127, 220, 221
Humanitarian aid 192
Hummers 185
Hummus 15, 182

Identity/ID cards/papers 42, 57, 59, 73, 87
Iftar, meal 162

Ighbariyyeh, Umar 168
Immigrants,
   Jewish 150
   Russian 16, 150
Im Tirtzu ("If You Will It") 210
'Imwas/Emmaus 167, 168
Incursions, Israeli 27, 48
Independence Day 172, 173
Indonesia 153
Ingersoll Rand, corporation 207
Institute for Market Ecology 157
International
   Committee of the Red Cross 195
   Conference for the Joint Non-violent Struggle Against the Wall 229
   Court of Justice 9, 199
   Criminal Court 192
   solidarity volunteers 46, 47, 48, 49
   Women's Day 185, 186
   Women's Peace Service 15
Intifada,
   cultural 21
   first 19, 22, 56, 81, 102, 127, 128, 165, 183, 192
   second 8, 13, 18, 23, 46, 56, 70, 119, 129, 140, 155, 165, 192, 201, 205, 219
   third 112
Invasions, Israeli 18–19, 20, 22–3, 27–8, 34, 44–5, 48, 103
   of Bil'in 215, 221, 222, 224, 229
   of Gaza (2008–09) 124, 206, 208, 211, 213
   of Lebanon (1982) 127, 139, 165, 213
   of Lebanon (2006) 123, 141–2, 145, 206
   of Nablus (2002) 53
Iran 202
Iraq 202
Iraqi Petroleum Company 114
Ireland 152
Ir Ganim-Kiryat Menahem 92
Iron Age 92, 95
Islam(ic) 51, 53, 114, 159, 167
Isaac (biblical figure) 136
Israel
   Antiquities Authority 90, 91, 92, 93, 96, 97
   Ballet 202
   Broadcasting Authority 56
   Forum for Promotion of Equal Share in the Burden 135–6

Israeli
    Apartheid 202, 213
        Week 212
    commandos 208
    Committee Against House
        Demolitions, ICAHD 30, 31–2,
        33, 34, 220
    Consulate, New York 202
    Defence Force, IDF 108, 129, 149,
        150, 194
    Jew(s)/Jewish Israelis 141, 165, 166,
        169, 170, 172, 176, 219
Israeli-Palestinian conflict 94
Issa, Mahmoud 159–60
Italy 152, 153, 161

Jabareen, Dr Yousef 80–8
Jaffa/Yafa 42, 44, 101, 105, 111, 139,
    149, 150, 180
Jaffa Gate 36
Jayyus 209
Jahshan, Shakeeb 80, 88
Jenin 18, 19, 102, 152, 154
Jerusalem 29, 30, 36, 38, 56, 64, 69,
    70, 85, 90, 91, 92, 105, 112, 123,
    131, 140, 150, 157, 166, 171,
    182, 183, 219, 223, 225
    Boulevard 105
    history 95
    Municipality 32, 93, 98
    next year in 73
    Old City 89, 90, 97, 99
    Syndrome 32, 33
    West 92
Jesus 80
Jewish
    Agency 83
    Defence League 211
    holidays 186
    Israelis 204
    municipalities 81
    National Fund, JNF 166, 167, 168
    religion 81
    state 87, 122, 174, 175
    Voice for Peace, US 209
Jew(s), 104, 105, 114, 118, 119, 120,
    122, 124, 165, 175, 186, 201
    Ethiopian 105
    Oriental 180
    Orthodox 100, 123, 135
Johannesburg 149
Jordan 43, 49, 53, 54, 108, 183, 210,
    217

Jordan Valley 54, 58–9, 60–1, 62–3,
    64–5, 66
Joshua, biblical figure 164
Journalism(ists) 116, 117, 118
Judaism(aic) 67, 121, 166, 211
Judea and Samaria 166, 208
Judeans 91
Judenstaat, Der 201

Kababir 114
Kairos 211
Kalandia 58, 62, 66–7
Kafr Qassem 8
Kaminer, Matan 129
Kharbatha 204
Keffiyeh 152
Keller, Hava 168
Kerem Shalom 191
Khamis, Arna Mer 19–20
Khamis, Juliano Mer 20, 23
Khatib, Khaled 221, 222
Khatib, Mohammed 215, 216–18, 219,
    220, 221, 222, 223, 224, 225,
    226, 228–30
Khatib, Ward 221, 222
Kjaergaard, Thomas H. 214
Kibbutz 127, 130, 165, 169, 170
    Amir 169, 171
    Bahan 165
    Ha'Ogen 126
    Sa'ar 168
    Yad Hannah 100
    Yakim 101
Kidron Valley 89
Ki-Moon, Ban, UN Secretary General
    59
King David 91, 92, 93, 95, 96
Kiryat Arba 7
Kiryat Gat 179
Kisch, Dr Eldad 103, 104–5, 108–11,
    112
Klaxons, the 209
Knesset 9, 34, 35, 110, 120, 121, 123,
    131, 137, 173, 184, 211
Kommunal Landspensjonkasse, Norway
    214
Kufr Qara 177, 178, 179, 184, 188
Kuwait 43, 48

Labour, party 142, 193
Labour for Palestine, Canada 203
Land confiscation(s) 77, 216, 217, 218,
    221

Land of Israel 78, 79
Land of Symbols: Cactus, Poppies, Orange and Olive Trees in Palestine 154
Laski, Gabi 223, 227
Law,
  British 220
  Canadian 216, 224
  humanitarian 194
  human rights 194
  international 14, 71, 94, 194, 197, 199, 200, 209, 211, 213, 216, 218, 220, 221
  Israeli 218, 224
  Jordanian 220
  Ottoman 220
Law of Return 174
Lebanon 126, 157, 169, 200
Leena 215, 226
Lieberman, Foreign Minister Avigdor 35, 86, 87, 172, 211
Livni, Tzipi, former foreign minister, Israel 122
London, UK 131, 209
Los Angeles Times 210

M16, rifle 140
Machsom (checkpoint) 216
MachsomWatch 54, 55, 56–7, 60, 61, 205, 206, 210
Mada Al-Carmel 211
Madison, Wisconsin 155, 163
Madrid, Spain 209
Mandela, Nelson, former president, South Africa 81, 223, 225
Manpower companies 177, 182
Maor, Adam 129
Marda 16
Margalit, Meir 29–41, 140, 150
Marton, Dr Ruchama 102
Martyrs 27
Maryland, US 203
Mas'ha 8–10
Masri, Haneen 49–51, 52
Massachusetts, US 219, 220
Massoud, Robert 157–8
Master plans 32, 37, 69, 131, 137
Matar, Haggai 128–9, 134–5, 137–8, 144–5, 150
McGill University, Montreal, Canada 170
Mediterranean
  coast 126
  sea 103, 105, 190, 216

Meir, Golda, former prime minister, Israel 142
Mekorot, Israeli water company 12
Meretz,
  party 30, 34, 35, 142, 220
  youth 141–2
Middle East 157, 171, 172
Milhim, Awad 159–60
Military
  court(s) 56, 82, 83, 145, 223, 227
  culture 140
  helicopter 160
  induction 127, 129, 134, 144, 145
  judge 225, 227
  prison 139, 144, 210, 223
    Ofer 222, 225
  prosecutor(s) 223, 227
  reserves 165
  rule 153, 183
  service 127, 134, 142, 170, 183
  state 126, 128, 217, 228
  vehicles 227
Ministries/Ministers, Israeli
  Construction & Housing 40
  Defence 75, 127, 141
  Education 87, 135, 136, 173
  Finance 124
  Foreign 204–5
  Interior/Internal Affairs 35, 118, 127
  Justice 75, 117
Ministries, Palestinian
  Health, 44
Mishly, Netta 139–49
Miska 55
Mizrachi, Yonathan 89, 90–2, 93–4, 95–7, 98, 99
Montreal, Canada 157, 221, 223
Morocco 46, 179
Moshav 130, 186–7
Mosque(s) 158, 168
Mossad 18
Mossawa Centre 114, 116, 118–25
Motorola, corporation 205
Mount Jerzim 42
Mount of Olives 89
Mount Zion 89
Mubarak, Hosni, President, Egypt 197
Muezzin 160
Mukhtar 168
Musih, Norma 171

Muslim(s) 50, 51, 91, 96, 108, 114, 149, 150, 167, 209

Nablus 11, 14, 23, 42, 44, 45, 46, 48, 49, 53, 102, 205
  circus school 49
Nablusi(s) 44, 46, 48, 49, 52
  soap 52
Nahal, Young Pioneers 29
Nakba 86, 101, 130, 167, 168, 169, 171, 172, 173, 175, 176, 201
  curriculum 169
Naor, Dorothy 5–16, 132, 133, 137, 206
Naor, Eric/Israel 6, 132
National
  Committee for the Rights of the Internally Displaced in Israel 166
  Insurance Institute 120
Nature and National Parks Authority 90
Nazareth 80, 85, 200
Nazi(s) 115, 219
Negev, the 106, 192
Neoliberal(ism) 121, 170, 180, 207
Netanya 101
Netanyahu, Prime Minister Binyamin 34, 40, 66, 78, 79, 86, 122
Neve Shalom 165
New England, US 219
New Israel Fund/Shatil, NIF 82, 85, 118
New Profile 126–38, 143, 146, 150, 206, 210
  counselling network 134, 136
  listserv 132, 137
  registered non-profit 132, 136
NGO(s), nongovernmental organizations 47, 48, 84, 107, 110, 118, 124, 166, 195
Non-violent(ce) 13, 141, 148, 216, 217, 223, 224, 226, 227, 228
North America 71, 133–4, 157, 158, 161, 171, 193, 200, 201
Norway, Norwegian 207, 210
  Ministry of Finance 199
  officials 205
  State Pension Fund 199, 205, 214
Nuclear
  disarmament 130
  power 202
  weapons 202, 228

Oakland, California 208

Obama, President Barack 40, 79, 193
  administration 112, 202
Occupation, the 42, 53, 57, 60, 66, 70, 82, 98, 101, 103, 106, 108, 111, 112, 127, 131, 139, 143, 146, 148, 149, 151, 152, 153, 155, 159, 160, 161, 166, 175, 180, 183, 191, 192, 197, 200, 203, 205, 206, 207, 208, 209, 216, 218, 219, 223, 227, 228
Occupied (Palestinian) Territories 55, 72, 103, 105, 107, 117, 128, 130, 131, 142, 144, 146, 150, 175, 191, 199, 201
Occupation Magazine 35
Olive(s) 153, 154, 159
  farmer(s) 155, 156, 158, 160, 161, 163
  grove(s) 153, 160, 196, 207, 221
  harvest 141
  oil 52, 152, 154, 155, 156, 157,158, 159
    extra virgin 153
  pressers 155, 156
  trees 140, 154, 217, 226
Olmert, Ehud, former foreign minister and prime minister, Israel 122, 193
One state 15
"Only democracy in the Middle East, the" 72
Open Shuhada Street 150
Open University 188
Or Commission 119
Oregon, US 208
Organic
  certification 156, 162
  farming/growing 159
Organization
  for Democratic Action, ODA 180, 184
  for Economic Cooperation and Development, OECD 123, 202
Oslo Accords/process 43, 90, 117, 184, 200, 201
Othman, Mohammad 209–10
Ottawa, Canada 212
Ottoman empire 164
Outposts 69, 70, 71, 75, 206

Pacifist(s) 126, 128, 146

Palestine 31, 52, 53, 100, 101, 105, 130, 146, 152, 153, 154, 157, 158, 163, 170, 172, 199, 200, 203, 213, 229
  Fair Trade Association, PFTA 155–6, 157, 159, 160, 161, 163
  Liberation Organization, PLO 115, 157, 183, 184
  (National) Authority 17, 27, 44, 102, 211
Palestinian
  Campaign for the Academic and Cultural Boycott of Israel, PACBI 199, 201, 202
  Centre for Human Rights 193
  citizens of Israel 200
  -Israeli 55, 84
  Medical Relief Society, PMRS 103, 107, 190, 191, 196, 197
  Territories 18, 42
Parasitic infections 195
Paris Accords 184
Parks, Rosa 223
Partition, UN 8
Peace negotiations 122
Peace Now 30, 69, 71, 72, 78–9, 140, 141, 142, 220
  Settlement Watch 70–1
Pensions 189
"People of the book" 134
People of the Wall 91
Permits 32, 107, 159, 160, 225
Persian period 92
Phalange militia, Lebanon 200
Phosphorus ammunition 193
Physicians for Human Rights – Israel, PHR 14, 100–11
  Occupied Palestinian Territory Department 101, 105, 106, 107
Pioneers 71
Pixies, the 209
PKA Ltd, Denmark 214
Pogrom(s) 219
Poland 100, 170
Popular committees 203
Presbyterian Church, US 208
Priest(s) 115
Privatization(ing) 135, 170
Project Hope 42, 44, 47–50, 53
"Promised Land, the" 219
Propaganda 148, 157
Prosthetics 195–6
Psychiatrist(s), military 147

Purim 139
"Purity of arms" 127, 129

Qabatiya 102
Quebec (Canada)
  Province of 216
  Superior Court 215, 221, 223
Queers Against Israeli Apartheid, Canada 203
Qur'an 62, 114

Rabbi(s) 105, 220
Rabbis for Human Rights 141
Rabin, Yitzak, former military commander and prime minister, Israel 7, 100, 117, 128, 167
Racism(ist) 120, 128, 149, 166, 176, 180, 210
Ramadan 17, 24, 43, 54, 64, 89, 98, 100, 104, 110, 162, 177, 188
Ramallah 22, 42, 46, 48, 54, 75, 82, 215, 216, 221, 224, 226, 227
Rape 146
Refugee camp(s), 129, 180, 191, 192, 200
  Askar 44
  Balata 44
  'Ein Beit el Ma 44
  Jenin 17–19, 21, 24, 27–8, 116
  Jisr el-Basha 200
  Nur Al-Shams 102, 103, 108, 110
  Shuafat 33
  Tulkarem 20, 100, 101, 105
Refugee(s), 17, 49, 130, 140, 150, 168, 170, 172, 173, 174, 176, 183, 190, 191, 200, 211, 213
  African 150
Refuse(rs) 134, 140, 142–3, 144, 145, 146, 147, 148, 151, 175
Reut Institute 209
Reuters 59
Right Living Award 20
Right of/to return 173, 174–5, 201, 213
Robinson, Mary, former president, Ireland 223
Rockets 192, 194, 195, 197
Roman(s) 91, 167
Rosh Ha'ayin 8, 12
Rumania 130
Russian(s) 16, 181
Rwanda 194

Sabra(s), prickly pear 113

Sadaka Reut, organization 55, 149
San Francisco, California 209
Santana, Carlos 208
Sarah (biblical figure) 136
Saskatchewan, Canada 45
Sasson, Talia, former head, State Prosecution Criminal Department, Israel 68
Saudi Arabia 45
Save the Children 195
Schaeffer, Emily 215, 216, 219–21, 222, 223, 226, 229, 230
Scotland 208
Sebastia 102
Second Temple (period) 95, 96
Sedek 169
Segev, Tom 170
Segregation, US 83
Senior letter 142, 150
Separation fence/barrier/wall 9, 35, 39, 58, 75, 91, 106, 137, 138, 140, 164, 185, 216, 226, 229
Settlement(s), 39, 40, 69, 70, 71, 76, 78, 94, 132, 160, 183, 200, 201, 202, 206, 207, 208, 211, 216, 217, 218, 221
    Amona 76
    Ariel 15–16
    Gilo 40
    Katzir 83
    Kokhav Yaakov 78
    Kiryat Sefer 216
    Mattityahu-East 218
    Mitzpe Shalem 208
    Modi'in Illit 215
    Modi'in-Maccabim-Re'ut 164
    Netzarim 30
    Nigron 76
    Ofra 74–6, 77, 78
    Roi 58, 64
Settlers 13, 16, 65, 69, 72, 73, 77, 90, 96, 112, 133, 139, 141, 150, 160, 207, 218
Seventh Million, The 170
Sexual harassment 147
Sfard, Michael 75, 220
Shabbat/Sabbath 76, 89, 114
Shabak/Shin Bet, General Security Service 98, 113, 115, 225, 227
Shahrori, Wala 43
Sharia court 73
Sharon, Ariel, former prime minister, Israel 68, 141

Shawamreh, Salim and Arabiya 33
Sheikh Jarrah 40
Shekels 58, 68, 77, 155, 159, 161, 177, 178, 189
Shiloah pool 97
Shministim (refusers) 139, 143, 146, 148, 150
Short Wave 195
Shubi family, Nablus 51
Shuhada Street, Hebron 150
Shwartz, Michal 177–8, 179, 180, 181, 182, 183–4, 185, 186, 188
Silwan/Wadi Silwan, 39, 89, 90, 92, 93, 94, 96, 99
    residents/citizens committee 97, 99
    Silwanis 97
Siyam, Jawad 97–9
Snitz, Kobi 203–5, 210
Snoop Dogg 209
Social change 180
Solomon, temple of 92
Souf, Issa 12, 13–15
Sound barrier, the 160
South Africa(n) 37, 137, 148, 150, 201, 204, 209, 213
    Apartheid 199, 201, 208, 209
    Constitutional Court 194
    Transport and Allied Workers Union 208
Soviet Union 115, 150, 183
Spain 161
Spiegel, Brigadier General Baruch 68, 74, 75
Staiti, Mustafa 1–2, 17–19, 20–22, 27–8
Stanczak, Jonatan 20, 27
Star of David 114
Stolen Beauty, campaign 208
Stone Theatre 20
Stop the Wall (Grassroots Anti-Apartheid Wall Campaign) 209–10
Strathclyde University, Scotland 208
Students Against Israeli Apartheid, Canada 203, 212
Subcontractor(s) 177, 178, 179, 180, 187, 189
Suicide bombers 9, 17, 144
Swedish 208
    International Development Cooperation Agency 24
Synagogue(s) 158
    reform 219
Syria 105

Ta'ayush 140, 220
Talbiyyeh 29
Talmud 33
Tamun 63
Tantura 130
Tayara, Wafa 177, 178–9, 185–6, 187,
    188, 189
Taybeh 100, 101
Tear gas 117–18, 148
    canisters/projectiles 218, 219, 227
Tel Aviv 5, 6, 16, 42, 66, 85, 102, 105,
    126, 128, 130, 139, 141, 143,
    149–50, 161, 169, 180, 186, 215,
    230
    University 80, 92
Temple Mount 36, 37
Territory, occupied 220, 221, 224
Terror, 61
    terrorism(ist) 3, 51, 115, 157, 183,
    211
Thai(s), Thailand 177, 187
TIAA-CREF (pension fund, US) 209
Timna 215, 226, 229
Tira 55
Toronto, Canada 203, 215, 220
Torture 110
Torture in Israel and Physicians'
    Involvement in Torture (report) 110
Traitor(s) 184
Trucks, truck drivers 180–1
Tubas 64
Tulkarem, city 103, 112
Turkey 98, 153, 161
Tutu, Archbishop Desmond 223
Two states 15, 72

Ukraine 130, 219
Umm Al-Fahm 80
Union(s), trade 180, 182, 188
United Nations, UN 44, 145, 159, 174,
    183, 192
    General Assembly 194
        Resolution 194 174, 213
    Human Rights Commission 194
    Human Rights Council 211
    International Criminal Tribunals 194
    Office for the Coordination of
        Humanitarian Affairs, OCHA 46
    Relief and Works Agency, UNRWA
        18, 27, 192, 196, 211
United States, US 36, 46, 69–70, 82,
    83–4, 90, 94, 122, 127, 148, 149,
    154, 156, 158, 162, 163, 171,
    183, 192, 193, 197, 202, 204,
    210, 211, 220
    Agency for International
        Development, USAID 161
Universal Declaration of Human Rights
    174
University of Wisconsin, Madison 154

Vardi, Sahar 140–50
Vatican 96
Viva Palestina 132
Volvo, corporation 207

Wadi Al-Hilweh 89, 90, 99
Wadi Nisnas 113, 114, 116
Wailing Wall 97
Wales 55
Wall, the 9, 158, 160, 162, 176, 199,
    200, 203, 206, 218, 222, 223
    apartheid 9
War,
    1948 8, 19, 124, 130, 170, 172, 173,
        174, 184, 186, 191, 192
    1967/Six-Day War 19, 69, 90, 94,
        101, 130, 174, 183, 192
    1973/Yom Kippur War 30
    crimes 132, 139
    resisters 127
Warqawi, Rawand 22–4
Warsaw Ghetto 9
Water 159
    control of 12, 18, 153
West Bank 6, 8, 33, 40, 44, 46, 54, 57,
    60, 68, 69, 70, 72, 74, 75, 78, 79,
    81, 84, 103, 108, 110, 129, 132,
    137, 140, 142, 143, 152, 153,
    161, 166, 182, 183, 200, 203,
    205, 206, 208, 215, 217, 219,
    227, 228
West Jerusalem 39
White supremacy 83
Whole Foods 161
Who Profits from the Occupation? 205,
    210
Wildeman, Jeremy 45–6, 47
Wind, Maya 148
Wisconsin Plan 171
Women in Black 127, 131
Workers Advice Centre, WAC 177, 178,
    179, 180, 181, 182, 184, 185,
    186, 187, 188, 189
    pension plan 189
Workers 188

Working class 182, 184
World Bank 12, 206–7
World Council of Churches 89
World Health Organization, WHO 12, 195
World War, Second 104

Yafa/Jaffa 42, 44, 192
Yaghi, Dr Aed 190–1, 194–5, 196, 197
Yalu 167, 168
Yaron, Ran 105–7, 108, 111
Yassin, Lamyaa 215, 221–2, 224, 228, 229
Yedioth Ahronoth 119
Yerushalaiyim Street 139
Yesh Din 69, 72, 75, 76, 77, 78
  Settlement Policy Judicial Advocacy Project 72

Yesh Gvul 127
Yiddish 77
Yihyeh, Salah Haj 100, 101–2, 103, 107–8, 109–10, 111–12
Yisrael Beitenu, party 87, 172
York University, Toronto, Canada 201, 212
Yousef, Hiba 49, 50–1, 53

Zatoun 157–8
Ziadah, Rafeef 200–1, 202, 209, 211, 212–13
Zionism, Zionist(s) 5, 7, 31, 55, 66, 69, 71, 77, 79, 81, 104, 127, 141, 142, 144, 148, 149, 158, 166, 169, 181, 201, 211, 212, 213
Zochrot 3, 126, 164, 165, 167, 168, 169, 171, 173, 174, 176
Zu'aiter, Adel 42

Milton Keynes UK
Ingram Content Group UK Ltd.
UKHW030837020824
446441UK00005B/91